The
ENNEAGRAM
MOVIE &
VIDEO GUIDE

THOMAS CONDON

The Changeworks

PUBLISHED BY

THE CHANGEWORKS
P. O. BOX 5909
BEND, OR 97708-5909

Cover design by Doug Thompson
Typesetting and editing by the Changeworks Staff
Printed in the United States of America

Library of Congress Cataloging-in-Publication Data:
The Enneagram Movie and Video Guide/
Thomas Condon   p. cm. includes bibliographical references
ISBN 1-884305-85-7 : $14.95
1. Psychology   2. Enneagram   3. Self-Discovery   4. Movies

For Katharine, Nicola, Kate,
and ma belle Nick

Acknowledgements

The genesis of the Enneagram is generally credited to Oscar Ichazo. He developed the material as a spiritual tool, giving the model its bones and internal organs. Chilean psychiatrist Claudio Naranjo gave it flesh when he took the Enneagram's character descriptions and cross-referenced them with the distinctions of modern ego-psychology. Author/therapist Kathleen Speeth is said to have been involved at this phase too.

I first encountered the Enneagram in 1979 when it was being widely taught in the San Francisco bay area. I took workshops from Helen Palmer, Claudio Naranjo and others during this time. Many of my friends were psychotherapists and knew about the model; we colluded with and inspired one another. Past these student days I took the material and went off on my own with it.

Each author of a book adds a perspective to the Enneagram. I especially like works that concentrate on descriptions *of* people rather than theories *about* them. The two works closest to textbooks on the Enneagram are *The Enneagram*, by Helen Palmer and *Personality Types*, by Don Riso. Both have theoretical trimmings but offer solid core descriptions of the styles. Palmer's writing is born from years of passionate research and practiced observation of real people. Don Riso I've not met but his descriptions of healthy-to-unhealthy expressions of each style are helpful to people who might otherwise find the model damning. Riso's insights on the wings are excellent. I also liked Richard Rohr's book, *Experiencing the Enneagram*, Claudio Naranjo's *Ennea-type Structures* and Margaret Frings Keyes's *Emotions and the Enneagram*. From all these people I have learned and extend my sincere thanks.

Enneagram teachers are like blind people describing an elephant, each clueing into a different aspect of the same animal. As far as possible, I've tried to stick to my own wording and point of view but some influence is inevitable. I apologize for any overlap in my listings of real people and the listings in other books, notably Riso's and Palmer's. Some famous people that we agreed about were just too pertinent to leave out.

This book is partly based on a regular column that I continue to write for the *Enneagram Educator* magazine. Clarence Thomson is my editor and friend, and he provided both the context and enthusiastic support for the development of the material. Clarence and I knew we had something when we learned that *Educator* readers were forming study groups just to watch the movies recommended in the column.

The physical production of this book has benefited greatly from the coaching of my friend, publisher David Balding. Thanks also to Lori "Bob" Stephens for her phone-tech support.

Finally, this book owes a lot to a broken hip. I had a sports accident followed by surgery and a long passive recovery. I searched hard for the accident's possible usefulness before one day realizing, "Hey! I can review 300 more movies!" This book is thicker and better thought-out than it would have been for that calamity.

Contents

Foreword

Movies are bigger than life, but they are not different from life. If they were, we could not see ourselves in them and we would lose interest. They reveal us to ourselves whether we know it or not, whether we like it or not.

With a few spoken lines, movie characters can express the inner geography of their psyches with a clarity and force that people in real life usually lack. A good movie becomes clearer than life, because in two hours it can reveal the essence and true motivations of a human being.

In reviewing movies for their Enneagram styles, Condon has crafted his own art form. A spoken line here, a telling gesture there, reveal to this skilled teacher the underlying moods and motives of a movie character. Reading his reviews is like having a gifted observer show you where to look through a microscope, or having a docent point out an artist's logic as you stand and see what you never saw right before you. The reviews in this book will show you Enneagram types writ large and writ vividly. Condon points out the obvious and suddenly you see it.

The dramatic evidence of the presence of Enneagram styles in films will encourage students of the system. It appears that, regardless of the imaginative process involved, when writers create a character, that character can often have an Enneagram style.

The clarity of the reviews and the sheer number of examples in this book will reinforce the confidence so many people place in the system. Using the book will also give you your own confidence at recognizing the outward signs of each style.

So may I humbly suggest that you gather around a good movie, read its review and tuck away Condon's stylish observations for later verification. Then sit back, relax, and watch the most enjoyable audio-visual aids in the history of education.

Clarence Thomson
Editor, *The Enneagram Educator*

INTRODUCTION

The Enneagram is about people — how we are the same, how we are different, what makes us tick. It presents a system of psychology that describes nine core personality styles that human beings tend to favor. The descriptions of these styles are both profound and comprehensive, detailing the inner motivations, thought patterns and basic beliefs of each one. Newcomers to the Enneagram are often astonished to discover clear, accurate portraits of themselves, their friends, parents and intimates.

Part of the power of the Enneagram is that it recognizes how human beings have sincerely different versions of reality. No version is presented as better than another. Each of the nine styles has its own internal logic and integrity. Each correctly perceives part of reality and has an area of "expertise." Each style has strengths, talents and advantages as well as limits, pitfalls and blind spots.

Enneagram styles are like nationalities. While we are all unique individuals, we belong to a larger group of which we are individual examples. If you have friends from other cultures, you know that on one level you are very aware of the differences between their culture and yours. The fact may contribute much to your relationship. On other levels, you and your friends connect affectionately in a way that bypasses how your cultures make you different.

Studying the Enneagram will reveal the differences between your psychological orientation and those of other "nationalities." With this awareness you can also connect more compassionately or usefully to others who have world views distinct from your own.

The major advantage to learning the Enneagram, of course, is to discover your own personality style. This can be a startling experience at first, but its usefulness soon emerges. Once you identify your core style, baffling aspects of your own behavior may suddenly make sense. You might see more clearly why you sometimes think and act the way you do. As you tune further into your own inner workings, you might sense deeper beliefs, plus a way of seeing the world that shades your daily actions and relationships.

You might initially be aware of the ways you are caught up in the pitfalls of your style and cause yourself suffering. There could be little psychological traps you set for yourself, limits you place on your experience or habitual ways that you react to events without much choice.

These learnings can be helpful in that they provide motivation to work on one's self. Some responses that you now have may be outmoded and carried over from childhood. You may act blindly at times. To an extent, you may find that your Enneagram style amounts to something like a hypnotic trance, as though part of you sleepwalks through life, relating to an *idea* of the world, rather than the world itself. Seeing the map but not the territory, this is called.

Most psychotherapists would say that having insight into your behavior is not enough to change it. Learning about the Enneagram won't magically transform you, but it will give you a tool that is greatly clarifying and uncannily useful.

Just as the Enneagram will show you how you are caught, it also points to your higher capacities — what you are good at, what creative resources are present when you are happiest and most awake. It will direct you toward the source of your personal power and give you a major tool for living more fully in the present-day world, basing your choices on your actual needs.

The Enneagram is a system of psychology. It is neither inherently esoteric nor spiritual. You might, however, find that it has deep spiritual implications in that it helps diagnose how you get in your own way and block the most free and soulful expression of your being.

On everyday levels, knowledge of the Enneagram is helpful in dozens of ways, from understanding relationships to improving communication to handling difficult people. You may discover that your friendships reflect affinities for certain Enneagram styles. You will also better pinpoint types of personalities that have been difficult for you to deal with. You may realize that the behavior of some people that you always took personally never was personal; they were just acting blindly out of the limits of their own world view.

The Enneagram is also useful in any professional context where communication is important. Attendees at my workshops have included psychotherapists, teachers, lawyers, counselors, business people, artists, plumbers, filmmakers. Anyone who needs to deal effectively with other people benefits greatly from studying the styles.

The premise of this book is that the Enneagram's nine personality styles are highly visible in certain movies, and that through study you can learn about them rather easily and enjoyably. The subtitle of the book might be "seeing the psychology in front of you." If you use the movie reviews to gain greater familiarity with the different "nationalities," chances are you'll recognize how visible they are in the people you interact with daily. Learning about the styles is like buying a new car — suddenly you start seeing them everywhere.

The medium of movies provides a fun way to learn and VCRs are widely available, even for rent. You can use the reviews to pursue whatever aspect of the Enneagram you are interested in. You can skip around the styles or work your way steadily through each chapter.

Some Enneagram workshops are taught by assembling representatives from each style. A panel of Sevens, for instance, will discuss their lives and perspectives, and it's fascinating to see how at once alike and yet different they are. The same themes and preoccupations will run through each panel member's life, yet they are obviously individuals, each with their own identity and soul. With the *Video Guide* you can create your own panel of film characters for a similar result.

Friends and couples interested in the Enneagram can use this material to great advantage. You and a friend or an interested group could read a description of, say, Twos, then screen a film, eat popcorn, have arguments and learn a lot.

If you are new to the Enneagram and use the *Video Guide*, you'll recognize a core pattern and basic point of view for each style. If a movie character reminds you strongly of someone you know in real life, the chances are good that they share the same Enneagram number. The same may be true for you and movie characters that you personally identify with.

As a reference book, the *Guide* is deliberately dense with detail. It is designed to be useful for all levels of acquaintance with the Enneagram. You can dip into it according to need. If you are a beginner, I'd encourage you to go lightly and try to get the gist of the thing first. Go for a general comprehension of all the styles or of those you are especially interested in. You can always backtrack and later study finer distinctions such as wings, connecting points and subtype themes.

The *Video Guide* is a companion to my other book, *The Everyday Enneagram*. *The Everyday Enneagram* offers tools for changing and growing within the recognition of your Enneagram style. The *Video Guide* is designed to give you practice and skill at spotting the different styles in the first place.

When I teach workshops, some of the nicest moments come when participants watch demonstration interviews and suddenly "see" a personality style in an indelible way. Someone will say, "I've read the descriptions over and over but this time I could really see and feel what Fives are like!" This is said in the astonished tone that comes with recognizing the obvious — consciously seeing something you may have unconsciously sensed all your life.

Video is a logical medium to illustrate the Enneagram, but there's not been much available for interested students. Accordingly, in workshops, I used to show movie clips to introduce the styles and this worked really well. Many students found it additionally useful to rent movies for further study so, over time, I'd developed a list of films that illustrated each character type. I had always intended to do something more with the list but wasn't sure what.

Clarence Thomson, editor of *The Enneagram Educator*, attended one workshop and suggested a column about the nine types as they appear in films. The first few reviews I tossed off from memory based on the workshop list. Then I screened a few new movies and wrote about what I generally saw. I knew the Enneagram well and had always enjoyed movies, so the task seemed a pleasant, lighthearted thing to do.

Shortly, though, something changed. I rescreened some of the movies from the workshop list and realized that a few of the character listings were wrong. I thought I had seen something that wasn't there or I had confused one type of character with another. It also seemed that, in a given story, many secondary characters also had Enneagram styles and that there were other levels of detail that I wasn't quite catching.

Then I noticed that there were routine tensions between similar kinds of characters in totally different movies. There was some kind of hidden architecture to film stories and it related to the Enneagram. I felt as if I was looking at something I couldn't quite see.

Gradually, I decided to disrupt my usual way of watching a movie. Like anyone else, I had always responded to them subjectively. I'd enjoyed stories and characters, the mood of a film and maybe its message. I decided to start watching movies with a narrow quality of attention, one in which I looked solely for evidence of personality styles. I began to look for the Enneagram first and let the story's mood, plot and message drop into the background.

This new perspective made it easier to screen a lot of films because I knew what I was looking for. I had a "half hour" rule: if there was no clear evidence of Enneagram styles after half an hour, I stopped the movie and went on to the next. Some films had it and some didn't.

Several friends of mine initially thought the idea of finding Enneagram styles in movies was a misguided, oddball enterprise. Some who knew the Enneagram said that a film story just couldn't show a character style with much accuracy or visibility. Others said that the collaborative nature of moviemaking would prevent an Enneagram style from ever being realized in the finished product. The idea was that a character would be written one way, interpreted by an actor differently, and perhaps the film's director would further influence how the character played finally on the screen.

As it develops, Enneagram styles are not only plentiful in films, but they are sometimes more obvious than in real life (Alfred Hitchcock once said, "Movies are like life with the boring parts cut out"). Stories are constructs based on human experience and one good way to propel a story is to give its characters vivid traits and attitudes.

A lot of movies with well-drawn characters take them through some change — a "character arc," this is called. Thus it's possible to see someone initially mired in the traps and excesses of their Enneagram style. As the story progresses you see the style's higher capacities evoked as the character goes through experiences that help them change and grow. Another character could decline through the course of a movie, but either "arc" will be interesting for what it shows about an Enneagram style and core point of view.

Some plots pit two characters with different Enneagram styles against one another for high contrast. Other stories are about characters who set out to do something and get in their own way because of neurotic complexity. What a character *wants* can be a telling reflection of his or her inner psychology. In some stories a character's Enneagram style is revealed in how a character responds to unforeseen circumstances.

When I first began this project I figured that movie stories were either plot-driven or character-driven and that the latter films were more likely to contain Enneagram styles. This has been generally true, though it has been surprising when certain stories that *seemed* character-driven didn't yield styles. Two recent (excellent) films, *Mississippi Masala* and *Menace II Society*, are like this. Both feature a small number of closely studied characters but somehow don't capture an essential *something* about them.

What the two films are really about is <u>context</u>. *Mississippi Masala* is about black and East Indian people trying to deal with oppression and culture shock in the USA's deep south. *Menace II Society* is a heartbreaking story of a smart, sweet teenager who can't quite transcend his brutal urban environment. The context is Los Angeles ghetto life and it overwhelms the young man's character and is ultimately the film's subject.

Good storytellers have to be part-time psychologists. Screenwriters, directors and actors all must keep track of a character's motivation during the course of a story for the finished movie to be coherent. Core motivations are highly related to a character's Enneagram style and how that character sees reality. Writers, directors and actors are far more likely to agree about a character's core in a good film than in a bad one.

Sometimes screenwriters are biographers as well, basing a movie character on a real person the writer has known. If the real person had an Enneagram style unconsciously apparent to the writer, then it gets written into the movie role. Sometimes a movie story is a deliberate biography, a character study of a real person who had an Enneagram style. At least one Hollywood screenwriter has said publicly that he and his writer friends use the Enneagram when constructing screen characters. They consider it a "well-kept secret" and have attended workshops.

Then there's casting. I've seen a number of film biographies where the movie's subject and the performer who plays the role *have the same Enneagram style*. Directors often know whether a role is right for an actor. The wisdom is that certain performers will bring a quality to a particular role that another won't. People in charge of movies are intuitively on the lookout for qualities of personality that they try to match to roles.

My contention is that Enneagram styles are a strong unconscious factor in how performers are matched to the characters they play. As we shall see, makers of movies often sort for the Enneagram styles without explicitly realizing it.

A few words about this book's layout. Each Enneagram style has its own chapter which includes a number of full-length movie reviews and additional listings of movie characters. The presentation of each is organized in the following sections:

FAMOUS REAL-LIFE EXAMPLES

These are examples of well-known people and their Enneagram styles that I've noted over the years. The list is fairly eclectic with an emphasis on actresses and actors. Some of the listings are of very famous people while others are quite obscure, but included in case they trigger recognition. The value of such listings is subliminal; you might realize the similarities between highly different individuals and maybe see a pattern that you have unconsciously sensed.

I've tried to make the lists somewhat international but probably haven't succeeded. For better or worse, though, American culture is exported all over the world, especially via our movies. The Cable News Network (CNN) is seen in about 210 countries. NBC is now all over Europe.

Generally, I've identified well-known people's Enneagram styles through watching filmed interviews, reading books and articles. A handful I have met. Unless someone was hugely blatant within their real-life style, I usually needed three or four sources before their Enneagram number came clear. If I got an idea from another Enneagram author, I still needed independent confirmation as we didn't always agree. I read a number of perfectly dreadful show business biographies to this end.

Since there is an emphasis on real-life performers, there are some imbalances to the lists. It's probably logical that there would not be as many real-life performers who are Fives since it's a relatively shy style. I was also surprised by the number of Sevens who work in films rather than, say, Threes.

INTRODUCTIONS

Each of the nine chapters begins with a brief overview of a specific Enneagram style. The sketches are only meant to set the context for the movie reviews and are aimed at people new to the Enneagram. As such, they are deliberately limited in scope.

Here and there in the *Guide*, I have used terminology from my other writings, specifically when I discuss healthy and unhealthy expressions of each style. I use the terms "awakened" and "entranced," as they relate to my thesis that having an Enneagram style is similar to being in a hypnotic trance.

For far more comprehensive descriptions of the styles, see *The Enneagram* by Helen Palmer, *Personality Types* by Don Riso and my own *The Everyday Enneagram*. If you are a sheer beginner, I'd highly recommend *The Enneagram Made Easy* by Renee Baron and Elizabeth Wagele.

ENNEAGRAM STYLES IN THE MOVIES

In this chapter section I discuss the types of roles that are often associated with each Enneagram style. Also included are familiar actresses and actors who have played roles related to the specific style. The intersection between performer and role is often fascinating.

As we will see, movie characters from each Enneagram style can be heroes or villains, although their motivations and actions will differ greatly. The same qualities that make a character virtuous can be magnified to villainous proportions.

I want to mention a few odd discoveries I made about the relationship between performers' real-life Enneagram styles and the roles that they play. There are surprising consistencies that are very confirming of the system.

Years ago, leaving the movie *MacArthur*, a friend of mine remarked: "Well, that settles it — Gregory Peck can't act." What he meant was that Peck had been unable to shed his usual screen persona sufficiently to play the character as written. Peck's usual character in movies was a principled One, although he sometimes played the persona for its dark side.

General Douglas MacArthur was written for the movie as an unhealthy Eight — an aggressive egomaniac — but Peck kept giving the character an honorable, principled aura. Thus after the film it seemed to my friend that Peck had been playing Peck rather than MacArthur.

The more I studied movies, the more I learned incidentally about real-life actors and actresses. After I began to identify their personal Enneagram styles, I was surprised to realize how many performers played their real-life Enneagram styles in movie roles. Gregory Peck turned out to be a real-life One. John Wayne was an Eight in real life and played an Eight character in probably every movie he made. Tom Cruise is a more current example. He is a Three in real life and in nearly all his movies, he plays Threes.

Other screen performers who have tended to play their real-life styles include: Woody Allen (Six), Gary Cooper (Nine), Harrison Ford (One), Tom Hanks (Seven), Katharine Hepburn (One), Charlton Heston (One), Diane Keaton (Six), Jack Nicholson (Seven), Dennis Quaid (Seven), Winona Ryder (Four), Sharon Stone (Three), Kathleen Turner (Three), Robin Williams (Seven). Throughout the book I mention Enneagram similarities between actors and their roles and I've named this phenomenon "Enneatype casting."

MOVIE REVIEWS

The movie reviews are meant to speak for themselves and be companions to your viewing experience. A lot of people keep the review of a film handy while watching, reading it before the film, afterwards, or both. The reviews can also be read on their own as a collection of stories about people who have core similarities.

When I first began the column in *The Enneagram Educator*, I warned readers that if Enneagram styles proved to be scarce, they might have to sit through some really rotten movies. Fortunately, this hasn't been true; Enneagram styles show up more often in good movies, usually because the filmmakers have paid extra attention to character.

I've tried to indicate what a reviewed film's general quality is, although no movie is truly bad for our purposes. I think I have reasonably good critical powers, but you'll have to decide that. Professional critics disagree with each other all the time and there's no accounting for taste. The Dustin Hoffman/Warren Beatty comedy *Ishtar* was a notorious, reviled bomb. I thought it was a little dumb but also sweet and surprisingly funny.

If a film has steamy sexual content, I'll mention it. Otherwise I'm going to assume that you're adult enough to handle the sight of actors and actresses pretending to have sex. If a film is especially violent, I'll also mention that. A few of the reviewed movies are suitable for children and this is indicated when relevant.

The book works hard to offer a balanced presentation of each Enneagram style, including healthy and unhealthy examples. Since movie stories are rooted in conflict, they often feature characters who are not so psychologically healthy. Sometimes a style is clearer in its neurotic expression, so this is emphasized in the reviews. The purpose of the *Guide* is to give you skill and practice at seeing the Enneagram, so sometimes it will focus on what's exaggerated or pathological. Remember, though, that each of the nine styles has its healthy side and a certain unique set of advantages.

Some Enneagram numbers are barely represented in films while others are everywhere. Fives, for instance, are pretty scarce in American movies so I had to turn to Europe where character studies of shy, withdrawn people are much more common. I could have written entire books on the more "photogenic" styles. Eights, for example, are usually blatant and declarative in their behavior and therefore drive story lines. In movies, they show up everywhere.

It's also true what film actresses say about the dearth of good roles for women. It took extra research to find clear female examples for some of the styles. Lady Fives, for instance, are so unusual in movies that I wrote up nearly every one I found. Male Twos are not that common either, probably because screenwriters don't know how to draw people-oriented male characters without making them seem effeminate.

One theory of film says that it has to deal with the "apprehendable universe." This means that a movie can't really portray the inner life of a character because the nature of the medium shows us only external behavior. This theory says that fantasy and dream sequences that attempt to show us a character's inner thoughts don't really work because they violate the rules of the film medium. If filmmakers want to illustrate a character's inner life, they must find a way to dramatize it in external terms.

This has relevance to learning about the Enneagram because many people wrongly assume that the system describes external behavior traits. They could look at, say, the achievement-oriented behavior of American tycoon Donald Trump and assume he is a goal-oriented Three. Trump talks about winning and wanting to be the best, so this sounds like stronger evidence. Sometimes, though, you have to dig deeper. The Enneagram is not about traits, but about world views and core motivations. You have to look past a person's external behavior and ask what internal need motivates it.

In Donald Trump's case, the desire to win is tied to a deeper need to seem and act strong, to dominate and prevail over events. This is a different motivation than a Three, who needs to win in order to know who they are. In interviews, Trump is often trying to seem invulnerable, which is not necessarily the same as being a winner. Though he has similar outward behavior, his inner logic and motivation would be very different. Trump is actually an Eight rather than a Three. *

For this book, I've handled this problem by reviewing movie characters whose Enneagram styles are flagrant. I've included characters who act out of their Enneagram styles and then talk about their motivations. They have to seem it, say it and do it.

As you apply your learnings to real life, though, remember that an Enneagram style is more than the sum of someone's behavior. You are looking for a basic inner stance and world view out of which someone's behavior flows. A person's traits can give you clues about their inner process, but you might have to go deeper at times. There are no magic formulas or automatic equations. Although it's fun to figure people out, remember that the Enneagram describes something about us that is rather profound.

   * This exact contrast between styles Three and Eight is on display in the movie *Wall Street*. The Michael Douglas character was modeled on Donald Trump.

ADDITIONAL LISTINGS

These film characters are included in case you want some additional possibilities for follow-up. Some of the roles are more vivid than others; some are large, some small. You may have seen some of these movies already. It's sometimes fun — and very different — to watch a film again with the perspective of the Enneagram.

FINER DISTINCTION NOTES

WINGS

Your core style has a built-in relationship to the numbered styles on either side of it. This is part of the theoretical formulation of the Enneagram, but I've found it to be a really accurate and useful distinction.

So if Two is your core style, you will have an intuitive connection to Ones or Threes or both. Within being a Two, you would have a basic orientation to other people. This will be influenced and modified by a preoccupation with principle and idealism (1 wing) or an extra sociable, achievement-oriented drive (3 wing). These are inherent connections; they are just *there*.

If you know your core style and think about it further, you can usually identify a wing that you favor. The healthy qualities of your wings are available to you almost like talents. The unhealthy qualities exist as potential pitfalls. Depending on your focus, you can tap the high side resources of your wings or unconsciously fall to the un-healthy side.

Somewhere between 60 and 70 % of the population have just one active wing, and will have an obvious connection they can identify. This means that their other wing is unconscious and latent. The remainder of the population have both wings active and will have a combination of motivations that reflect their joint influence.

Throughout the reviews, I discuss various characters who illustrate particular wings. At the end of each chapter is a reference section called "Finer Distinction Notes." This includes mini-profiles of wings, connecting points, and subtype themes as they influence the specific Enneagram style. These are written impressionistically, just to give you the flavor of each. For further descriptions of all the Finer Distinctions, see *The Everyday Enneagram.*

CONNECTING POINTS (Stress & Security)

Within your core style you also have a built-in connection to two other Enneagram styles. These connections are often called stress and security points. Just as with wings, you can recognize an intuitive, unconscious link from your core style to your connecting points.

The words "stress" and "security" are used as neutral descriptive terms. When you are under pressure, for instance, you will tend to temporarily access the attitudes and motivations of your stress point. So under stress a principled One might begin to act like a self-pitying, melancholy Four. When relaxed, she would begin to manifest the attitudes of her security point, the playful high side of Seven. As a neutral description of what sometimes happens this is true as far as it goes.

A lot of writers have taken these connecting points to mean something more. In book after book, the stress point is called an unhealthy direction in general and the security point is portrayed as the general path to psychological health. The security point is called the direction of growth, integration, redemption, while the stress point is called the direction of decline, disintegration, breakdown, etc. These are presented as correct and incorrect directions for you to go in when attempting to work on the dilemmas of your core Enneagram style.

I understand a teacher's desire to provide direction and a theorist's need to create a complete and unified theory. Unified theories about human behavior never hold together very long, though. Our personal psychology is a messy, complex process and theorists usually have to ignore contradicting facts to keep their theories intact. It would be nice to think that within your Enneagram style there was one sure direction out, a royal road to health and well-being. It's just not what happens.

When people are unhealthy or under stress, they manifest the neurotic behavior and defenses of *both* their stress and security points in a kind of cycle. They will also manifest the unhealthy elements of their wings; not to mention their core style. These become the ingredients of being stuck or lost in a downward spiral and they all tend to reinforce one another. No one element offers a magic direction out and how people change and grow is a *whole other subject.*

The same is true when someone is healthy or relaxed within their being. The high side qualities of both their stress and security points will be evident and will contribute to a kind of upward spiral. The powers and resources of both your wings will also be available as you operate out of the healthy perspective of your core style.

Two films in the chapter on Ones put the case quite succinctly. Joan Plowright's character in *Enchanted April* is on an upward spiral and manifests the high side qualities of both her connecting points. Fredric March's character in *Dr. Jekyll And Mr. Hyde* is sinking into decline and his two connecting points reinforce each other negatively.

These generalized connections — both healthy and unhealthy — are evident in many, many films listed in this book and are discussed as we go.

SUBTYPE THEMES

The original formulation of the Enneagram states that within each style there are three possible suborientations that people tend towards. Your subtype is determined by whether you are unconsciously preoccupied with personal survival (self-preservation), whether you incline towards one-to-one relationships (intimate) or whether your style of relating includes a lot of people (social). Most politicians, for instance, would likely be social subtypes.

Author Margaret Frings Keyes describes these subtypes with the phrase "the One, the Few and the Many." The subtypes relate to three key realms of life — survival or how we take care of ourselves, the realm of close relationships and then how we relate socially to the larger world. We all have portions of our attention and energy focused on these three realms. Within your core Enneagram style, however, you might habitually favor a particular realm more than the others.

As with wings, it's possible to have more than one subtype theme in your life. The content of the themes is different for each Enneagram style and explained both in the reviews and at the end of each chapter.

Subtypes are especially useful for recognizing what further motivates you within the core framework of your style. Movie stories favor some subtypes far more than others, as we shall see.

MORE ABOUT PERFORMERS AND THEIR ROLES

When I was in college and took an acting class, the professor used to say, "If you play a role in real life, you won't be able to act." What he meant was, if you were image-conscious and had a social persona in real life, you would have a difficult time in letting yourself go and becoming someone else within a role. The idea was that the actress has to surrender her personal self and give herself over to a totally different point of view and way of being.

The professor was talking about what is called "character acting," where an actor seems to take on a new character with each role. He omitted what's called "personality acting," which is when a performer develops a persona that they essentially play from role to role. Huge film careers are built by personality actors and they almost always are considered movie stars rather than character actors. They also almost always play their real-life Enneagram style.

After I realized that personality actors tended to play their real-life Enneagram styles, I began to wonder if there was any relationship between the roles character actors played and their personal Enneagram styles. I doubted it — the words of my college professor lingered. Character acting meant jumping completely out of your own skin and becoming a totally different person.

What I found instead was slightly amazing. Character actors don't exclusively play their real-life Enneagram style the way personality actors do. Character actors do, however, routinely play their *wings and connecting points* — Enneagram styles for which they have built-in affinities. Only once in a while does a performer play a style that is completely unconnected to their own. Movie roles are directly related to a performer's real-life Enneagram style *even when it seems like they aren't*.

This demystifies character acting a little; playing a character who has your wing or connecting point is not the same as slipping completely out of your own skin. Another built-in affinity that everyone has is to the Enneagram styles of their parents. We all carry our mother and father around inside us. I wouldn't be surprised if character actors were playing a parent's Enneagram style in roles that otherwise have no connection to their core style.

These are subtle distinctions but you might find it intriguing to keep track of them as you use the *Guide*. The connection between performer and role is almost eerie in its consistency and I mention examples throughout the reviews. There are even consistent patterns to scripts that directors choose to film; they sometimes will make several very different movies that nonetheless contain the same Enneagram character tensions.

ENNEAGRAM TOP TEN LIST

To get you started — listed below are ten good "beginner" films that each feature several vivid Enneagram styles:

Batman Returns — Four, Five, Six, Eight
Crimes And Misdemeanors — One, Two, Six, Seven, Eight
Dangerous Liaisons — Three, Eight, Nine
Little Murders — One, Two, Six, Seven, Nine
Mermaids — Four, Seven
Mr. And Mrs. Bridge — One, Six, Nine
My Dinner With Andre — Seven, Nine
Out Of Africa — Four, Seven
Postcards From The Edge — Two, Six, Seven, Eight
sex, lies and videotape —Three, Five, Eight, Nine

Note that the entire Enneagram is visible in just three films — *Crimes And Misdemeanors, Out Of Africa* and *sex, lies and videotape*.

MOVIES WITH MULTIPLE ENNEAGRAM STYLES

To follow up on the best Additional Listings, turn to the second index, "Movies With Multiple Enneagram Styles." The index will give you choices of movies with several characters who demonstrate the Enneagram. Sometimes a film will contain several of the Additional Listings and may be more worth your time and study.

The index also notes when there are typical dynamics or conflicts between styles. For instance, you can see a Four and a Seven in relationship in several different films. In some stories they might be in conflict, while in others they get along well. This is a useful tool for understanding your own relationships and also seeing the persistent consistency of the Enneagram in movies. Most movies offer contrasting Enneagram styles to make the story more interesting. This mirrors real life, though — long marriages between people with the same style, for instance, are relatively rare.

ONES

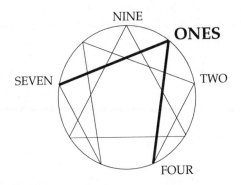

PEOPLE WHO COMPARE REALITY TO A SET OF STANDARDS. MAY BE OBJECTIVE, BALANCED AND MORALLY HEROIC OR REPRESSIVE, CRITICAL AND PERFECTIONISTIC.

FAMOUS REAL-LIFE ONES

Actress Jane Alexander, the culture of the Amish, Julie Andrews, Hanan Ashrawi, St. Augustine, Author/Politician William Bennett, Father Phillip Berrigan, Ambrose Bierce, Psychologist John Bradshaw, NBC's Tom Brokaw, Sierra Club founder David Brower, Feminist author Susan Brownmiller, William F. Buckley, John Calvin, Cesar Chavez, Singapore President Ong Teng Cheong, Hillary Clinton, Confucius, Actress Jane Curtin, Angela Davis, Michael Dukakis, Christian Scientist Mary Baker Eddy, Activist Daniel Ellsworth,

Harrison Ford, Jodie Foster, Barry Goldwater, Author Lillian Hellman, Katharine Hepburn, Charlton Heston, St. Ignatius, Glenda Jackson, Peter Jennings, Author Samuel Johnson, CNN's Myron Kandel, U.S. Senator John Kerry, Dr. Jack Kevorkian, Ted Koppel, NRA Vice President Wayne LaPierre, Martin Luther, Nelson Mandela, Miss Manners, Thurgood Marshall, George McGovern, Playright Arthur Miller, Author Jessica Mitford, Sir Thomas More, Ralph Nader, the cultural aura of New Zealand, Leonard Nimoy, John Cardinal O'Connor, Pope John Paul II, Gregory Peck,

H. Ross Perot, Sidney Poitier, Emily Post, Colin Powell, the culture of the Puritans, Marilyn Quayle, Yitzak Rabin, Tony Randall, Actress/Activist Vanessa Redgrave, Actor Cliff Robertson, Conservative author Phyllis Schlafly, George Bernard Shaw, CNN's Bernard Shaw, the cultural aura of Singapore, Film critic Gene Siskel, Alexander Solzhenitsyn, Actor Peter Strauss, Meryl Streep, the cultural aura of Switzerland, Margaret Thatcher, Emma Thompson, Harry Truman, Mark Twain, Dragnet's Jack Webb, Joanne Woodward, Actress Jane Wyman.

INTRODUCTION

At the core of Enneagram style number One is a strong unconscious tendency to compare reality with what *should* be. Ones generally have a set of standards by which they evaluate themselves, the behavior of others, and the world around them.

These ideals differ from person to person. Some Ones are preoccupied with spiritual standards while others, like advice columnists, might be focused on good manners. Others might be social reformers of some kind while others still might simply be intent on living an upright life or doing a good job at work.

The healthy side of this point of view is that a One can easily specialize in accurate moral perception and objective evaluation. More than other Enneagram styles, Ones can be ethically discerning, dispassionate and fair. They can make great priests and judges, for instance, or constructive social commentators.

Awakened Ones can be selfless and morally heroic, willing to sacrifice a great deal for principle. If they have a cause or mission, they might work hard and responsibly towards its fulfillment. Ethics and personal integrity are put above expediency, profit or easy solutions. An awakened One might display a balanced, cheerful perfectionism that is tempered by forgiveness and compassion.

For Ones who are more defensive or entranced, the preoccupation with principles and high ideals might degenerate into a mundane concern with the rules. The person might still be crusading for a cause but have more ego-involvement than they realize. Higher morality gets confused with *moralism*, discernment changes into *judgment*.

An entranced One might still sacrifice for the rules but a level of resentment begins to emerge. Ones can become openly critical, angry when their reforming zeal isn't shared by the world at large. They might still work hard and hold themselves to strict standards of behavior but their speech could be punctuated by sharp-tongued remarks, as anger breaks through. Their calm, ethical perspective gives way to dualistic thinking — "either/or" propositions, right/wrong dilemmas that reduce complex situations down into black and white choices.

A One's attempt to be good is a tense enterprise, sometimes leading to rigid behavior and a tendency to obsessive worry. A lot of entranced Ones fight their desires, especially the "bad" ones. These are often sensual but, otherwise, "bad" impulses are the opposite of whatever the One considers good and virtuous behavior.

Social problems can emerge because Ones have trouble knowing when they are angry and don't realize how scolding or repressive they can sound to others. When insecure or feeling criticized, a One's defensive reaction is to start judging. They simply don't accept reality as it is and don't think you should either.

When deeply entranced, people with this style can grow obsessive, paranoid and zealous. They may be capable of profound cruelty in the service of "goodness." Moral vanity and hypocrisy are likely, and unhealthy Ones can also grow obsessed with the fulfillment of insane missions.

Whatever a One disapproves of within their own behavior is what they will condemn in others. They may not allow themselves to act out "badly" but that doesn't mean they don't want to. Ones in this state tend to beat down or contain their desires and then project them outward.

So a One might see an inviting place to swim on a summer's day and suddenly begin to talk about the evils of laziness and the skimpy bathing suits people wear nowadays. The One's sensual desire to swim is "reverse projected" onto the environment and then a case is built against it. This case-building is called "reaction formation" and it's something we'll see Ones do a lot of in the movies. The One's emotional tendency towards anger is shared by Eights and Nines (see "Eights: Introduction").

ONES IN THE MOVIES

One characters play a variety of roles in movie stories. Heroic Ones started in the movies as uncomplicated virtuous figures. Thirty to forty years ago people like Charlton Heston and Gregory Peck (both real-life Ones) played moral stalwarts in role after role. Heston played biblical roles — Moses, for instance — while Peck played principled crusaders or slightly stiff leading men. Sidney Poitier played similar roles, too.

Actors like James Stewart and Henry Fonda were also going strong. Both men were Nines (1 wing) in real life but played Ones periodically. Kevin Costner now plays roles in the same range, always as a Nine or a One.

Katharine Hepburn is a One in real life and for much of her long career she played One characters who were spunky, argumentative, and chastising of men. Many of her roles as a barking One had a comic edge and her judgmental quality created a friction that drove story lines. Recent One movie actresses tend not to play their own style. Meryl Streep, for instance, has often played Twos (her wing) and Fours (connecting point).

Heroic movie Ones used to be priests, military leaders, social reformers and representatives of the establishment. Over the decades, though, such characters became more ambiguous, partly because public perception changed about the institutions that movie Ones stood for (imagine in the 1990s a biblical epic about a moral figure who is sure he knows the absolute truth). Also, heroes or heroines who are solely virtuous are dull.

The closest thing we have to a One movie star currently is Harrison Ford, also a One in real life. He tends to play morally decent men caught up in corrupt circumstances. His Oneness is implicit — we know he's a good guy and couldn't be responsible for the trouble he's in. Ford otherwise underplays his style's tendency to preach out loud or appear too one-dimensionally virtuous.

The dark side of the One style has always been represented in the movies, too. As I said, the same qualities that can make a heroine or hero can be magnified to villainous proportions. There's a fine line between moral certainty and madness, and One villains range from flawed perfectionists to mean figures of repression to obsessed, merciless characters who have gone mad with morality.

Gregory Peck played Captain Ahab in *Moby Dick* as a crazy One. Harrison Ford is a ranting semi-psychotic One in *The Mosquito Coast*. Dramatic figures like Captain Bligh *(Mutiny On The Bounty)* or the Big Nurse *(One Flew Over The Cuckoo's Nest)* represent Ones in positions of authority who abuse their power, often without realizing the extent of their cruelty. Milder unsympathetic One roles are reserved for crabby old faultfinding ladies, disapproving ministers or difficult, eccentric subjects of character studies.

Perhaps because this style can be so adamant and absolute, movie Ones have loads of conflict with other Enneagram styles. I must have screened fifty movies that featured Ones and Sevens in conflict. The party pooping moralism of Ones and the exuberant, fun-loving tendencies of Sevens are high contrast and collide visibly. The next most frequent contrast is between Ones and Threes, generally a conflict between principle and expediency. The third most common conflict is between virtuous Ones and rule-breaking Eights.

MOVIE REVIEWS

Agnes Of God

"I know what you are! I don't want that mind cut open. She's an innocent; she belongs to God!"

That's Mother Superior Anne Bancroft ranting to Sixish psychiatrist Jane Fonda about a nun, Agnes (Meg Tilly), whose sanity Fonda has come to evaluate. Tilly is under investigation for the murder of a baby on church grounds and Bancroft, the One, is out to protect the nun from the antispiritual premises of modern psychiatry.

Bancroft and Fonda go several noisy rounds debating the merits of their respective world views (spiritual vs. psychological). The actresses have a mutual love of scenery chewing and these arguments get plenty repetitious.

Gradually they soften their positions, become friendlier, and the film starts to get a little better. As Bancroft comes off her Oneish rigidity, she reveals a more relaxed human being who is more muddled in her certainties than she would like to seem. The resolution of the murder mystery is of this world but points beyond it.

Meg Tilly is quite persuasive as the nun subject to visions. She speaks in a breathless, childlike voice and beams with God-intoxicated pride. Her fantasies and visions are filled with competition and repressed sexual content. The stories she tells about her history of physical abuse are usual for the background of some phobic Sixes. Actress Tilly is a Six in real life and mostly plays them. I originally thought she was a Two in *Agnes*, but took another look and saw a character mired in fear and dependency on authority.

Jane Fonda often sounded like a One in her film roles but her basic screen persona was more of an edgy counterphobic Six, and that's what she's like here. Fonda's screen characters frequently fought with Ones. You can see it with Gregory Peck in *Old Gringo* (page 28) and especially between Fonda and her real-life father Henry in the film *On Golden Pond*.

The Bridge On The River Kwai

This David Lean film is set in an Allied POW camp in Burma during World War II. The Allied prisoners, led by Alec Guinness, are ruled by Japanese camp commander Sessue Hayakawa.

Both Guinness and Hayakawa are Ones. At the start of the film they lock horns over a point of law and neither one will give in. Guinness is thrown into an outdoor cage to suffer until he relents his position in the conflict. He will not. "Don't you see that it's a matter of principle? If I give in now all will be lost." Guinness is willing to die for a point of law.

Hayakawa is too. Guinness is needed out of the cage to help build a bridge for the Japanese across the nearby river Kwai. Hayakawa explains that if the bridge is not completed by its deadline, he will have to kill himself in dishonor. Guinness, still stubborn, replies, "I do not think you understand; I have my orders."

Eventually Hayakawa gives in and Guinness sets about supervising the construction. Guinness insists that it is a point of British honor that this bridge for his enemies should be exceptionally well built. He gets so carried away with this new principle that he very nearly thwarts an Allied attempt to destroy the finished product. Right at the end, he realizes how far off beam he has gone ("What *have* I done?") and redeems himself heroically.

This 1957 film is still splendid, a story told with epic texture and great simplicity. William Holden plays a Generic American, probably a Three. He's cynical, pragmatic and opportunistic ("This is just a game, this war").

Guinness's One has a 9 wing, which brings an emotional coolness and detachment. He is impersonal, abstract and wrongheaded in the service of social principle. The difference between the 9 wing and 2 wing is almost that of temperature.

Ones with a 2 wing have warmth and, when defensive, heat. Hayakawa, by contrast, has a 2 wing and is more easily upset. He yells and screams while Guinness remains calm. People with this style can be volatile — they may give hot-tempered, finger-shaking lectures or display a kind of contained emotionalism.

Enchanted April, Dr. Jekyll And Mr. Hyde

Enchanted April is a warmhearted, surprising story of a month's vacation at an Italian villa organized by two suffering Victorian women from gray, sodden London. Film begins with Josie Lawrence (a nervous Six) talking acquaintance Miranda Richardson (Nine) into the scheme:

"I'm sure it must be wrong to go on being good for so long that you become miserable. I can see you've been good for years and you aren't happy. I've been doing things for other people ever since I was a little girl and I don't believe I'm any better!"

More than just needing a vacation, the two share a spiritual malaise. We see them struggling within pinched, pious lives and sterile marriages. To make the excursion affordable, they recruit two strangers (Joan Plowright and Polly Walker) to share the villa. All of the women initially agree that the arrangement is to exclude men.

After some bickering and settling in to the lazy pace of life, a spirit overtakes the visitors one by one. Each kind of melts, both into the redolent sensual environment and towards each other. What overtakes them is like *agape*, nonsexual, nonsentimental love. The best comes out in everyone and this is very believably evoked.

"I have this obsession with justice, you see," Six Lawrence says, "I wouldn't love him unless he loved me back exactly as much. The emptiness of it all." Now calmed-down, she's explaining why she has invited her husband to Italy after all. Played by Alfred Molina, he's a status-seeking Three who comically blunders about the villa trying to make deals before relaxing into his wife's warmth.

Nine Richardson's transformation is also sweetly credible. We watch her surrender her piety (1 wing) to a quiet sensuality. She emerges with a tender, firm sense of her own priorities, especially towards her Sevenish husband, who shows up at the villa too.

The most interesting and obvious change, however, is in Joan Plowright's upper-crust One character. She's a very good example of a social subtype, characterized by inadaptability. As a social One she moralizes at others from a position that she is convinced *should* be true. Plowright judges present events against what would be proper in her remembered literary circles. She grew up around famous authors and acts like their representative. "All I wish to do is sit in the shade and remember better times and better men," she says.

As the villa's atmosphere works its strange magic, Plowright begins to recognize the trap she's in: "All my dead friends don't seem worth reading tonight. They always say the same things, good things, but always the same ... they were — they are — great. But they have one terrible disadvantage, they're all dead. I'm tired of the dead. I want the living." Note the melancholy cast of these statements. As Plowright gets more in touch, we hear her emotional connection to 4 (see "Finer Distinction Notes").

Her playful, sensual connection to 7 also emerges, although not without a fight. It starts with small clues like forgetting to walk with her cane. We see little laughs trying to break through her armor but, at first, she suppresses them with judgments: "Ridiculous! This feeling that I'm going to burst out! At my age! I won't have it!" (This is "reaction formation.")

By day, Plowright moralizes about propriety and rails against "unbridled license." At night, however, she feels something more: "Why am I so restless? I haven't been this restless since I was a child. I feel something is going to happen ... I won't let it, I won't let it!"

Despite her best suppressive efforts, something does happen to Plowright — she lightens up. She starts painting (connection to 4). She also plants her cane in the ground and leaves it there. She makes jokes, gets playful and, at one point, muses: "Isn't it better to feel young somewhere than old everywhere?" The change is both delightful and vivid and at the heart of this subtle, gracious film.

The kindly villa owner (Michael Kitchen) is a Nine with a 1 wing. Polly Walker's character is the most sketchy; she seems like a Three, a Seven and a Nine at different times. What she's struggling with is a life of surfaces and she responds strongly in the end to a desire for inner substance. Her early conflicted exchanges with Plowright have a One/Seven flavor, but Walker could also be a vain Nine caught up in her connection to 3.

I know it sounds unlikely, but **Dr. Jekyll And Mr. Hyde** (1932 version) makes a perfect double bill with *Enchanted April*. The stories have no similarities but Joan Plowright and Fredric March display identical character tensions as Ones. March's are much more extreme and amazingly clear; this is a perfect portrait of what's called a "trap-door One."

March's virtuous, idealistic Dr. Jekyll is too good to be true, but he does make scientific speeches about the dark side of human psychology and the virtues of instinct. Maybe he suspects something about himself for he also refuses invitations to enjoy night life: "A gentleman like me *daren't* take advantage of London's amusements." Instead he stays in his laboratory dutifully mixing instinct potions until he gets one right. This he drinks down in the spirit of science and in a matter of moments virtuous One Dr. Jekyll is transformed into Mr. Hyde — *a Seven.*

The change is so total and clear that it's actually kind of stunning. Mr. Hyde is a Seven with a strong 8 wing. His first words as he looks at himself in the mirror are: "I'm free! I'm free! Free at last!"

Mr. Hyde is the kind of Seven that a One would dread turning into. He's a walking Id — pure narcissistic appetite — and he knocks down anyone in his way on the path to pleasure. Most unhealthy Sevens with 8 wings take the word "no" badly because they have little impulse control. Mr. Hyde tells a woman, for instance, "I want you! And what I want, I get!" He throws tantrums when his manic, greedy enthusiasm is opposed. He wants to hear what he wants to hear.

Hyde is very oral, as his protruding teeth suggest. He gulps at fresh rain, loves alcohol and good food. He's fairly irresponsible too: when he beats people up who won't give him what he wants, he quickly turns back into Dr. Jekyll so as to escape consequences.

When One Dr. Jekyll comes to and realizes what havoc Mr. Hyde has made, he's horrified. In fact, he immediately plunges to the low side of 4 and becomes self-pitying, tormented and melodramatic about his defect. He's full of regrets and apologies for Mr. Hyde's bad behavior and vows more strongly each time to repress his Seven streak ("I'll fight the monster! I promise to defeat it!"). The harder he suppresses Mr. Hyde, of course, the more easily the latter comes out (repression just makes these things worse). Jekyll again gets Fourish: "I'm beyond help! I'm in hell! I have no soul. I'm beyond the pale. I'm one of the living dead!" The cycle continues downward to the end.

I really recommend this film for how clearly it shows a One in tension to stress and security points. Dr. Jekyll's fiancée's father is also a One. A further wrinkle is that author Robert Louis Stevenson was a Seven in real life. Sevens have a connection to One, going the other way, so Stevenson personally would have known the conflict he was fictionalizing (see "Sevens: Seven's Connection to 1").

Dr. Jekyll And Mr. Hyde is well made with art direction inspired by German Impressionism, and March's dual performance is masterly.

Missing

Superb, poignant fact-based story about the disappearance of a young American (John Shea) during a coup in a nameless South American country.

Jack Lemmon gives an excellent, restrained performance as a Calvinist One. He's Shea's intolerant religious father, forced to follow the mystery of his son's vanishing when official searches come up clueless. Lemmon arrives in the country cranky and sarcastic, spitting disapproval at daughter-in-law Sissy Spacek (a Six).

He radiates judgment and righteous anger and especially refuses Spacek's assertion that the government might be responsible for Shea's disappearance. "I don't want to hear any of your antiestablishment paranoia! I've had enough of that from my son. If he had settled down where he belongs, this never would have happened in the first place!"

Spacek alternates between fighting with him and making peace. Lemmon gets so nasty with his judgments that even he realizes he's gone too far and apologizes. He's not uncaring, just dour and controlling.

This is more reaction formation. Lemmon's trying not to feel a growing anguish that his son may be dead. He's also polarized in a One/Seven conflict. Shea appears in flashback and it's clear that he's a Seven; he's fun-loving, jaunty and antiauthoritarian (counterphobic 6 wing). It's easy to imagine their estranged relationship, based on Lemmon's judgmental comments. You can tell he's been *dis*identifying with his son's Sevenness for years. As Lemmon and Spacek continue their search, Father begins to appreciate his son; he surrenders to their similarities and starts liking the very qualities he formerly disapproved of.

This film also shows a moral tension between Ones and Threes. David Clennon plays the U.S. Embassy representative, a calculating fellow. American foreign policy is the real villain of the piece and most of the Embassy representatives are unhealthy Threes. The Ambassador says, "There are 3000 U.S. firms doing business here; I'm pledged to protecting a way of life and a damn good one." To this end he justifies his means. Lemmon's final reply to the lot of them is: "I just thank God that we live in a country where we can still put people like you in jail!"

Another movie with similar themes is *The Killing Fields*, a well-staged, harrowing account of the 1970s war in Cambodia. Fact-based story is from the writings of *New York Times* reporter Sidney Schanberg (Sam Waterston), an excitable, self-righteous One. He has a 2 wing and is prone to loud anger and moralistic rages. The U.S. military machine is personified by creepy, cold-eyed Craig T. Nelson, a representative Three.

The Mosquito Coast

Critics passed on this well-made movie partly because it's a downer and has a couple of notable flaws. Harrison Ford, however, is wonderful as a misanthropic One going gradually mad. He's a brilliant inventor who is supremely nonadaptable to the tenets of civilization.

As the film begins, Ford is loudly building a case against modern life, partly, it seems, because he can't fit into it. His blistering, defensive diatribes are funny, accurate and yet crazily off. He convinces his wife and family that life in modern America is a hopeless compromise and that the only solution is to sail south to raw jungle and there create an ideal civilization.

Once there, Ford builds ingenious structures, but human realities get in the way of his realizing utopia. The film shows how loony a One can get while thinking that he makes sense. Ford is impersonal, cruel, reckless and brilliantly self-justifying. He has a strong 9 wing, and his degeneration reflects the One's connection to the low side of 7. You might also see similarities betweeen Ford's character and Alec Guinness in *The Bridge On The River Kwai*.

The story is told through the eyes of Ford's son (the late River Phoenix), a Nine. Helen Mirren, a fine actress, has a nothing role as Ford's Niney wife. Andre Gregory plays a preachy One minister whom Ford loathes, but they are similar characters and shadows for each other. Gregory's a real-life Seven so he's playing a connecting point. Ford is a One and Phoenix was a Nine, so this is Enneatype casting.

The Official Story

Quiet, intense film set in 1970s Argentina during a time of horrific political repression. Norma Aleandro gives a moving, dignified performance as a sheltered, upper-class school teacher who slowly awakens to the idea that her adopted daughter may be the orphan of parents murdered by the country's military regime.

She's a One and the more she learns about her daughter's background, the more she has to pursue the true story ("It's important to me as it is to any moral being"). Chief perpetrator of the official story is her husband (Hector Alterio) who arranged the adoption in the first place and still knows a secret or two. He's also a One, but a different kind — he's a self-preservation subtype which makes him an overwrought worrier.

The difference between Aleandro and Alterio that emerges is between moral courage and moral cowardice. Alterio is worried about losing all he has and tries myriad ways to dissuade Aleandro. He's a deeply unpleasant man, but something of a torn villain and oddly sympathetic by the end. His frantic will to preserve his status and material well-being has a ranting Oneish cast. But it blinds him to larger moral issues and turns him almost accidentally against his wife.

Also interesting are the scenes between Alterio and his father. The father is a liberal, freethinking One who douses his son with disapproval. You can almost see how Alterio would have formulated his conservative principles in direct reaction to the father's imposing ideals.

This deserved its Academy Award for best foreign film. It's really a good one.

Old Gringo

Gregory Peck plays a character based on the One American writer Ambrose Bierce who vanished and presumably died in turn-of-the-century Mexico during the Mexican Revolution. He begins the film by angrily renouncing his work at a press conference and vowing to disappear from the public forum.

It's a corny role — the Crusty Old Disillusioned Idealist — but Peck makes the most of it. He manages to suggest a broad, open, philosophical cast of mind even as he tends towards judgment and categories. When Ones relax, they get curious and interested in things (high side of 7). Peck stays flexible and suspends judgment as he tries to comprehend perspectives of war that confound moral categories. He also grows wistful and full of feeling (connection to 4).

At other times, Peck's Oneishness asserts itself: "You're so eloquent but you say such appalling things," Jane Fonda tells him. In Mexico a wounded soldier asks if he's going to die. "Yes," Peck replies. When later criticized for not offering a dying man comfort, Peck says, "He deserved the truth at least once before he died."

Overall this is a lavish, uneven melodrama. It features 50-year-old Fonda improbably cast as a 30-year-old virgin. Jimmy Smits plays an Eight revolutionary and the film vacillates between showing him as a brooding, violent idealist and a sexy hunk who looks good in white muslin. Peck's performance, though, is really worthwhile.

One Flew Over The Cuckoo's Nest

This adaptation is more naturalistic and less clichéd than its source novel by Ken Kesey. It is basically about a One and a Seven squaring off in a state run psychiatric hospital. The One is the head nurse who oversees a ward of severely disturbed men, including Jack Nicholson's manic Seven character. In the book she is a figure of conscious, angry, rule-bound repression. In the movie she is brisk and calm, like a One who doesn't know she is angry.

While the Big Nurse is unable to comprehend the madness that surrounds her, she does understand management. Louise Fletcher plays her as orderly, even cheerful — like Mary Poppins with steel teeth. When an inmate commits suicide she is genuinely upset and oblivious to her role in bringing it about. The anticreative, antisexual tendencies of the One style also figure in the story.

The character of Billy Bibbit is a phobic Six and Chief Broom, the taciturn Indian, is a Nine. He's played by Will Sampson.

Summertime, Rooster Cogburn

Katharine Hepburn is a One in real life and for much of her long career she played Ones, Twos or Sevens. These are respectively her core style, her wing and her connecting point. In real life Hepburn speaks in brisk epigrammatic sentences and has been known to be perfectionistic and severe. In interviews, she is funny, self-critical and judgmental of others. More than one interviewer has claimed they were castigated for being just minutes late for their appointment.

Profilers have often described Hepburn in terms of her New England roots. The cultural cliché for people from that part of the USA describes a One. New England Yankees are thought to be moralistic, stern, hardworking and rule-bound. Part of this image is probably based on legends about the early pious Puritan settlers. The term "Banned in Boston" refers to strict community standards that have led to the occasional censoring of public performances in that New England city. The license plate for the state of New Hampshire carries the uncompromising motto, "Live Free or Die."

In some of her better roles Hepburn has played a variation on this cultural image. Two of many examples are the 1955 David Lean film *Summertime* and the 1974 comedy *Rooster Cogburn*.

Summertime features Hepburn as a lonely One spinster off on a solitary vacation to Venice, Italy. She's middle-aged, never married, and melancholy (connection to 4). She romanticizes marriage ("Two — that's the loveliest number in the world!") and doesn't want to be a burden to other traveling couples.

This vulnerable condition makes Hepburn ripe for the peeling by shopkeeper smoothie Rossano Brazzi. He acts like a romantic Four, but sounds more like a Seven, with his live-for-today credo. He's a cliché Italian male and less well-drawn than Hepburn, but his invitation to her is to abandon her rules and fling herself at the moment and him.

She gradually does, but irritably resists Brazzi several steps of the way mainly on moral grounds. He's married but counters her objections with "European" arguments — he and his wife have an understanding, Americans are just prudes, etc. Anyway, she relents, goes a little wild, dances barefoot and surrenders to the romantic atmosphere (Lean films Venice as sensual rather than spooky). She loses her self-consciousness, becoming more in touch with her needs (high side of 4), and also more playful and funny (high side of 7). Part of this character change can be measured in her treatment of a pesky street boy who adopts her. At first she is stern with him, but she grows more soft-hearted and generous towards the boy as the story moves along.

The film is corny, stately, and yet well done. Despite its cruel prognosis for an unmarried woman, we see a One learning how to enjoy life in a way that's realistic for the style.

Rooster Cogburn pairs Hepburn with John Wayne in an amiable, chatty adventure-comedy that kids might enjoy. This was Wayne's next-to-last movie and he was getting good at broad self-parody. He was an Eight in real life and played them always in films (see *The Shootist* in "Eights"). In *Rooster*, he's got a comic 9 wing and has gone mellow and slovenly with haphazard flashes of the old aggression. These come up in response to Hepburn's lectures and hectoring (she's a Minister's daughter).

Some of their arguments are quite funny as she levels Wayne with cold-eyed, accurate criticism and he blusters and swaggers helplessly in defense. Defending his love of whiskey, Wayne says, "Life ain't easy, Sister. It don't hurt to make a fool of yourself once in a while." Hepburn replies evenly, "Yes, once in a while ... but not more often than not. Marshal Cogburn, you're in a sorry state: you're unsteady on your feet, untidy in your person and rank with the smell of sweat and spirits. Cleanliness and abstinence are next to Godliness, or had you forgotten?" Wayne loses every round, of course ("she's frightening!"), but somehow they find each other appealing.

This movie is also notable for Wayne's kind, respectful treatment of a young Indian sidekick. Maybe he was trying to make up for all his early Westerns... This Eight/One dynamic is also visible in *Class Action* (see "Sixes") and *Malcolm X* (see "Eights").

Other good One roles for Katharine Hepburn are in *The Philadelphia Story* and *The Corn Is Green*. She played Twos in *Suddenly Last Summer*, *Long Day's Journey Into Night*, *Guess Who's Coming To Dinner* and, I think, *The African Queen* (Humphrey Bogart was a Nine). She plays a Seven in *On Golden Pond*. An exception I found was Hepburn's role in *The Lion In Winter*, where she plays a ruthless Three.

The World According To Garp

Adaptation of John Irving's picaresque novel about a writer's life. The writer is a Four (Robin Williams, giving the role a Sevenish cast) and his One mother figures prominently in the story.

Glenn Close plays the mother and she's a lot like the Big Nurse (*One Flew Over The Cuckoo's Nest*), only nicer. Her big beef is with men; she's shown to be on a lifelong crusade against the lustful nature of the opposite sex. Here's how she explains to her young son why he has no father: "I always wanted a child but you need a man. You know what men are like; full of lust. (Your father) was dying. I wanted a child. It seemed like a good arrangement. He wouldn't be hanging around with legal rights to my body." Elsewhere she goes on about another man: "He's full of lust. I can smell it a mile away." When someone replies, "Attraction is just natural," Close says, "Diseases are natural too; it doesn't mean we have to give in to them."

She starts a suffrage-like movement to minister to the needs of abused women. Close has a 2 wing and is another social subtype.

The movie is overlong, but well-constructed. It makes a consistent and warped equation between feminism and man-hating. John Lithgow is funny as an ex-football player who's had a sex change operation. He's a Seven though at first he seems like a Two.

OTHER MOVIE ONES

Dan Ackroyd, *Dragnet*; Julie Andrews, *Mary Poppins*, *"10," Tchin Tchin (also called A Fine Romance)*, *That's Life!*; Ingrid Bergman, *Cactus Flower*; Roberts Blossom, *Resurrection*; Wilford Brimley, *The Stone Boy*; Pierce Brosnan, *Mr. Johnson*; James Cagney, *Mr. Roberts*; Tsai Chin ("Lindo"), *The Joy Luck Club*; Kevin Costner, *American Flyers, Bull Durham, JFK, The Untouchables*; Hume Cronyn, *Conrack*; Willem Dafoe, *Mississippi Burning*; Lolita Davidovich, *Leap Of Faith*; Bette Davis, *The Corn Is Green*; Robert De Niro, *A Bronx Tale*; Melvyn Douglas, *Hud, I Never Sang For My Father*; Henry Fonda, *On Golden Pond*; Carlin Glynn, *The Trip To Bountiful*;

Rex Harrison, *My Fair Lady*; Eileen Heckart, *Butterflies Are Free*; Wendy Hiller, *The Elephant Man*; Judd Hirsch, *Running On Empty*; Anthony Hopkins, *The Bounty, Howard's End, The Remains Of The Day*; John Houseman, *The Paper Chase*; Glenda Jackson, *House Calls, Women In Love*; Burt Lancaster, *From Here To Eternity*; Karl Malden, *Patton*; Fredric March, *Inherit the Wind*; Matthew Modine, *And The Band Played On*; Demi Moore, *A Few Good Men*; Leonard Nimoy, *Never Forget*; Laurence Olivier, *A Voyage Round My Father*; Michael O'Keefe, *Nate And Hayes*;

Gregory Peck, *To Kill A Mockingbird, Other People's Money*, most any film; H. Ross Perot, *Straight Talk*; Sidney Poitier (as Thurgood Marshall), *Separate But Equal*; C.C.H. Pounder, *Bagdad Café*; Cliff Robertson, *Picnic*; Rosalind Russell, *Picnic*; Paul Scofield, *A Man For All Seasons*; Tom Skerritt, *A River Runs Through It*; Kiefer Sutherland, *Flashback*; Jessica Tandy, *Driving Miss Daisy, Used People*; Philip Terry, *The Lost Weekend*; Eli Wallach, *Nuts*; Oskar Werner, *Ship Of Fools*; James Whitmore, *Nuts*; Shelley Winters, *An Unremarkable Life*; Joseph Wiseman, *Dr. No, Seize The Day*; Edward Woodward, *Breaker Morant*; Daphne Zuniga, *The Sure Thing*.

FINER DISTINCTION NOTES

WINGS: Ones can have a 9 wing, a 2 wing or both wings.

One With a 9 Wing

Ones with this wing can have an aura of 9-like calm although eruptions of temper are possible. Often have a detached quality and can be mistaken for Fives. Tendency to formulate and embrace principles that have little human content, but this is also their strength. When awakened, may be objective and balanced, cool and moderate in their evaluations. More entranced, might have perfectionistic expectations that are not humanly possible to meet. May hold social or political opinions that are supremely logical but ultimately heartless. Draconian. The rules come first, could be merciless or unwittingly cruel.

Often a little colorless in their personal appearance. Many Ones with this wing are plain dressers, preferring functional clothing that is appropriate to context but not flashy. The emphasis on function may extend to their general lifestyle. Practicality is highly valued.

Real-Life Ones With a 9 Wing: The culture of the Amish, David Brower, Angela Davis, Michael Dukakis, Harrison Ford, Ralph Nader, John Cardinal O'Connor, Colin Powell, the culture of the Puritans, Yitzhak Rabin, Vanessa Redgrave, Bernard Shaw.
Movie Ones With a 9 Wing: Henry Fonda, *On Golden Pond*; Harrison Ford, *The Mosquito Coast*; Alec Guinness, *The Bridge On The River Kwai*; Katharine Hepburn, *Rooster Cogburn*; Anthony Hopkins, *The Remains Of The Day*; Jack Lemmon, *Missing*; Lilia Skala, *Lillies Of The Field*; Tom Skerritt, *A River Runs Through It*.

One With a 2 Wing

This wing generally brings more interpersonal warmth. High standards are tempered by humanism. May understand and partly forgive humanity for not doing its best. Work hard to improve the conditions of others, sacrificing time and energy to do good works.

When more entranced, can be volatile and self-righteous. Authoritarian inflation and moral vanity on the low side. Can give scolding lectures or display a kind of touchy emotionalism. "Do as I say, not as I do" attitudes possible. Hypocrisy likely because the person is so convinced they have moral good intentions. Overlook inconsistencies in their own behavior. Dependency in relationships. Far more likely to be a jealous intimate subtype than Ones with a 9 wing.

Real-Life Ones With a 2 Wing: Jane Alexander, William Bennett, John Bradshaw, Susan Brownmiller, Hillary Clinton, Barry Goldwater, Lillian Hellman, Glenda Jackson, Miss Manners, Gregory Peck, H. Ross Perot, Sidney Poitier, Marilyn Quayle, Meryl Streep, Joanne Woodward.
Movie Ones With a 2 Wing: Norma Aleandro, *The Official Story;* Glenn Close, *The World According To Garp;* Katharine Hepburn, *Summertime;* Glenda Jackson, *House Calls;* Gregory Peck, *To Kill A Mockingbird;* Joan Plowright, *Enchanted April;* Sam Waterston, *The Killing Fields.*

CONNECTING POINTS (Stress and Security)
Ones connect to the high and low side of 4.
Ones connect to the high and low side of 7.

One's Connection to 7

Healthy connection to 7 supports qualities like playfulness, flexibility and good cheer. Ones relax their judgmental stances, let themselves play. Sensuality can emerge plus an improved sense of humor. Creative imagination is enhanced, an appreciation of paradox develops. Begin to enjoy life, loosen the rules and look for what's going right.

When more entranced, Ones fight their Sevenish feelings. May feel a desire for freedom which they squelch in the service of being good. "Illegal" impulses come through anyway. Ones having this struggle become less reliable, more hypocritical and escapist. Addictive appetite a factor, could drink alcohol to relax, for instance. Extreme version is episodic escapes, breaking completely free of the rules to go on illicit adventures. Called "trapdoor Ones."

Movie Ones who demonstrate this connection: Julie Andrews, *Mary Poppins;* Harrison Ford, *The Mosquito Coast;* Anthony Hopkins, *The Bounty;* Glenda Jackson, *House Calls;* Jack Lemmon, *Missing;* Fredric March, *Dr. Jekyll And Mr. Hyde;* Michael O'Keefe, *Nate And Hayes;* Joan Plowright, *Enchanted April;* Paul Scofield, *A Man For All Seasons;* Kiefer Sutherland, *Flashback.*

One's Connection to 4

Healthy connection to 4 brings Ones access to inner feelings and a romantic, sometimes poetic streak. Experience soulful, sometimes contradictory, feeling states. Discover how they really feel in contrast to the way they "should" feel. Creative artistic imagination combines with playful high side of 7. Attraction to art, however latent. Make place for the aesthetic and spiritual in their lives.

Down side can reinforce dissatisfaction with reality. Ones can get morose and feel sadly alone in their efforts to reform others. Fourish yearning to live in a better, more ideal society. Sense of defect that may sink into self-loathing and self-indictment. Turn their standards violently against themselves. May remorsefully vow to suppress their flaws which sets up the next episode of "bad" behavior. Self-indulgent Fourish sense of being exempt from normal consequences reinforces "trapdoor" syndrome mentioned earlier.

Movie Ones who demonstrate this connection: Katharine Hepburn, *Summertime;* Anthony Hopkins, *The Remains Of The Day;* Raul Julia, *Kiss Of The Spider Woman;* Fredric March, *Dr. Jekyll And Mr. Hyde;* Paul Newman, *Mr. And Mrs. Bridge;* Gregory Peck, *Old Gringo;* Joan Plowright, *Enchanted April;* Rosalind Russell, *Picnic;* Tom Skerritt, *A River Runs Through It.*

SUBTYPE THEMES

Self-Preservation

Characterized by a tendency towards worry and negative anticipation, especially as it relates to material well-being. Can seem a little like Sixes. They fret about how to avoid making mistakes that could jeopardize survival. Petty, finicky quality; could seem "penny-wise and pound-foolish." Sense of being undeserving or inadequate — try to compensate with worry. As a parent or friend, they might be critical and nurturing by turns, wanting to protect you from the same negative consequences they worry about.

Self-preservation Ones are not plentiful in movies, but some good examples are Hector Alterio in *The Official Story*, Melvyn Douglas in *I Never Sang For My Father*, Joel McCrea in *Ride The High Country*, and

Jessica Tandy in *Driving Miss Daisy.*

Intimate

May be preoccupied with their romantic partner. Have high expectations based on having idealized their beloved. Their partner is supposed to be perfect man or woman. One's reaction is jealous judgment if their beloved acts in less-than-ideal ways. Jealous Ones may drive partners away with endless criticism.

Can have a dependent tendency related to the low side of 2. Most intimate Ones have a 2 wing. Also there's a melancholy yearning and fear of abandonment fueling the One's criticism. Connection to the low side of 4.

I found very few intimate Ones in movies but Geraldine Page in *The Beguiled* displays some of this theme. In *The Official Story,* Hector Alterio's basic subtype is self-preservation but he has eruptions of jealousy that are based on his high expectations of his wife. Also Cliff Robertson shows this theme to a degree in the movie *Picnic.*

Social

Social subtype Ones are everywhere in the movies, probably because they create dramatic friction. Characterized by a preoccupation with rules and how they should apply to (other) people's behavior. Tend to moralize and apply old standards inflexibly to each new situation.

Believe they are representatives of a larger social order or tradition. They're not, of course — acting as if they represent the rules is their psychological defense. Usually had great uncertainty in childhood, at least one undependable parent. Made themselves rigid to feel strong, aligned with the rules to contain their anxiety. Tend to depersonalize their own feelings, hope to be above criticism.

Social Ones can have either wing, though a 9 wing brings rules that are more abstract and inhuman-sounding. Examples in the movies include Glenn Close in *The World According To Garp,* Louise Fletcher in *One Flew Over The Cuckoo's Nest,* Alec Guinness in *The Bridge On The River Kwai,* Raul Julia in *Kiss Of The Spider Woman,* Joan Plowright in *Enchanted April,* Jack Lemmon in *Missing,* Katharine Hepburn in *Rooster Cogburn.*

TWOS

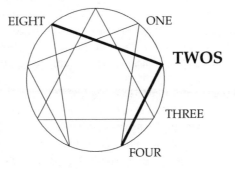

PEOPLE WHO SEE THE WORLD INTERPERSON-ALLY AND DEFINE THEMSELVES THROUGH SER-VICE TO OTHERS. MAY BE SELFLESS, LOVING AND GIVING OR DEPENDENT, PRIDEFUL AND HOSTILE.

FAMOUS REAL-LIFE TWOS

Alan Alda, Yasser Arafat, Tammy Faye Bakker, Child psychologist T. Berry Brazelton, Actress Ellen Burstyn, Barbara Bush, Jesus Christ, Glenn Close, Bill Cosby, Self-help author Barbara de Angelis, Feminist Betty Friedan, Kathie Lee Gifford, Danny Glover, Roosevelt Grier, Melanie Griffith, U.S. Ambassador Pamela Harriman, Leona Helmsley, Psychologist Karen Horney, Actress Anne Jackson, Author Erica Jong, Actress Sally Kellerman, Actress Sally Kirkland,

Jessica Lange, Jerry Lewis, Sophia Loren, Actress Susan Lucci, Madonna, Alma Mahler, Imelda Marcos, Maureen O'Hara, Merlin Olsen, Yoko Ono, Jack Paar, Dolly Parton, Fitness author Susan Powter, Priscilla Presley, Sally Jessy Raphael, Nancy Reagan, Mr. Rogers, Family therapist Virginia Satir, Rod Steiger, Sally Struthers, Mother Teresa, Marlo Thomas, Tiny Tim, Actress Lesley Ann Warren, Brazilian singer Xuxa.

INTRODUCTION

In the organization of the Enneagram, Twos, Threes and Fours form an "emotional trio," in that they share some general tendencies and undercurrents. People within this trio of styles can experience a kind of ongoing confusion about their identities, confusing *who* they are with the *roles* that they play and *images* of who they seem to be.

All personality styles do this to some degree, but Twos, Threes and Fours are most deeply prone to confuse *seeming* with *being*. They share a general tendency to lose track of how they actually feel, in favor of how they imagine they feel within the roles they are playing. People with these styles have the most conflicts in relationships and matters of the heart. They are least well-developed in the realm of core emotions.

Two is the most purely interpersonal of all the Enneagram styles. Twos are most apt to conceive of life as a fundamental give and take between people, regarding all human beings as members of one vast family. Within this point of view, giving love becomes the most important thing a Two can do.

People with this style have a well-developed capacity to identify emotionally with the needs of others. They have a strong unconscious habit of "sending" themselves over to other people and intuitively divining what another might be feeling or needing. Healthy Twos practice this habit voluntarily; they willingly identify with others as an act of love and can also then return to their own point of view. They are able to care for the needs of others and yet return to their own emotional truth and attend to their own needs. The phrase "lend yourself to others but give yourself to yourself" describes what Twos do when healthy.

The high side of this style is expressed through truly selfless love and exceptional ministerial skills. The Catholic nun Mother Teresa is an example of a Two who dedicates her daily life to the relief of suffering among the poor. Portraits of saints often describe the behavior of devoted Twos and descriptions of Jesus Christ read the same way. Whether or not it has succeeded, the classical intention of Christianity is fundamentally Twoish.

Living to give to others is tricky because you must be very honest about your motives and recognize that you have personal needs that may impact on your desire to give.

When Twos are more entranced, they begin to repress their own true needs and funnel their energies towards taking care of others — whether the others need it or not. Something happens to the Two's strategy of identifying with outside people; they still "send" themselves over to others, but now they forget to return to their own position. Instead, Twos form a codependent bond with another person and give in hopes of being recognized. Twos also can begin to fear abandonment and being alone. When overly identified with others, they lose their sense of themselves and, in a way, compulsive giving is an attempt to take care of their own lost self. Through others, Twos try to give back to themselves.

Flattery, manipulation and seduction are all used by Twos in the service of getting others to respond to and define them. The Two need to give is so strong that it becomes selfish and what is "given" comes with an invisible price tag. It's often a high price as the Two, in compensation for having lost their real self, begins to inflate and exaggerate the importance of their contributions.

Not surprisingly, Twos can have struggles in relationships because it's important to know your own true feelings and motives in order to relate cleanly to others. Their exaggerated self-importance is otherwise known as pride and when Twos are really unhealthy, pridefulness becomes their most striking feature.

What maddens others about unhealthy Twos is the way they package what *feels* like hostility as love. When Twos are deeply entranced, they are usually quite deluded about their motives. They replace their real feelings of selfish desperation and aggression with the image of an altruistic martyr who is owed big sums for their wonderful efforts.

The saintly high side of this style is very high indeed while the lowest expression can be drastically destructive. The motif of stalking an objectified "loved one" goes with the unhealthy side of this style as does the metaphor of the vampire, who lives on the blood of others.

TWOS IN THE MOVIES

Twos in the movies are a little difficult to generalize about. They tend not to be main characters but a few decades ago this wasn't true. Actresses like Bette Davis and Joan Crawford used to play romantic heroines who gave of themselves, usually to the wrong man. Elizabeth Taylor played tempestuous Twos in many movies and Natalie Wood had a string of roles where she played the style. A lot of actresses who had Twoish auras on screen had other Enneagram styles in real life.

For a long time, Two was an acceptable style for lead female roles in American movies but the roles were shaded to the submissive side of the style. As portraits of women became stronger and more complex, screenwriters began to feature fewer subservient Twos. This is culturally influenced as well; French films, for instance, still routinely have Two heroines. In current American movies, large roles for female Twos are usually in character studies.

I haven't mentioned male Two movie stars because I never really found any who play the style overtly. Two is generally identified with the feminine and male Two actors, at most, play a disguised version of the style. Actors like Danny Glover and Bill Cosby, for instance, project an interpersonal sensitivity that's appealing, yet their roles carefully emphasize worldly capabilities.

Other real-life Twos tend to be character actors and actresses. They either don't play their own style or they stick to supporting roles. It makes sense that the Two capacity for projective identification would fuel good character acting.

The most recent female star who invariably plays Twos on screen is Barbra Streisand. Early in her career, in role after role, she was the proud nurturer of others but a woman who also had an independent streak. Critics used to complain about her schizophrenic screen persona; one minute she was gooey over her man and in the next scene she was a militant feminist. Actually this split is very consistent with an intimate subtype (see "Subtype Themes"). Streisand brought this aura to nearly every role she played.

As we shall see, the healthy and unhealthy aspects of the Two style are often used in movie stories. Types of roles include: good mothers, exasperating mothers, mean mothers, saintly selfless helpers, interpersonal assistants (to main characters), clingy or histrionic lovers, seductive bimbos, egomaniacs, stalkers, and spoiled princes or princesses. Two is the style associated with the Jewish Mother stereotype but Two movie mothers come from all cultures, just as they do in real life.

MOVIE REVIEWS

Kiss Of The Spider Woman

This film features a well-detailed relationship between a Two and a One so it's a nice transition. *Kiss Of The Spider Woman* is about what happens when a gay window dresser (William Hurt) and a straight Marxist militant (Raul Julia) are thrown together in a South American jail. Story traces the evolution of their friendship from initial hostility to acceptance to mutual caring. Both learn from the other, Julia coming to admire Hurt's capacity for personal love while Hurt wakes to respect for Julia's commitment to social reform.

Hurt's character is effeminate, wears makeup and is highly identified with his mother. He passes prison time by narrating a shallow, glamorous love story that he keeps adding romantic chapters to. Julia listens, half carried away, but inevitably attacks Hurt for his triviality. Julia is serious about his politics — "What life offers me is a struggle. The most important thing is a cause." Hurt is capable of deceit (3 wing) but turns out able to sacrifice for a cause especially as it relates to people he cares for. The abstract Julia gradually relents his rigidities and begins to appreciate Hurt's ethos of personal love.

In an indirect way, the characters bring out each other's latent wing. Responding to Hurt, the impersonal, big-pictured Julia moves from his abstract 9 wing to his more caring, personal 2 wing. Hurt, in turn, moves from the vain, trivializing side of his 3 wing to an ethical, idealistic course of action consistent with his 1 wing.

Film is very good. Hurt won an Oscar for a brave performance. It's brave not because he's gay, but because the role steers so close to caricature yet Hurt still communicates the character's humanity. His exaggerated, dramatic mannerisms are essentially those of a drag queen. Yet, underneath, he perfectly captures a Two with a 3 wing.

Postcards From The Edge

Shirley MacLaine plays an overbearing Two mother to Meryl Streep's Six daughter. They are both film actresses, MacLaine a faded one while Streep is on a troubled drug-addicted rise.

As the story begins, Mother is highly competitive and intrusive towards Daughter. She has their identities thoroughly confused, wishes Streep would have the career that she failed to, and has unwelcome opinions about every aspect of her daughter's life.

Shirley MacLaine played a similar role in *Terms Of Endearment*. This time her character's motives are blatantly prideful — she inflates her own importance in her daughter's life to brighten up her own fading alcoholic star. She's unconsciously self-centered and rationalizes her motives away. She flirts with Streep's dates and talks over her with self-glorifying monologues. The more she denies her alcoholism, the more she nags her daughter about the latter's drug problems.

Progress comes late in the film after MacLaine has a car accident while driving drunk. She's shaken open. In the hospital, she begins to own up to her jealousy towards Streep and sees how tangled her motives have been. As this gets sorted out her genuine caring for her daughter begins to come through.

Streep's grandmother also plays a role in the emotional unfolding. She is a bossy, intrusive, bellicose Eight. MacLaine's character is suddenly shocked to recognize the similarity in their mothering styles. She is able to *see* and *hear* herself — something Twos can have trouble doing.

Meryl Streep is quite good in this comedy-drama. "I can see my life happening all around me but I can't feel it." "I know my mother loves me but I can't believe it." These statements of Sixish doubt reflect Streep's ambivalent turmoil throughout the film. She's afraid of her own power and addicted to drugs as a dependent reaction to anxiety. She is passive/aggressive, nervous, edgy and sarcastic.

Her mother both spoils and undercuts her, which is one way to create a Six. Someone who is pampered and hamstrung by turns is likely to have questions about their own strengths. MacLaine's prideful, blind domination is both resented *and* appreciated by Streep's character. A Six may rebel against authority but then depend upon the same authority for a sense of security and identity.

By the film's end, Streep starts to claim some of her own power. Streep has a 7 wing. Dennis Quaid shows up as a Seven and Gene Hackman plays a gruff but kind Eight.

REAL NICE TWOS

A lot of movie portrayals of Twos are mixed to negative so I wanted to highlight some characters from different films that show off the likable sides of the style. Some of these roles are larger than others but each is plenty distinct.

In The Spirit is a daffy New Age comedy-mystery with Marlo Thomas and Elaine May fleeing a murderer and learning to live by their underused wits. Thomas is a lovable, hapless interior designer who talks daily to her dead husband and has esoteric explanations for the most minor of events. She's scattered and fuzzy about her boundaries — "Let me help you!" is her mantra. Some of her more Twoish comments include:

"I try to see my sister-in-law once a week — she needs me, she smokes!"

"I don't know you and maybe I have no right to say this but you've *got* to stop eating meat."

"I've never gotten tired of or left anyone in my life! They've *always* had to leave me!"

Thomas really sparkles in this role, and as the plot unfurls the character remains lovable but also grows more grounded and sensible. Elaine May plays sort of an angry Nine, basically receptive but with flashes of 8 and 1. She's exasperated by Thomas but grows to like her. She takes on a little of Thomas's mystical world view as Thomas becomes more practical and humble.

Men Don't Leave features Jessica Lange in a sweet, small story about a Nine widow coping with single motherhood after her husband's sudden death. She has to move to a city to find work, gets involved with a musician and winds up working for Kathy Bates, an Eight. Her son (Chris O'Donnell) begins dating a slightly older neighbor, Joan Cusack, and she's the Two.

"I'm pretty good at helping people," Cusack likes to say in her odd, sweetly overbearing way. She's a little batty, off-center and regularly runs over O'Donnell ("Can we do something about your shirt? It's really not that flattering on you").

Cusack and Lange clash at first, but when Nine Lange suffers some setbacks, she gives up on life and goes to bed for a week. Cusack takes it upon herself to drag Lange out of bed and force her back into the world. Lange ultimately appreciates this intrusive gesture and it's obvious that Cusack is a sweetie.

Kathy Bates is very vividly Eightish. She is bossy, patronizing, dismissive, domineering, obnoxious and yet ultimately sympathetic. Blinded by narcissism, she has little idea of the effect of her communication style and yet underneath she's softhearted. The musician, by the way, is a Nine and he's played with dry, sleepy understatement by Arliss Howard.

Punchline casts Tom Hanks and Sally Field as neophyte nightclub comics fishing for their big breaks. They work out of a comedy club managed by Romeo (Mark Rydell), a Two. While this film doesn't quite come together, it has several excellent elements.

Field is a Six housewife and her side of the movie is about her conflict between pursuing comedy and being loyal to her family. Loyalty is a strong pull, but so is ambition. How she resolves the conflict is also very Sixish. John Goodman plays her husband with his usual Nine (8 wing) aura.

Tom Hanks gives a wrenching, sometimes brilliant performance as a bitter, competitive Four who has flunked out of medical school and draws humor from his own considerable pain. He falls, naturally, for the unavailable Field.

Rydell, the Two, is supportive and encouraging and tries to be equally helpful to his entire stable of comics. What's nice about the character is his honesty; part of what he offers is level criticism in addition to encouragement. He probably has a 1 wing. It's not what he gives, it's the way he gives it. Romeo's rooting for everyone and always happy when they succeed.

Call this film the "War of the Twos." **Zelly And Me** focuses on an orphaned little girl (Alexandra Johnes) sent to live with her grandmother (Glynis Johns) and watched over by governess Isabella Rossellini. Johns is a confused, somewhat mean Two, and Rossellini embodies the well-intentioned, loving high side of the style. In a way, they represent two aspects of the same character.

Rossellini has the capacity to love selflessly — "Whatever happens," she tells the child, "I am always with you and you are with me." She is merged with the child and is tender and straightforward in her concern.

Johns is a lot more confused about her motives. She thinks she is loving but she's actually demanding, punitive and jealous (low side of 4). At one point she browbeats the child:

"Say that you love me more than Mademoiselle (Rossellini)!"

The child refuses: "No, I love Mademoiselle."

To which Johns replies, "You're a bad girl. I take you into my house. I clothe you. I teach you manners. Don't you understand?

You're all *I* have in the world!"

This is called "giving to get," and it's the opposite of what Rossellini does with the girl. Johns goes to the nasty low side of 8 and the melancholy low side of 4.

The little girl is something of a budding Four. She lives in her creative imagination and is wistful for another life. She also internalizes Rossellini, "introjects" her. This means carrying a beloved person around inside of you and it's a specific habit of Fours (see "Fours").

She-Devil, Sophie's Choice

Meryl Streep double bill with the actress playing Twos in both films — one a comedy, the other a tragic-toned drama.

She-Devil is a brisk, feminist comedy about Roseanne Arnold (probable Nine, 8 wing) losing her flaky husband (Ed Begley Jr.) to rich, beautiful romance novelist Streep. Arnold spends the film slowly ruining their lives while rebuilding hers.

This film didn't do well because word got out that comedienne Arnold had the straight role and Streep was supposed to be funny. Actually she's *really* funny, playing a spoiled princess who lives in a tasteless, kitschy palace and can't stand too much reality. She has a strong 3 wing and lives very much within her romantic images. She speaks in a high, breathless voice, has exaggerated, melodramatic reactions and turns angrily Eightish when facts frustrate her glamorous expectations. This is a good comic portrayal of a Two and the rest of the film is reasonably fun. Linda Hunt has a small role as a friend of Roseanne's. She has the aura and manner of a Five with a 4 wing.

Sophie's Choice takes place in post-World War II America and focuses on Sophie, a Polish concentration camp survivor. Character study essays Sophie's relationship to a manic-depressive Seven (Kevin Kline) and writer/narrator Stingo (Peter MacNicol). Latter is a sort of Nine-by-default in that he plays the audience, but the character is not well developed. We witness events through his eyes and he is a reporter of stronger personalities than his own.

Streep's Sophie accents the codependent quality Twos can have ("Sophie loved to tell how Nathan had saved her life"). She's full of appreciation for Kline: "Thank you for making me to bloom like a rose." She also tends to romanticize her parents: "My father was a civilized man living in an uncivilized world," or, "No child ever had a more wonderful father and mother."

Sophie is exceedingly Fourish partly because it's a connecting point for a Two and partly because she's haunted by her concentration camp experiences. The story contains flashbacks so lengthy that it's really like two films. The one about the concentration camp is powerful and the other a bit draggy. Combined they are quite affecting.

The abusive quality of the Sophie/Nathan relationship is clear. She's hysterical and he's manic and they have lots of highs and lows. Still, Sophie is among the nicest of our movie Twos; you get the sense of a well-intentioned person who was overwhelmed and broken by ghastly events.

Nathan is described by Stingo as "utterly, fatally glamorous," and possessing a "generous mind." Kline vacillates between cheery Seven expansiveness and angry paranoia. This is partly what manic-depression is like and partly the behavior of a Seven with a 6 wing.

Star Trek V - The Final Frontier

The *Star Trek* series is generally enjoyable for its ensemble acting and busy space operatics. For those unfamiliar with the series, this installment is as good as most. *Star Trek IV- The Voyage Home* is faraway the best of the bunch.

Star Trek V features that movie rarity, a noneffeminate male Two. A renegade Vulcan kidnaps the Starship Enterprise and leads the Star Trek crew past the Great Barrier in search of a planet believed to be inhabited by God. God turns out not to be who He seems and even has an Enneagram style, that of an unhealthy Eight.

Based on the tenor of his comments, most Enneagram teachers agree that the historical Jesus was probably a Two. Sybok, the Vulcan, is an explicit Christ figure but without the self-transcendent quality. This is Jesus with an ego: Sybok is prideful, self-justifying, flamboyant and deluded about the loving purity of his motives. Mr. Spock describes him as "a passionate Vulcan who believes that the key to self-knowledge is emotion."

Actor Laurence Luckinbill is wisely allowed to steal the movie; he plays Sybok with the charisma and messianic zeal of a cult leader. You might notice the wet-eyed, earnest way he focuses in on people. His tone of voice is seductive but not sexual, inviting intimacy and offering soothing help. Sort of a siren song of codependency.

One of the Vulcan's tactics is to merge with another person and to draw them into a kind of therapeutic ritual. He sets it up by saying, "Your pain runs deep. Let us explore it together. Each man hides a secret pain. It must be exposed and reckoned with. Share your pain with *me* and gain strength!" The result of this "sharing" is a melted-down, vulnerable convert who believes that Sybok is a savior and will follow him anywhere. (This is how cult leaders do it, folks.)

Elsewhere Sybok says, "I don't control minds — I free them!" and charges on with naïve certainty about the goodness of his mission. This confusion about motive and blindness to self-interest can be a problem for Twos. Far from being altruistic, Sybok seems lonely, longs for approval and is searching for a symbolic father in his quest to find God (connection to 4). He tells Captain Kirk, "I so much want your respect." After Kirk replies that Sybok is insane, the latter looks genuinely wounded.

When things go rather badly in the meeting with God, Sybok realizes his blindness, and repents his pride ("This is my arrogance, my vanity!"). He makes an authentic sacrifice that reflects a jump from the low to the high side of Two.

For *Star Trek* fans, Captain Kirk is a Three with a 4 wing. He's competitive and performance-oriented, yet thoughtful and humanistic. I've read and seen interviews with actor William Shatner and he too is a Three with a 4 wing, so this would be Enneatype casting. * Dr. McCoy is a One with a 2 wing. He's cranky, rigid and judgmental. Much humor is mined from his principled eruptions.

The other regular characters are underwritten. Chekov might be a Six. Scotty, the Chief Engineer, is likely an extroverted Nine with an 8 wing. He plays the kind of sidekick role usually reserved for movie Nines, but he's grumpy and aggressive at times.

In Enneagram books, Mr. Spock has been pegged as both a One (9 wing) and a Five. In the old (and truly awful) TV show, Spock was definitely a One. He was rigid, principled and logical — a kind of preachy know-it-all.

In the subsequent movies, actor Leonard Nimoy drolly underplays the character and it's written differently. The movie emphasis is on Spock's emotional reserve and uninfluenceable quality ("I am not predisposed to reveal things of a personal nature"). He still values logical courses of action but not necessarily the *right* course of action. He seems more like a Five in the films, but confusion is possible because a One with a 9 wing can be very impersonal and withdrawn like a Five. What cinched it for me was seeing actor Nimoy interviewed at length;

he's a real-life One and based Spock on his own character.

If you have seen the *Star Trek* spinoff, *Star Trek - The Next Generation*, Spock's rough equivalent is an android named Data. This character is a Five (6 wing), a living computer who is forever trying to find human feeling within himself (latent 4 wing). Captain Picard is an inventive, flexible One. He sorts for multiple options (high side of 7), has a melancholy streak (connection to 4), but Picard's basic commitment is to ideals. His second in command, Commander Riker, is a Three with a 4 wing just like Captain Kirk.

The Klingon Worf is a One with a 9 wing. He is sharp-tempered but has the abstract, removed quality of a Nine. Counselor Deanna Troi, the ship's psychotherapist, is a passive, receptive, empathic Nine. She has the Good Girl/Model Child aura that Nines with 1 wings often display.

* Just about a week after I first published this review, excerpts from Shatner's reminiscences about *Star Trek* were published. Here is what he says about the Captain Kirk role and his own personality:

"I always played Kirk fairly close to home. Kirk's wisdom, courage and heroic capacities were all fictional, but at his core he was, for the most part, me. I wasn't so much acting as I was reacting. We were basically one and the same although Jim was about perfect and I, of course, am perfect."

STUPID CREEPY THRILLERS (SCTs)

Unhealthy Twos can be maliciously selfish, all the while believing they are acting in the name of love. A number of suspense movies have based their plots on this tendency. An unhealthy Two character will fasten their "love" obsessively on the main character and plague them dangerously, invading the boundaries of the other's life, until the Two has to be stopped with force. The Twos show lots of hostility (low side of 8) and usually some melancholy yearning (low side of 4).

Fatal Attraction is a good example of the genre. Clearly made by men, this film put the women's movement back a few years with its portrayal of career woman as nutso succubus. On another level, though, Glenn Close is playing a very accurate Two. Almost immediately after bedding down with married man Michael Douglas, she starts invading his life at every turn.

"I'm not going to be ignored!" she screams histrionically. Her character's initial lack of definition is the flip side of her later hostile self-inflation. She does it all for pride and to stave off a yawning emptiness. This is a good portrait of what's called a borderline personality — an unhealthy Two with big boundary problems.

Douglas is playing a Niney character but it's not really clear. Film is slick and skillful but also hollow as a drain pipe. It is almost a remake of 1971's **Play Misty For Me**. Jessica Walter played the crazy Two (scarier than Glenn Close) and Clint Eastwood had the ambivalent Nine role.

Misery is more intelligent than *Fatal Attraction* and Kathy Bates won an Academy Award for her role as the "Number One Fan" of writer James Caan. Latter has a horrible car accident in the middle of winter and is rescued by Bates and kept in her mountain home.

"I'm your Number One Fan. You're going to be just fine," she tells him. "You've got a lot of recovering to do and I consider it an honor that you will be doing it in my home."

"We're put on this earth to help people, Paul, as I'm trying to help you. Help me to help you, Paul."

He does need help — his legs are broken — and it's only gradually that he recognizes that the flattering, helpful Bates is actually murderously hostile.

This highly exaggerated character embodies the split Twos can have between ostensible giving and hidden selfishness. The more she waits on him, the more demanding she grows, even to the point of burning his latest manuscript and making him rewrite it. She's not seductive like Glenn Close was; Bates's character would be more a self-preservation subtype who expects special treatment in return for all she gives.

Bates masks her hostility with a disassociated good girl role. She has a warped 1 wing, and plays at an image of goodness. She's not sexually seductive, but instead acts like a prepubescent child. She talks in baby talk, objects to swearing and says things to Caan like: "Forgive me for making you feel all oogie." As her hostility more openly emerges she starts to swear. She later breaks Caan's foot with a hammer as she says, "God, I love you."

This is a high grade SCT that builds its suspense in small increments. Caan has a Niney, passive-reactor role but he also seems a little like a Four. Richard Farnsworth, who always plays Nines, is a sheriff looking for Caan. Frances Sternhagen, who always plays Ones, is Farnsworth's scrappy wife.

Unlawful Entry mixes up *Fatal Attraction*'s ingredients and pours them into a different pie pan. This time the Two is a male cop (Ray Liotta) who fastens his obsession onto a scared Six (Madeleine Stowe), who's married to Eight architect played by Kurt Russell. They are a troubled yuppie couple, victims of a burglary, who first take comfort in the overly solicitous Liotta.

When hotheaded Russell sees through Liotta's manipulations, the cop begins to invade the couple's life and uses the force of law against them. Russell is framed for a crime and jailed so that Liotta can move in on Stowe.

The story gets *really* stupid, but since it's character-driven, there are some worthwhile Enneagram dynamics. Russell is a decisive Eight and scaredy-cat Six Stowe lets him take care of her. Under stress, however, Russell gets loud and authoritarian and Stowe goes defiant. She also yo-yos in her loyalties, a weakness that the seductive Liotta plays upon. He offers her police protection, especially appealing to a scared Six.

Liotta acts little-boyish with Stowe, pretending to be shy and speaking in a baby voice. This is part of the seduction: Twos will sometimes make themselves seem childlike to ingratiate and appear nonthreatening. Later their voice tones can change ... Liotta, like all the villain Twos, is destructively Eightish.

Truth Or Dare

This is the film that unconsciously asks the question: "What if you were paid $30 million a year to blindly act out your Enneagram style?" This documentary about singer Madonna follows her on tour and shows us a thoroughly flaming Two. The prideful, interpersonal tendencies of the style are evident in most everything Madonna says and does.

Within the intensity of show touring it's quickly clear that the singer has structured her world so that it reflects entirely back on her. She has a strong need for positive feedback from others and assigns herself the role of mother hen to her crew and group of dancers. Of the latter she says: "By the time we left Japan I found myself growing really attached to the dancers and I started feeling like a mother to them. When we finally got to America I got the chance to meet the mothers of all the children I had temporarily claimed as my own."

As a mother, Madonna is pretty confused in her motives. Most of her statements reflect the sincere desire to give fused with patronizing self-interest. Here's how she talks about the dancers:

"They're innocents — they haven't been anywhere — this tour was the opportunity of their lives. They've suffered a great deal, whether with their families or being poor or whatever, and I wanted to give them the thrill of their lives. I wanted to impress them. *I* wanted to love them."

She reflects a little later on her own motivations, but even her insights are fraught with pride:

"I think I've unconsciously chosen people who are emotionally crippled in some way or need mothering in some way because I think it comes very naturally to me. It fulfills a need in *me* ... to be mothered."

Mixed-up Twos mother by metaphor. That is, they give to someone else in a confused attempt to give to themselves. This is what Madonna's talking about, and she demonstrates it constantly. "Let Momma get her makeup done," she tells one hovering adult dancer. When he leaves, she says, "Oh God, I just love having children to watch over." Later she holds a prayer before a show that *she's* anxious about and says: "All my little babies are feeling fragile and I just want you to know that I love you all and I appreciate everything that you are doing for me and I'm here if you need me."

Madonna has a strong 3 wing which brings ambition and social effectiveness as well as an extra dose of vanity. Her 1 wing is smaller; it comes out in her concern about AIDS victims and also in her reaction to censorship. Madonna's father asks her if she could tone down the sexual content of her show and she replies, "No, because that would be compromising my artistic integrity!" She's also histrionic on the subject of being an artist, a trait related to the low side of 4. When it rains in Japan, she says, "I think the only thing that kept me from slashing my wrists was the thought of coming back to America and doing the show as it should be done." Some of Madonna's slow-paced songs are very melancholy, a Two connected to her own Fourish emotions. Offstage she also shows flashes of 8.

There are three subtype themes within the Two style and Madonna demonstrates a mash of them all. Intimate Twos act seductive as a means of eliciting sexual attraction and therefore approval. A seductive Two may have little actual interest in following through on an attraction and in Madonna's case, her sexuality is channelled into her public persona. She wants to attract you to know that she's worthwhile and she switches on the persona almost constantly. This subtype can also get aggressive to get attention or break through to deeper relationship.

The main subtype theme she has is ambition. Twos, especially with a 3 wing, can affiliate with powerful people or will have their own ambitions as they lead to being seen and accepted (Madonna's tour is called "Blonde Ambition"). Madonna's deliberately provocative style is also consistent with this subtype. She doesn't care if you like her as long as you notice her.

A third subtype theme for Twos takes a "Me First" attitude and acts out of a sense of haughty entitlement. Madonna would feel justified acting like a prima donna considering how much she believes she gives to others.

OTHER MOVIE TWOS

Isabelle Adjani, *The Story Of Adele H*; Bibi Andersson, *Persona*; Anne Bancroft, *'Night Mother*; Shirley Booth, *Come Back, Little Sheba*; Betty Buckley, *Tender Mercies*; Leo Buscaglia, *Politics Of Love*; Leslie Caron, *Damage*; Glenn Close, *Meeting Venus*; Tom Courtenay, *The Dresser*; Jaye Davidson, *The Crying Game*; Geena Davis, *The Accidental Tourist*; Maynard Eziashi, *Mr. Johnson*; Iain Glen, *Fools Of Fortune*; Danny Glover, *Lonesome Dove*; Joel Grey, *Man On A Swing*; Linda Hunt ("Billy Kwan"), *The Year Of Living Dangerously*;

Glynis Johns, *Mary Poppins*; Lainie Kazan, *My Favorite Year*; Lila Kedrova, *Zorba The Greek*; Angela Lansbury, *The Manchurian Candidate*; Piper Laurie, *Carrie*; Shirley MacLaine, *Being There*; Bette Midler, *Down And Out In Beverly Hills*; Helen Mirren, *The Comfort Of Strangers*; Kate Nelligan, *The Prince Of Tides*; Marisa Paredes, *High Heels*; Priscilla Presley, *The Naked Gun*; Diana Ross, *Mahogany*; Isabella Rossellini, *Blue Velvet*;

Michel Serrault, *La Cage Aux Folles*; John Shea, *A New Life*; Martin Short, *The Big Picture*; Rod Steiger, *Guilty As Charged, The Loved One*; Margaret Sophie Stein, *Enemies: A Love Story*; David Strathairn, *Judgment*; Barbra Streisand, *The Way We Were*; Elizabeth Taylor, *Little Women*; Lee Tracy, *Dinner At Eight*; Lesley Ann Warren, *Songwriter, Victor/Victoria*; Charles White Eagle, *Three Warriors*.

FINER DISTINCTION NOTES

WINGS: Twos can have a 1 wing, a 3 wing or both wings.

Two With a 1 Wing

This wing brings conscience and emotional containment to the basic Two style. When healthy, they act from general principles about the value of serving others. Ethics come before pride. May hold themselves to high standards. More discreet and respectful of other people's boundaries. When upset, tend to go quiet and experience strong emotions internally. More melancholy than Twos with a 3 wing.

When less healthy and entranced, tend to confuse their sense of mission with self-centered needs. Go blind to their own motives; invade and dominate others. Believe their actions are perfectly justified by their ethic of helping. May repress their personal desires and focus on others as a way to avoid guilty dilemma between the rules and their inner needs. If really blind they will warp their ethics crazily to justify personal selfishness and prideful hostility.

Real-Life Twos With a 1 Wing: Yasser Arafat, T. Berry Brazelton, Barbara Bush, Jesus Christ, Bill Cosby, Betty Friedan, Danny Glover, Pamela Harriman, Jerry Lewis, Mr. Rogers, Virginia Satir.
Movie Twos With a 1 Wing: Kathy Bates, *Misery*; Joan Cusack, *Men Don't Leave*; Piper Laurie, *Carrie*; Laurence Luckinbill, *Star Trek V - The Final Frontier*; Kate Nelligan, *The Prince Of Tides*; Barbra Streisand, *The Way We Were*; Marlo Thomas, *In The Spirit*; Charles White Eagle, *Three Warriors*.

Two With a 3 Wing

This wing brings Twos an extra measure of sociability and the capacity to make things happen. When healthy, can be charming, good-natured and heartfelt. Really get things done, serve effectively on projects that involve the well-being of others. Thrive on group process and are generally good communicators. Enjoy keeping several threads or projects going at once.

Entranced Twos with a 3 wing can be quite emotionally competitive and controlling. 3 wing brings a double dose of vanity. Strong tendency to live in one's images. May grow brazenly deluded, preferring their glamorous, self-important scenarios to reality. Tendencies to deceit and emotional calculation. Highly manipulative. This wing is also more extroverted; dramatization of feeling in the form of hysterical snit-fits is far more possible.

Real-Life Twos With a 3 Wing: Kathie Lee Gifford, Leona Helmsley, Sally Kirkland, Susan Lucci, Madonna, Imelda Marcos, Dolly Parton, Susan Powter, Nancy Reagan.
Movie Twos With a 3 Wing: Glenn Close, *Meeting Venus;* Maynard Eziashi, *Mr. Johnson;* Joel Grey, *Man On A Swing;* William Hurt, *Kiss Of The Spider Woman;* Angela Lansbury, *The Manchurian Candidate;* Shirley MacLaine, *Postcards From The Edge;* Madonna, *Truth Or Dare,* Michel Serrault, *La Cage Aux Folles;* Meryl Streep, *She-Devil.*

CONNECTING POINTS (Stress and Security)
Twos connect to the high and low side of 4.
Twos connect to the high and low side of 8.

Two's Connection to 4

Like Ones, Twos have an emotional connection to 4. Their feelings also tend to have a melancholy flavor. Healthy connection to 4 helps Twos develop their inner life and maintain an independent, possibly artistic point of view. Shift focus off roles and other people, search for themselves within. A need for self-expression and creative release often follows. Connection helps with emotional honesty as Twos start to see the dark side of giving and their own tangle of mixed motives. Admit their emotional complexity and personal needs.

When more entranced, this connection brings a tendency towards self-pity, obsessive love and depression. May become guilt-inducing martyrs haunted by melancholy. Disown their capacity to be alone. Begin to fear abandonment. Can slip into unrequited love scenarios or develop romantic obsessions. Low side of 8 fuels aggression in the pursuit of a romanticized other. The low side of this connection can also bring a haughty artistic pretentiousness and, occasionally, a streak of morbidity.

Movie Twos who demonstrate this connection: Isabelle Adjani, *The Story Of Adele H;* Linda Hunt, *The Year Of Living Dangerously;* William

Hurt, *Kiss Of The Spider Woman*; Laurence Luckinbill, *Star Trek V*; Madonna, *Truth Or Dare*; Isabella Rossellini, *Zelly And Me*; Meryl Streep, *She-Devil, Sophie's Choice*; Barbra Streisand, *The Way We Were*; Marlo Thomas, *In The Spirit*; Charles White Eagle, *Three Warriors*.

Two's Connection to 8

Healthy connection to 8 helps a Two make stronger personal boundaries and assert their own needs. Develop and express an appropriate honest selfishness. Brings self-confidence and a direct, almost blunt communication style. Have force of personality for getting things done, especially projects related to their inner sense of mission. May care less about other people's opinions. Can be quite decisive; do well in leadership positions.

The low side of a Two's connection to 8 brings anger and aggression in the service of self-importance. Vengeful blaming. Demanding, prima donna behavior. If a Two's pride is insulted or they feel underappreciated they can act out nastily like an unhealthy Eight. Two then goes on thinking they are a caring, giving person and blocks out evidence of their own hostility. If more unhealthy, they can turn persecutory, using their sensitivity to others to gather ammunition for outbursts of Eightish cruelty. True hatred and acts of violent retribution possible.

Movie Twos who demonstrate this connection: Kathy Bates, *Misery*; Glenn Close, *Fatal Attraction*; Jaye Davidson, *The Crying Game*; Glynis Johns, *Zelly And Me*; Ray Liotta, *Unlawful Entry*; Laurence Luckinbill, *Star Trek V*; Shirley MacLaine, *Postcards From The Edge*.

SUBTYPE THEMES

Self-Preservation

Self-preservation Twos often harbor a striking sense of entitlement. May act superior to others and expect preferential treatment that reinforces their pride. Can seem shameless in their expectation of pampering. Behind this attitude is a logic that says, "I give and do so much for others, I deserve to be treated as someone special." Like an unconscious collection of fees for sacrifices made. Others who encounter this attitude are often amazed at a self-preservation Two's self-importance and diva-like behavior.

Real-life people with this subtype often have a 3 wing. Dip easily to the low side of 8 when angry. Not many movie examples, but Kathy Bates displays some of this theme in *Misery*. Glynis Johns has some of it in *Zelly And Me*, as does Madonna in *Truth Or Dare*. A notorious real-life self-preservation Two is American hotelier Leona Helmsley.

Intimate

Tend to act seductive and aggressive by turns. Basic interest is in finding romantic union. Generally confuse sexual desirability with being loved and valued. Act receptively interested in others, use inviting touches. May ooze some combination of charm and sexuality.

When they encounter resistance will begin to push and challenge. Try to find a way around the other's objection. May go militant and angrily blame (connection to 8). Behind these flare-ups is a melancholy desire for total enmeshed connectedness to another. Yearning is related to the low side of 4.

Barbra Streisand in *The Way We Were* is an exact depiction of this subtype. Other examples include William Hurt in *Kiss Of The Spider Woman*, Ray Liotta in *Unlawful Entry*, Glenn Close in *Fatal Attraction*.

Social

Twos with this subtype are notable for their ambition, particularly to be publicly recognized as someone special. Seek attention either directly from their own efforts or via affiliation with powerful people. In the former scenario, a Two works to draw an audience through socially useful works or some kind of performing. Confuse being noticed with being loved. Can sometimes act provocative or obnoxious as this is better than being ignored.

Might also marry someone influential and concentrate their energies on the spouse's ambitions. Can groom their children to become achievers. Stage mothers and political spouses are possible roles. Often have a 3 wing but a 1 wing is possible.

Video examples include: Madonna, *Truth Or Dare*; Angela Lansbury, *The Manchurian Candidate*; Laurence Luckinbill, *Star Trek V*; Shirley MacLaine, *Postcards From The Edge*; Marisa Paredes, *High Heels*; Rosalind Russell, *Gypsy*.

THREES

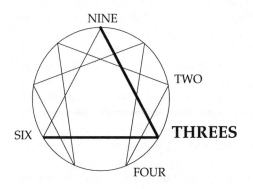

NINE

TWO

SIX

THREES

FOUR

PEOPLE WHO MEASURE THEMSELVES BY EXTERNAL ACHIEVEMENT AND THE ROLES THAT THEY PLAY. MAY BE ACCOMPLISHED, HONEST AND EXCELLENT OR CONNIVING, COMPETITIVE AND FALSE.

FAMOUS REAL-LIFE THREES

The cultural aura of America, Former U.S. Secretary of State James Baker, David Bowie, Jimmy Carter, Dick Clark, Joseph Cotten, Joan Crawford, Tom Cruise, Rebecca DeMornay, Nora Ephron, Werner Erhard, F. Scott Fitzgerald, NBC's Bryant Gumbel, Actor Mark Harmon, the (modern) cultural aura of Japan, Michael Jordan, Mary Kay, Carl Lewis, Rob Lowe, Joan Lunden, Ali MacGraw, Singer Reba McEntire, Football commentator Don Meredith, Joe Montana,

Demi Moore, Martina Navratilova, U.S. Senator Bob Packwood, Reporter/author Sally Quinn, Businessman Summer Redstone, Burt Reynolds, Self-help author Anthony Robbins, Political strategist Ed Rollins, Reporter Diane Sawyer, Arnold Schwarzenegger, William Shatner, Cybill Shepherd, O.J. Simpson, Wesley Snipes, Reporter Lesley Stahl, Sylvester Stallone, Sharon Stone, Kathleen Turner, Jean-Claude Van Damme, Austrian President Kurt Waldheim, "Father" of America George Washington, Raquel Welch, Author Marianne Williamson, Oprah Winfrey, Natalie Wood.

INTRODUCTION

Unlike Twos, people with the Three style identify less with ideals of helpfulness and instead with images of success and productivity. Threes often expect to be loved for what they *do* rather than who they are. Their image-confusion is between *seeming* accomplished and *being* true to their less-than-perfect inner self. Entranced Threes most tend to cut off deeper feeling in favor of outer appearance. They deny their imperfections and present a public image they hope the world finds laudable.

Healthy Threes are often highly accomplished and practice a credo of excellence and professionalism in whatever they do. They are extremely strong at setting and meeting goals and will usually have mastered a number of life skills. Threes learn fast, make good leaders, and do well in high-profile, socially established occupations where performance is measured by results. Most are organized, flexible and industrious. When healthy, they usually make excellent role models and teachers of the skills they have mastered.

Awakened Threes can be energetic and cheerful, with a positive eye to the future and a self-confident, open approach to challenges. Their actions are often governed by a sense of honor; family and friendship are valued in addition to work. These priorities are sometimes arrived at after a struggle with moral expediency and through a Three's conscious search for values.

When Threes are more entranced, the strategy of *being* successful and well-rounded yields to a desire to *seem* that way. Corners start getting cut in the quest to maintain an image. A Three can slip into impersonation and play a role of themselves, adopting chameleon-like poses to seem noteworthy in many different contexts. Personal feeling begins to be denied as a Three increasingly identifies with their mask. Most have an "Achilles Heel," a sense of inadequacy that they compensate for with achievement and role-playing.

Intimate relationships can suffer as the Three reroutes their feelings through their image of who they *should* be. They may present a persona to intimates; hiding a deep sense of flaw and instead offering a feelingful mask for others to love. Expediency and efficiency become more important and an entranced Three may begin to enjoy the feeling of nonfeeling. They may think of themselves as high-performance engines whose purpose is to race with speed from task to task, securing outcomes before dashing on to new finish lines. It's not uncommon for entranced Threes to talk in sports metaphors and make themselves believe that life is only a game, a game that's played to win.

To win, they may push themselves harder, enjoying the hyperactivity, now using their relationships mainly as springboards for professional gain. Their once healthy flexibility might degenerate into arrogant calculation and amoral strategizing. Entranced Threes comfortably operate in occupations where appearance and persuasion are all — public relations, sales, advertising, etc.

When deeply entranced, winning becomes everything and a Three's mask just eclipses their soul. They sell out completely to *seeming* and make themselves into a commodity to market. A core of malicious hostility replaces their true identity at this stage.

Unhealthy Threes can be amoral, Machiavellian, heartless, slick, and plagiarizing. They believe their own lies and con people without conscience. They work hard to best or deceive others. The aim is to maintain an illusion of superiority from which they derive a hollow, vindictive sense of triumph. Anyone who has ever been deliberately and maliciously lied to has felt the sting of this attitude.

The Three's defensive tendencies towards playing roles, masking their true motives and identifying with success are on display in many of the movies below.

THREES IN THE MOVIES

Real-life Three performers tend to practice what is called "personality acting." This means that they establish a screen persona that they essentially play from role to role. Once in a while they may break out of the persona to play a much different character but inevitably they return to their core style.

There are obvious economic reasons for this pattern, but there's another level that is related to the psychology of Threes. A real-life tendency to project a persona and play a role of one's self would be perfect practice for becoming a personality actor on film. Most successful personality performers have loads of screen presence but lack range. They are almost always considered movie stars rather than character actors.

If the objective in acting is to play characters distant from your own personality, then Three performers don't really act. They make up for it, though, with star power. Joan Crawford, Natalie Wood and Burt

Reynolds are good examples of former Three movie stars. All had limited talent but projected a charisma that they made the most of. Currently, actress Demi Moore is someone with much movie star chemistry who might have to work extra hard at character acting.

Tom Cruise is a good example of a real-life Three who almost always plays them in the movies. In most of his films he's cast as a callow young man who cuts ethical corners and is either preoccupied with winning (*Days Of Thunder, All The Right Moves*), or is seduced by success and then acquires integrity (*A Few Good Men, The Firm, Rain Man*). These stories are peculiarly American and reflect the fact that American culture is essentially Threeish in its values and preoccupations.

A lot of movie action heroes are real-life Threes, including Sylvester Stallone, Jean-Claude Van Damme and Arnold Schwarzenegger. Although their Enneagram style is usually implicit, they often play very focused, goal-oriented figures. Most of Stallone's movies are about coming from behind and winning. His *Rocky* movies show a Niney guy who gathers focus and turns into a winner Three.

Arnold Schwarzenegger is on display as a real-life Three in the documentary *Pumping Iron*, but his fictional roles have an odd connection to Three psychology. In the movie *Total Recall* he plays a Niney character who has amnesia for his true identity. He eventually discovers that his former self was a sleazy Three and that he's married to a Three woman who is also not who she seems to be. Not to put too fine a point on it, but Schwarzenegger's role as "The Terminator" — a goal-focused, hyperefficient, emotionless robot — actually reflects a neurotic ideal that Threes sometimes aspire to.

Unless they are hard-bitten career women who sacrifice love for ambition (Faye Dunaway, *Network*; Joan Crawford, *Mildred Pierce*), most female movie Threes are alluring, haughty beauties who are just out of reach, playing a role of desirability.

Three movie roles otherwise run the range from truth-questing heroes to scoundrel/heroes to fabulists to sociopaths. Special mention needs to be made of the Evil Corporate Three. This type of villain is present in lots of films; they are usually businessmen, sometimes politicians, and they always put profit over morality. There are at least twenty listed throughout the *Video Guide*.

MOVIE REVIEWS

Basic Instinct

Eightish Michael Douglas plays a troubled and deeply stupid homicide detective investigating an ice pick murder. Chief suspect is chilly, rich novelist Sharon Stone, a Three.

Stone is hard, manipulative and an actress in her own life. The character is similar to Kathleen Turner's below. Both are intimate subtypes, playing roles of desirable women (see "Finer Distinction Notes"). Though she's portrayed as aggressively seductive, sexuality is not what drives Stone's duplicity and game-playing. Rather, she has a heart that she's trying not to feel, and she spins illusions to control her emotions and environment. This emotional-management-through-scenario is reflected in the way she arranges life to imitate the story lines of her novels.

It helps to know that she's a Three because the story is both misogynistic *and* homophobic. *Basic Instinct* freely panders to the chuckleheaded notion that Stone's character might be driven to murder because she's a lesbian man-hater. This is the kind of movie where a woman who preaches sexual independence from men would just naturally turn out to be a serial killer.

Overall, the film is glossy, lurid and rather peculiar. It was a big hit, so go figure. The mystery is no great shakes either, but Stone is better than the movie and instructive as a Three. In an accidental way, *Basic Instinct* is about men's fears of women. Stone's deceitful, alluring character matches the archetype of the Siren. Female Threes who are intimate subtypes often have a specific function in movies — to lie to men and lure them to their doom.

Dangerous Liaisons, Valmont

These two films offer a fascinating contrast for our purposes. They tell different versions of the same story and were released within a year of one another. The story line — about deceit and vanity — is strongly driven by the main character's Threeness. The two actors — John Malkovich and Colin Firth — play Valmont quite differently but both nicely capture the style. Most of the other major characters are the same in both films, so this makes an interesting double bill. If you haven't seen either one, start with *Valmont* and then compare its characters with those in the more entertaining *Dangerous Liaisons*.

The story is about sexual gamesmanship among aristocrats in 18th century France. The main character Valmont (Malkovich, Firth) enters a competitive wager with an ex-lover (Glenn Close, Annette Bening). She challenges Valmont to deflower the virginal daughter of a friend because the daughter (Uma Thurman, Fairuza Balk, both Nines) is to marry Close/Bening's current lover. Her motive is revenge against the lover (who thinks he is marrying a virgin). She further challenges Valmont to seduce the virtuous wife of a minister (Michelle Pfeiffer, Meg Tilly, both Nines), a pious woman who is by reputation incorruptible.

Three Valmont sneeringly takes the challenge, the reward being the sexual favors of Close/Bening, whom he secretly loves. The scheme is set in motion but over the course of the story, everyone involved is tragically undone. Cunning Valmont's surprise flaw is that he has a heart, a fact he discovers when he falls in love with the woman he has set out to ruin.

John Malkovich invests his role with charisma and panache, and plays Valmont as an intimate subtype. He has lust for the game and arrogantly revels in his skills as a sexual imposter.

Firth lacks Malkovich's venom and tang. He plays Valmont as a social subtype, someone who thinks his status will improve if he wins the game. He seems more juvenile and accepts the challenge as though it were some larkish prank. With Malkovich there is the feeling that his whole personality is riding on his ability to win the wager. His subsequent undoing is all the more poignant for this reason.

The other interesting contrast is between the Glenn Close and Annette Bening roles. Both have identical functions within the story, but they have different Enneagram styles and different motivations for initiating the wager. Close is an Eight and her drive is to be strong and prevail over a world of men. She tells Malkovich: "I've always known that I was born to dominate your sex and avenge my own. In the end, I distill everything to one simple precept — win or die." She wants to win, as a Three would, but in a way that makes her strong. Elsewhere she mentions her determination to "never again be ordered around."

Bening's Three wants to win, but more to recover from a wounding of her vanity. Her desire for revenge is not specifically in the service of having a strong self so much as to maintain a narcissistic self-image. She's attached to her persona and her motive for ruining her ex-lover almost seems like revenge for his cracking her mask ("No one has ever left *me* before"). She's relentlessly false and duplicitous in all of her relationships. She has a 2 wing and is chameleon-like with each person she manipulates.

Stephen Frears, who directed *Dangerous Liaisons,* went on to make *The Grifters,* which is about Three con-artists who come to tragic ends. Then Frears made the movie *Hero,* about an imposter who has qualms about the role he plays.

Malkovich plays a decidedly similar character in *In the Line of Fire,* although the story couldn't be more different from *Dangerous Liaisons.* In *Fire* he's a sociopathic assassin trying to outwit Eight Secret Service man Clint Eastwood. He's crazier and not an intimate subtype, but otherwise a Three with a 4 wing with the same world view. Malkovich is very good and Eastwood gives a winning, endearing performance in an exciting thriller.

Downhill Racer

Early Robert Redford movie about a competitive cad, a Three who wants to qualify for the U.S. Olympic ski team in the worst way. Everything has been subsumed by his athletic goals and the film coolly shows the cost. He's hard, hollow and emotionally inarticulate.

Best moment comes when Redford goes home to Idaho and is asked by his farmer father why he even wants to qualify for the team. Redford looks uncomfortably bewildered and blurts, "If I win I'll be a champion!" Father thinks for a moment and says dryly, "World's full of 'em."

The father is stingy, uncommunicative, and Fiveish. He won't give his son a chance. It's not unusual for a Three to have an emotionally distant parent for whom the child performs. The achievements are an attempt to leap over the distance and try to get the parent's recognition.

In the end the skier wins but, of course, really loses. Camilla Sparv plays a glamorous, empty woman whom Redford takes up with, and she's pretty much a Three as well.

Good documentary style film with exciting ski sequences.

IMPOSTER MOVIES

There are many films about imposters and they often involve

Threes. Most of the story lines have similar tensions to *Dangerous Liaisons*. The main character falsely sells him or herself and then is undone, either by falling in love or because the impersonation backfires in some way. Sometimes the Three gets in touch with some genuine feelings, sometimes they get punished, sometimes they happily get away with the scam. The following short reviews start with sympathetic and comic imposters and then progress to the more villainous variety.

Bed And Breakfast features Roger Moore (the former James Bond) as a man on the run from a powerful gangster Moore has scammed. He hides out at a small-town bed and breakfast owned by Talia Shire (One, 2 wing). Sparks fly initially between them because Shire is Oneishly fighting her attraction to Moore, and besides, she knows he's up to something and ethically disapproves.

Moore asks her: "Have you ever told a lie?"

"No! Why would I?" she asks.

"For convenience, for profit, for fun!"

"Lying isn't fun!"

"Then you've not been telling the right lies."

He eventually confesses to his career as a con-man ("I've never been an honest man"), but it's clear that his developing affections for everyone in the household are genuine. He's truthful within his façade, a charmer yet well-meaning.

This is a slender film but it's kind of enjoyable, almost wholesome. Moore's no John Gielgul, but he's rather good in a modest role as a nice Three. Colleen Dewhurst is Shire's mother, something of a Seven with an 8 wing.

Sommersby stars Richard Gere as the maybe/maybe not husband of Jodie Foster who returns home just after the Civil War. It's been such a long time that nobody remembers Sommersby too well and Gere *seems* to know everyone. Gradually cracks appear in his sheen and it's clear that he's playing some sort of role. He's watched over and disapproved of by another One, fundamentalist Christian Bill Pullman.

Gere eventually goes on trial for crimes committed by Sommersby but the denouement has several interesting twists. Role-playing turns out to be his attempt at redemption and living truthfully. Gere's motivations are ironic and yet just right for a Three. He's also a good-hearted, if confused, guy, and has a 2 wing.

Australian actor Bryan Brown plays the title role in **Sweet**

Talker. We know from the start that he's a con-man. We watch him leave prison and settle into a small beach resort. There he hatches a scheme to convince the locals that a sunken galleon resides nearby. He works the scam from various angles, takes money from investors, and predictably gets involved with a Niney woman (Karen Allen) and her young son. He is eventually unmasked, Allen gets Oneish and Brown is torn between his scam and people he has come to care for.

Film is a little flat, but has its moments. Brown is transparently calculating rather than charismatic, a bit like Colin Firth in *Valmont*.

For a more criminal but still sympathetic Three, there's Jamie Lee Curtis in **A Fish Called Wanda**. This rollicking, expert comedy casts Curtis as a likable con-woman in cahoots with manic Seven Kevin Kline. They are partners in a London robbery that lands their English accomplice in jail. Since the jailed partner knows where the diamonds are, Curtis spends most of the story scheming and seducing her way to the loot's location. Her motives are simple; she wants the jewels and she's cheerfully shameless about what she'll do to get them.

Part of her strategy is to feign interest in the accomplice's lawyer, John Cleese, a melancholy, dutiful Nine (1 wing). Depressed about his dead-end career and marriage to a shrewish One, Cleese responds vulnerably to Curtis's overtures. He's so smitten with her that we worry that she will devastate him. Turns out Curtis grows truly fond of him and her authentic feeling *almost* steers her off her goal. It also becomes clear that Cleese as a Nine has his own connection to 3. He sees through Curtis but likes her anyway. A little bit of larceny actually suits him and becomes his ticket out of the misery of being good.

Kline is wildly funny as an inflating narcissist whose high opinions of himself are based on less than nothing. Michael Palin is another accomplice, a self-defeating, tormented Six.

John Cleese, who wrote the screenplay, said he thought it was about the difference between the Americans and the English. As a European, his image of Americans is Threeish, and Three is the Enneagram style that we as a culture most often prize. In any case, *Wanda* is wonderful obnoxious fun; comedies of any kind are rarely this good.

There's also a pretty good suspense comedy with similar tensions to *Wanda* called **Framed**. Jeff Goldblum is a Niney American artist enlisted in a scam by English con-woman Three, Kristin Scott-Thomas. She's also after cash but likable anyway.

A clever, unusual comedy returns us to (pre) Civil War times. **Skin Game** is something of a sleeper; it first seems breezily trivial but turns out to have a sharp anti-racist edge. James Garner and Lou Gossett star as con-men partners who work a scam where Garner sells Gossett as a slave and then later breaks him free. They have a jaunty, profitable time at this until the day the scheme backfires and Gossett actually does wind up enslaved. Garner teams up with con-woman Susan Clark and together they track down his lost partner. Gossett's from a rich family, is well-educated and has no reference for the bitter conditions he endures. His loyalties get more and more complex as he learns that what he's been playing at is no game.

Twin souls Garner and Clark are both Threes. They make a pragmatic scheming couple who enjoy each other's role playing. Clark is very similar to Jamie Lee Curtis in *Wanda*.

Garner and Gossett bicker and clash, but fondly. Gossett's pretty much a Six and has more integrity than Garner. He's also better at predicting what will go wrong. Garner is unchanged in the end but still quite genial. Story is witty, well acted and deceptively perceptive.

White Men Can't Jump faintly resembles *Skin Game*. It tells a tale of two basketball hustlers joining forces to win inner city games. The scam depends on opponents underestimating dim-looking white guy (Woody Harrelson) as he teams up with black sharp-shooter Wesley Snipes. Snipes is the Three and while he's ultra-competitive and a bit shifty, underneath his goals and loyalties are clear. He wants to take his family up and out of their poor urban neighborhood. To do this he works several jobs and will even hustle his partner if he has to. Snipes has a certain personal decency and grows to be a protective if unsentimental friend to the troubled Harrelson.

Latter is a Nine with an 8 wing. The contradiction between Nine and Eight is evident in how Harrelson first wins and then loses at whatever he does. He's focused enough to win games (connection to 3), but angrily hooked on proving himself. His girlfriend, Rosie Perez, a goal-oriented probable Three, demands that he commit wholeheartedly to their relationship. Sustained focus is precisely what Harrelson can't manage and his attempts to understand his failures are dogged by a Niney inability to see the obvious.

I was prepared to dislike this film, but found it disarming, raucous and full of energy. The endless ball-court hype and palaver is funny and the performances are all very good.

Now for the baddies:

The One/Three clash mentioned earlier is quite visible in a movie called **The Beguiled**. Geraldine Page and Clint Eastwood star in — of all things — a gothic feminist revenge fantasy. Eastwood plays a wounded Civil War deserter posing as a pacifist Quaker who finds refuge in an orphanage for young girls. Once inside, he sets about seducing one woman after another, changing his stories and manufacturing sentiments as he goes. Elizabeth Hartman plays a naïve Six whom Eastwood preys upon.

Page is the headmistress, an orderly, moral One. She's an intimate subtype and prone to jealousy, which is bad news for Clint. The women eventually compare notes, get angry and exact a rather gruesome revenge. As they do, we see the opportunistic hardness that motivated Eastwood all along. This film is another sleeper; both unusual and atmospheric.

Steamy, well-made film noir **Body Heat** has Three Kathleen Turner married to Three tycoon Richard Crenna. She initiates an affair with bored, small-town lawyer William Hurt, a Nine.

A self-acknowledged weakling, Hurt allows himself to be drawn into a plot to kill Turner's husband ("You're not too smart. I like that in a man"). She is alternately seductive and pleading by turns, matching his images of her and creating new ones of herself. She lures him with the promise to be together once the rich husband is dead, but Hurt finds multiple levels of deceit as the story unfolds. Behind it all Turner's heart is diamond-hard and her true motives are revealed in the denouement. She has a 2 wing and is another intimate subtype Siren.

House Of Games — David Mamet wrote and directed this story of a repressed, successful Nine lady psychiatrist drawn into an elaborate scam by Three con-man Joe Mantegna. The whole film is about deception and the illicit fascination the psychiatrist (Lindsay Crouse) has for Mantegna's sleight of mind. The psychiatrist is a self-muffled good girl who is excited by the social audacity of the con-man's lies and many false faces. As a Nine, she's connected to 3, in this case to the deceptive low side.

She's also a little dim, slow to catch on to how many ways she herself is being scammed. In the end, the Mantegna character's true motivations emerge, and they're none too pleasant. We see the venal, unapologetic hostility that drove all the games. Throughout the film, he is both charismatic and hollow, charming and calculated. His confederates all display the same attitudes, and several seem like Threes as well.

The film is engrossing though it feels truncated, like a two act play. Lindsay Crouse as the psychiatrist is deliberately stilted, like a Nine walking in her sleep. Lilia Skala is on hand as Crouse's supervisor and she's something of a nice Two.

If *House Of Games* portrays a netherworld, **Glengarry Glen Ross** is like a visit to one of Dante's levels of Hell, the one where everybody lies. Based on another David Mamet play, this film is an exhilaratingly good portrait of a group of sleazy salesmen working for a shady real estate company.

Al Pacino and Jack Lemmon both play Threes, the former successful while the latter is kicking and flailing down a greased slide to oblivion. They're Outcome Monsters; they'll say or do *anything* to make a sale. Work requires a constant impersonation, but it's a way of life for these men.

Pacino's style is smoother. As we watch him close a deal, he's like some silky prince of darkness enfolding his victim in his robes. He's elegantly groomed and laser-fast at switching masks and tactics.

Lemmon's character is more desperate and obsequious, sort of a parody of himself. Yet when he makes a big sale he turns gloating and abusive, preaching bankrupt salesman philosophy and one-upping the company's quiet office manager (Kevin Spacey). Despite his mean streak, we feel Lemmon's growing desperation; he's a crumbling phony who's probably lost the dubious skill he once had. The main office has pressured the salesmen and their jobs are at risk if they don't make more sales. They react like sewer rats; they eat family. Some fail, some succeed, but Lemmon's decline is inevitable.

This film is terrific in a tense-stomached sort of way. There's great individual and ensemble acting as the cast handles Mamet's foul-mouthed, stabbing dialogue. The salesmen's snapping exchanges sound like some nasty stacatto form of jazz.

Alec Baldwin weighs in as a sinister Eight. Alan Arkin and Jonathan Pryce both play placating, underdog Nines.

Network

This film was wildly praised and awarded when it came out, but it's really not very good. Its writer, Paddy Chayefsky, was a One, and his film characters tend to moralize, speechify and eat scenery. *Network* is supposed to be a dark, outlandish satire of television, but it's mostly just overblown.

Faye Dunaway plays a Three network executive who gets involved with One anchorman William Holden. While he's the movie's voice of moral virtue and integrity, she's amoral and predatory. Her name is Diana (The Huntress — get it?) and she describes herself thus: "I was married for four years and pretended to be happy. I was in analysis for six years and pretended to be sane. I seem to be inept at everything except my work, so I limit myself to that. All I want out of life is good ratings."

Away for a weekend with Holden, all Dunaway can talk about is TV programming, even during sex. She too lives in scenarios but is not an intimate subtype. Dunaway's character is more social, concerned with results and prestige as a measurement of self. She's totally identified with her job.

Holden the One gets to make smug, virtuous speeches. As Chayefsky's mouthpiece he passes easy judgment on Dunaway. He breaks up with her because she's heartless and measures herself by externals, two facts he recognized the nanosecond he met her. Holden's character also speaks in odd, self-conscious stereotypes, saying things like, "Dammit, I'm supposed to be the Romantic and you're supposed to be the Embittered Cynic."

Peter Finch plays a probable phobic Six, an anchorman who has a psychotic break on the air ("I'm mad as hell and I'm not going to take it any more!"). Robert Duvall is a nasty, ruthless Eight named Hackett ("Hack it" — get it?).

Rain Man

Tom Cruise is just fine as a shallow, opportunistic Three whose heart starts to thaw towards his autistic savant brother, played by Dustin Hoffman. Hoffman got all the attention for his performance but Cruise gives a subtle shading to Threeish narcissism. His character's emotional warming and ethical changes are gradual, believable, and consistent with how Threes grow. They do it for love.

Hoffman is a Six, often plays them and his autistic character here works out to be a Six, too.

Ride The High Country

Classic Western about two aging gunfighters hired to escort gold from a mining camp back to civilization. Some of the dialogue and all of the music is corny, but the film is otherwise kind of wonderful. Chief pleasure is watching old pros Randolph Scott and Joel McCrea playing a Three and a One respectively.

Scott has a slightly smaller role than McCrea's but he's plenty vivid. We first see him costumed, disguised as a Wild West Hero working a stand in a carnival. He signs on with McCrea to guard the gold but secretly intends to steal it. This necessitates role-playing with his old friend, but Scott's personal sentiments are real. He shows evidence of both wings and the two men spend a lot of time warmly reminiscing. Part of the tension of the story is guessing what Scott will ultimately do about the gold. He's charming but calculated, goodhearted but morally ambivalent. He behaves as though the end justifies the means, yet he does have loyalties. Sort of a scoundrel and yet very appealing.

McCrea, by contrast, is straight as a gun barrel. He's prone to judgmental speechifying that he punctures with amiable self-mocking humor. His 9 wing brings a steady and receptive quality. He searches for fair, balanced and legal solutions to problems. He polices Scott's unstable young protégé, a half-cocked, counterphobic Six. Faced with the religious zealotry of another One, McCrea calmly and wittily undercuts the man. Still, he turns merciless when he discovers Scott's plan to steal the gold. McCrea's character is probably a self-preservation subtype. He's a bit of a worrier and has survival on his mind.

James Drury, the miner who gets married, is a Seven with an 8 wing. At least one of his brothers is an Eight and the alcoholic justice of the peace is a Nine.

Wall Street

Director Oliver Stone's enjoyably trashy indictment of rampant greed. Charlie Sheen plays a young Three stockbroker climbing up the ladder of success into thin air. Early in the film he is competitive, ambitious, and outcome-oriented. He has a flimsy hold on conse-quence and strikes a Faustian bargain with ruthless tycoon Michael Douglas, an Eight. Sheen is another social subtype — he wants money, objects, trappings and totems of success.

Sheen's father (Martin Sheen) is a One against whom Charlie has modeled. In fact, the son is helping Douglas buy the airline his father works for in order to sell it off in pieces, corporate raider style.

The turning point comes when the father has a heart attack, brought on by the stress of his company being raided. This personal-izes the suffering Sheen is helping Douglas to cause and Sheen's own heart begins to open. He is arrested for his wheeling and dealing, and has a painful awakening of conscience.

Several things are noteworthy. The Three/One dynamic is active here. Sheen's father is an angry, intense One with a 2 wing. The clash between son's ambition and father's ethics is very explicit ("There's no nobility in poverty anymore, Dad"). This argument is echoed at the Wall Street firm where Charlie works. Hal Holbrook plays an older One broker who moralistically cautions Sheen about the consequences of actions. The young man dismisses him as the voice of antiquated principle ("I'm shooting for the stars").

On the other side of the moral moat is Douglas's Eight. The amoral corporate raider is concerned with strength rather than rules. Winning is important as a way to prevail and dominate events. At one point he makes a speech about how "Greed is good." It's an Eight speaking with narcissistic justification. Principles are for sissies, integ-rity is a luxury.

This attitude appeals to Sheen as long as his heart is closed. For a confused Three, winning can be a way to *be* somebody. For an Eight, winning would be a way to feel strong. Both styles are narcissistic but are motivated differently. Of course, a One would disapprove of either motive.

Douglas, by the way, is quite good and has a scene that is very telling about Eights. He's seen walking on the beach at sunrise ruthlessly scheming with Sheen over a portable phone. Suddenly he breaks off the war-talk and stands awestruck at the beauty of the sunrise. This may seem incongruent, but it shows an unguarded innocence of perception that Eights often have (see "Eights").

OTHER MOVIE THREES

Annette Bening, *The Grifters*; Lara Flynn Boyle, *The Temp*; Marlon Brando, *The Missouri Breaks*; Dabney Coleman, *Tootsie*; Tom Cruise, *The Color Of Money, Days Of Thunder, A Few Good Men, The Firm*; John Cusack, *The Grifters, True Colors*; Charles Dance, *Pascali's Island*; Mac Davis, *North Dallas Forty*; Rebecca DeMornay, *Guilty As Sin, Risky Business*; James Garner, *Barbarians At The Gate*; Richard Gere, *American Gigolo*; Robin Givens, *Boomerang, A Rage In Harlem*;

Tony Goldwyn, *Ghost*; Charles Grodin, *Ishtar*; Jean Harlow, *Dinner At Eight*; Mark Harmon, *The Deliberate Stranger*; Laurence Harvey, *Darling*; John Heard, *Deceived*; Anthony Hopkins, *The Elephant Man*; Jeremy Irons, *Betrayal*; Mick Jagger, *Freejack*; Michael Keaton, *Pacific Heights*; Nicole Kidman, *Malice*; Jack Lemmon, *Save The Tiger*; Shelley Long, *Outrageous Fortune*; Rob Lowe, *Bad Influence, Wayne's World*; Ali MacGraw, *Just Tell Me What You Want*;

Steve Martin, *Leap Of Faith*; Mary Tyler Moore, *Ordinary People*; Rick Moranis, *Parenthood*; Robert Morse (as Truman Capote), *Tru*; John Neville, *The Adventures Of Baron Munchausen*; Christopher Reeve, *Monsignor*; Paul Reiser, *Aliens*; Tim Robbins, *Bob Roberts*; Kurt Russell, *Tequila Sunrise*; Arnold Schwarzenegger, *Pumping Iron*; George C. Scott, *The Hustler*; Sting, *Bring On The Night*; Sharon Stone, *Total Recall*; Robert Urich, *Lonesome Dove*; Christopher Walken, *At Close Range, The Comfort Of Strangers*.

FINER DISTINCTION NOTES

WINGS: Threes can have a 2 wing, a 4 wing or both wings.

Three With a 2 Wing

Threes with this wing are often highly gregarious. They have a tendency towards persona — playing a role of themselves in real life. Social perception, prestige and recognition important. Healthy side brings personal warmth, leadership qualities. Sincere desire to do well by others; may be genuinely nice people. If they have achieved some measure of success they are generous in their mentorship of others.

When more entranced, they are preoccupied with seeming ideal to others. This can extend to friendships, family, as well as at work. Want to seem a perfect spouse, friend, parent, employee, good son or daughter. Strong social focus because they need so much validation from others. Preening and boastful behavior possible. Bursts of egotism. Wanting to be on top, better than others. Slip into impersonation easily, may falsify feeling and not know it themselves. Malicious intentional deceit possible. Behavior of con-artists and sociopaths.

Real-Life Threes With a 2 Wing: Dick Clark, Joseph Cotten, Joan Crawford, Tom Cruise, Ali MacGraw, Reba McEntire, Joe Montana, Demi Moore, Burt Reynolds, Anthony Robbins, Arnold Schwarzenegger, Cybill Shepherd, Sharon Stone, Kathleen Turner, Oprah Winfrey, Natalie Wood.

Movie Threes With a 2 Wing: Annette Bening, *The Grifters*; Tom Cruise, *Rain Man*; Jamie Lee Curtis, *A Fish Called Wanda*; Richard Gere, *American Gigolo, Sommersby*; Tony Goldwyn, *Ghost*; Jack Lemmon, *Glengarry Glen Ross*; Arnold Schwarzenegger, *Pumping Iron*; Cybill Shepherd, *The Last Picture Show, Texasville*; Sharon Stone, *Basic Instinct*; Kathleen Turner, *Body Heat*.

Three With a 4 Wing

May be slightly less image-conscious or project an image that is more implicit and subtle. 4 wing brings a degree of introversion. May measure themselves more by their creations, artistic or social. Tend to compete with themselves first more than with other people.

High side brings the motivation and ability to work on oneself. May accomplish everything they set out to do materially, then embark on a path of self-analysis. Artistic explorations or teaching possible. Will still like a challenge, but thoughtful, intuitive or humanistic concerns of prime interest.

The low side of this wing can bring a haunted, self-tormented quality or a haughty, competitive pretentiousness. Might be snobs or accuse critics of being too plebian to appreciate them. Cool, hard shell. In private, can lapse into Fourish self-questioning and melodrama. Instability and moodiness can be factors. Unrealistic grandiosity.

Real-Life Threes With a 4 Wing: James Baker, David Bowie, Werner Erhard, F. Scott Fitzgerald, Bryant Gumbel, Michael Jordan, Martina

Navratilova, William Shatner, Wesley Snipes, George Washington. **Movie Threes With a 4 Wing:** John Cusack, *The Grifters*; Charles Dance, *Pascali's Island*; Jeremy Irons, *Betrayal*; John Malkovich, *Dangerous Liaisons, In The Line Of Fire*; Robert Morse, *Tru*; William Shatner, *Star Trek V - The Final Frontier*; Sting, *Bring On The Night*; Christopher Walken, *At Close Range, The Comfort Of Strangers*.

CONNECTING POINTS (Stress and Security)
Threes connect to the high and low side of 9.
Threes connect to the high and low side of 6.

Three's Connection to 9

Three's connection to 9 brings a capacity for self-reflection and a partial slow-down of tempo. A Three may become more receptive to the people in their lives and appreciate "idle" time, especially when it's spent with family and friends.

The modest, unpretentious quality of 9 is inherent, if latent, in Threes. Connection helps them come out of roles and relax into being. Winning can become less all-important. Success is sometimes seen through as an illusion. Take time out from the world's races. New projects might be entered into because they look interesting, or will benefit others, or for intuitive reasons that can't be explained.

More entranced, a Three might go through periods of 9-like confusion. Could start racing around, going in circles at high speed. Lose sight of their goals. The 9 tendency towards emotional numbness reinforces emotional absence. Three's unhealthy habit of altering themselves for an environment can also get worse.

May flip from hyperactivity to paralysis. Sink into a nihilistic "What's the use?" attitude and a numb, 9-like apathy. Lacking motivation and direction they can go passively depressed and use drugs or alcohol to further deaden their feelings.

Movie Threes who demonstrate this connection: Tom Cruise, *Rain Man*; Jamie Lee Curtis, *A Fish Called Wanda*; John Cusack, *The Grifters*; Jack Lemmon, *Glengarry Glen Ross, Save The Tiger*; Roger Moore, *Bed And Breakfast*; Robert Morse, *Tru*; Cybill Shepherd, *Texasville*.

Three's Connection to 6

Healthy connection to 6 helps Threes drop masks, admit flaws, be seen for who they are. Their true emotions generally have a fearful cast; fear is a door to authentic feeling. Honest vulnerability. Make and keep commitments to ideals beyond winning and succeeding. Develop personal loyalties to family and friends as well as to spirituality. Ethical concerns become far more important, moral courage emerges. They stay faithful and keep their agreements, even at the risk of losing.

Unhealthy connection brings runaway anxiety that fuels the Three's desire to cut off or mask feeling. Fear motivates hyperactivity as the Three runs away from the "awful truth" about themselves. May go nervously ambivalent about relationships, unable to decide or commit.

Threes also overidentify with hierarchies and traditions like a 6 can do. May give their power away to authority figures. Play "good child" roles that get them approval within the dependency. Could become overly cautious. Stay within the confines of tradition or excel within its terms as a way to stay safe.

Movie Threes who demonstrate this connection: Tom Cruise, *Rain Man*; Richard Gere, *Sommersby*; Tony Goldwyn, *Ghost*; Jack Lemmon, *Glengarry Glen Ross*; John Malkovich, *Dangerous Liaisons*; Charlie Sheen, *Wall Street*; Wesley Snipes, *White Men Can't Jump*.

SUBTYPE THEMES

Self-Preservation

Have a preoccupation with acquiring material security as a way to calm core anxieties about survival. Some grow up poor and focus on amassing wealth. Concentrate on doing well, having enough, especially of the right things. Irony is that the strategy doesn't really work — a Three could amass millions and still, say, harbor a morbid fear of dying broke. Insecurity fuels a sense that enough money is never enough.

Movie examples include Wesley Snipes in *White Men Can't Jump*, Rebecca DeMornay in *Risky Business* and, a little bit, Charlie Sheen in *Wall Street*.

Intimate

Intimate Threes mask themselves with an image of what a sexually appealing man or woman is. They play roles in romantic relationships hoping to get love or admiration. Image is based on community or cultural standards of desirability or a given partner's expectations. If not committed to a specific partner then they will project an image generally and seek sexual conquests.

Intimate Threes in the movies can be sexual imposters or suave, attractive ideals of masculinity or femininity. Female characters tend to be beautiful out-of-reach Sirens. Examples include: John Malkovich, *Dangerous Liaisons*; Cybill Shepherd, *Texasville*; Richard Gere, *American Gigolo*, *Sommersby*; Sharon Stone, *Basic Instinct*; Kathleen Turner, *Body Heat*.

Social

Social Threes are often extremely status-conscious. Most confuse their inner self with the world's badges, honors and totems. Measure themselves by money, position, awards or results. Strive to match group standards and have the right credentials. How they rank in the eyes of others is most important. May be materialistic but with an eye towards the best brand names so as to be identified with the product's status.

The excesses of this subtype make for fine morality plays about the hollowness of fame and status. Movie examples include: Charlie Sheen, *Wall Street*; Robert Redford, *Downhill Racer*; Mary Tyler Moore, *Ordinary People*; Faye Dunaway, *Network*.

FOURS

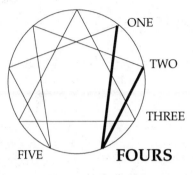

ONE

TWO

THREE

FIVE   **FOURS**

PEOPLE WHO LIVE IN THEIR IMAGINATION AND FEELINGS. MAY BE ARTISTIC, ARTICULATE AND INSPIRING OR WHINY, ELITIST AND NEGATIVE.

FAMOUS REAL-LIFE FOURS

Photographer Diane Arbus, Painter Francis Bacon, John Barrymore, Charles Baudelaire, Ingmar Bergman, Poet John Berryman, Director Peter Bogdanovich, Marlon Brando, Richard Brautigan, Jackson Browne, Raymond Burr, England's Prince Charles, Leonard Cohen, Judy Collins, James Dean, Robert De Niro, Director Brian De Palma, Neil Diamond, Novelist Michael Dorris, French novelist Marguerite Duras, Albert Finney, the cultural aura of France, Martha Graham, Singer Nanci Griffith,

Michael Jackson, Janis Joplin, Naomi Judd, Harvey Keitel, Poet Philip Larkin, Charles Laughton, John Malkovich, Steve Martin, Marcello Mastroianni, Author Mary McCarthy, Author Yukio Mishima, Joni Mitchell, Actor Michael Moriarty, Jim Morrison, Singer Morrissey, Edvard Munch, Liam Neeson, Stevie Nicks, Author Anaïs Nin, Nick Nolte, Laurence Olivier, Edith Piaf, Sylvia Plath, Edgar Allen Poe, Novelist Anne Rice,

Winona Ryder, Françoise Sagan, Poet Anne Sexton, Percy Shelley, Simone Signoret, Playright Neil Simon, Singer Paul Simon, August Strindberg, Edna St. Vincent Millay, Singer James Taylor, Spencer

Tracy, Actress Liv Ullmann, Vincent van Gogh, Suzanne Vega, Author Robert James Waller, Alan Watts, Australian novelist Patrick White, Tennessee Williams, Virginia Woolf, Neil Young.

INTRODUCTION

Like Ones, Fours compare reality with what could be. While a One will look for imperfection about them and maybe have a desire to correct what's wrong, Fours often turn away from reality and live in their imaginations, feelings and moods.

Along with Twos and Threes, Fours share the tendency towards vanity and image-confusion but they can express it paradoxically. Fours are more likely to identify with an image of defect especially as it confers on them a quality of uniqueness or exempt specialness. A Four might, for instance, bemoan their inadequacy to succeed in the everyday world, but within this complaint there could be a subtle quality of boasting. This is usually driven by a self-image that is romantically tragic but also elitist. They may take pride in what is unique or defectively unusual about them.

Because of the strength of their emotional imaginations, people with this style are often described as artists. Many of the world's most accomplished artists have been Fours and nearly all people with this style need or find creative outlets. Otherwise, Fours work in all kinds of occupations, although they will try when possible to make their work creatively interesting.

Awakened Fours tend to be idealistic, have good taste and are great appreciators of beauty. They filter reality through a rich, subtle subjectivity and are very good at "metaphorical thinking," the capacity to make connections between unrelated facts and events. The Four tendency to see things symbolically is enhanced by their emotional intensity. This creates raw artistic material that almost has to be given form. Self-expression and the pursuit of self-knowledge are high priorities for people with this style.

Fours value the aesthetics of beauty as much as they are attuned to the tragic nature of existence. When healthy, people with this style work to transmute the pain of living into something more meaningful. This can be done through creative work of all kinds. Fours are excellent at articulating subjective experience, and can be fine teachers and psychotherapists in this regard. They may also be empathetic friends, able to take in and understand the dilemmas of others and especially be willing to listen to a friend's pain.

When more defensive or entranced, Fours begin to focus on what is unavailable or missing in their lives. They can become negative and critical, finding fault with what they do have, seeing mainly misery in the present. They then turn inward and use their imaginations to romanticize other times and places. Fours can live in the past, the future — anywhere that seems more appealing than here. "The grass is always greener on the other side." Entranced Fours fall into a habit of envy for whatever it is they don't have now.

The need to be seen as someone special and unique may become more neurotically pronounced too. Fours can seem very in touch with their feelings but their defensive tendency is to translate authentic feeling into melodrama. They could be full of lament and nostalgia, demanding recognition yet rejecting anything good they get from friends. They might also grow competitive and spiteful, unable to enjoy their own successes without taking away from the achievements of others.

An entranced Four could be moody or hypersensitive while beginning to act exempt from everyday rules. Buoyed by their sense of defective specialness, they might give themselves permission to act badly, be selfish or irresponsible. They may refuse to deal with the mundane and the ordinary, reasoning that they are different and not of this world anyway. Entranced Fours incline towards feeling guilty, ashamed, melancholy, jealous and unworthy.

Deeply entranced Fours can inhabit a harrowing world of torment. They may be openly masochistic and extravagant in their self-debasement. The lives of spectacularly self-destructive artists often reflect this kind of scenario.

At this point, a Four could become unreachably alienated. Stricken by a profound sense of hopelessness, they can sink into morbid self-loathing and suicidal depression. Their "differentness" is now seen in entirely negative terms and they banish themselves into a kind of exile. The desire to punish themselves and others is also quite strong.

Fours have a specific defense that comes up a lot in movies, especially love stories. It's called "introjection," and it means carrying someone around inside of you in your imagination and feelings. A Four will introject a loved one, usually someone idealized and out of reach. Their beloved is romanticized from afar but the Four feels the absent person to be present. They then have a kind of relationship with their fantasy of the other person.

FOURS IN THE MOVIES

Unlike Three performers, who mostly play themselves in movies, real-life Fours mostly play Enneagram styles other than their own. Performers with this style are almost always considered character actors and actresses.

A list of Four performers includes some very creative people from movies past and present: John Barrymore, Charles Laughton, Spencer Tracy, Laurence Olivier, Marlon Brando, James Dean, Liv Ullmann, Albert Finney, Simone Signoret, Robert De Niro, Harvey Keitel, Nick Nolte, John Malkovich. All of these performers are capable of movie star roles but they generally are somewhat different from film to film.

Note the above list is almost all male — I'm sure there are more Four female actresses but for some reason I didn't find that many. Some who are known for Fourish roles — Meryl Streep for instance — have other Enneagram styles in real life.

Younger Four performers tend to play the style a little more often, usually in roles as misunderstood teenagers. The condition of feeling different, lonely, self-conscious and tormented, is well represented by performers like James Dean (*Rebel Without A Cause*) and Winona Ryder (*Beetlejuice, Mermaids*).

Another kind of movie story that strongly favors Fours is about unrequited love. Usually the Four is the lover-from-afar (*Blume In Love, Out Of Africa, New York Stories*) but sometimes the roles are reversed. In movies like *From Noon Til Three, Cherry 2000* and *The French Lieutenant's Woman*, the Four is loved from afar by someone else. Usually the Four doesn't notice because they are too self-absorbed or preoccupied with someone else that *they* are in love with from afar.

The other noteworthy type of role that especially applies to Fours is that of the Melancholy Monster. Stories like *The Phantom Of The Opera, Cyrano de Bergerac* and *The Hunchback Of Notre Dame* are exactly about Four psychology. The deformed hero is driven to hide his true feelings because of shame over his disfigurement. He's a pure-hearted romantic under the defect but unable to expose his real feelings or function normally.

Note that most of these stories are from France, a very Fourish culture. Other examples include lovesick vampires (*Bram Stoker's Dracula*) and the occasional mutant (Danny DeVito, *Batman Returns*). Anjelica Huston does a comic reversal of this motif as Morticia in *Addams Family Values*; she's deeply weird but believes she's normal.

The most obvious type of Four role, of course, is of the artist.

These range from the tormented to the struggling to the fulfilled. The list includes: F. Murray Abraham, *Amadeus*; Anne Bancroft, *The Turning Point*; John Barrymore, *Dinner At Eight*; Judy Davis, *Impromptu*; Tom Hanks, *Punchline*; Maria de Medeiros, *Henry And June*; Jack Nicholson, *Five Easy Pieces*; Nick Nolte, *New York Stories*.

Fours and Sevens conflict a lot in the movies that follow. For a movie where they get along see *Addams Family Values*.

MOVIE REVIEWS

Amadeus

This film contrasts the lives of classical composers Salieri and Mozart. Mozart is played as a Sevenish jerk and Salieri keeps asking the Big Philosophical Question: "How could God let such a jerk be so talented?" But it's not a philosophical question at all; Sevens are often gifted and Salieri is a competitive Four being eaten by envy ("I admit I was jealous when I first heard the tales of him").

The latter's monologues, well spoken by F. Murray Abraham, have an almost oral craving behind them, as if Salieri can taste what it would be like to have Mozart's talent: "Mozart's music filled me with such longing that I thought it was the voice of God. All I ever wanted was to sing to God but he made me mute. Why plant the longing in my heart and then deny me the talent?"

Abraham captures the preening "I-am-special" quality of the Four style as well as a certain whininess. His Salieri is a Four with a 3 wing; vanity and envy both motivate him. He is also an intimate subtype, with an especially strong tendency towards competition in relationships. The entire film is about his drive to measure up to Mozart.

The film is sumptuously shot and the music is great. It goes hollow dramatically, I think, because Salieri's conflict with Mozart is neurotic rather than philosophical. The latter is one-dimensional throughout, though Tom Hulce is good in the underwritten role. He plays Mozart as a Seven with bad social skills and worse impulse control.

Mozart's father is a One and the Emperor (Jeffrey Jones) is a Nine.

Blume In Love

Not very funny marital comedy told in flashback by ex-husband George Segal, a Four. His ex-wife is a Nine (Susan Anspach), notable for her ambivalent, receptive nature and physical beauty. Segal carries her around inside him (introjection) and projects romantic longing onto her indistinct soul ("I'm in love with her — that's my tragedy"). Segal continually plots to remarry Anspach, never mind that his memories of being together are mixed at best.

The less interested she is in remarriage, the more attracted he is. He can't live with her or without her, but he's mostly self-involved. He's in the trance of his obsession *about* her. The film has a ghastly rape scene that is nevertheless telling about his obsession and her passivity.

Look for a young Kris Kristofferson as a mellow hippie Seven.

Cherry 2000

So let's say you're driving and your car collides with a peach truck but only your critical faculties are damaged. During your recovery you could do worse than to rent this goofy, well-made B-Grade movie. It takes place in a bizarre but believable future and boasts some spectacular stunts. While not strong on characterization it has a funny plotline driven by the lead character's Fourishness.

Cherry 2000 is the name of a lifelike robot wife owned by Sam Treadwell (David Andrews). When an accident (during sex on the kitchen floor) disables her body, Sam recovers her computer memory and goes searching for a copy of her body to plug the chip back into. Turns out they don't make Cherrys anymore, so Sam must venture into the lawless Forbidden Zone where a stash of the robot bodies is rumored to be stored. He hires lady tracker Melanie Griffith (pretty good here) to guide him through the Zone to his beloved Cherry.

"There was tenderness, a dream-like quality about her ... you wouldn't understand," he tells Griffith. She hassles him throughout about being in love with a robot and as they grow closer, part of the suspense is whether he will cling to his Fourish dream of Cherry or wake up to the reality of his feelings for Griffith. Andrews keeps the sullen faraway persona of a Four throughout the film and has several good moments. At one point, fearing he may have lost Cherry's memory chip, he laments, "Her whole personality is on that chip! If we find a body now it would be just like finding a toaster!" The joke is that Cherry's personality is that of a bimbo, anyway. She talked to him in an adoring, vacant way and he romanticized the rest.

Melanie Griffith probably plays a Nine with an 8 wing though she's a Two in real life. Ben Johnson is on hand as a Nine desert prospector. Tim Thomerson is very funny as the leader of a paramilitary New Age community. A Seven with an 8 wing, he has lines like, "Hunt them down and kill them! And remember, men, be yourselves." Spoofy, mindless fun.

Cries And Whispers

A visit to Four Hell. This film from director Ingmar Bergman — at his most depressive — focuses on sisters in a Swedish household. Two out of three of them are Fours and their mother was too. This movie probes Fourish pain at its core and reveals something almost beautiful. It is, however, heavy going and intensely morbid. The household's interiors are almost entirely white and bloodred — intrauterine colors that make the story seem like it's staged within a womb.

Harriet Andersson plays the dying sister who's full of reminiscence of early abandonment — "I always felt frightened and left out. I was the only one who couldn't join in the merriment. Mother has been in my thoughts every day even though she's been dead for 20 years. I remember that I used to spy on her without really meaning to because I loved her to such a jealous extreme. I wish I could see her again to tell her of what I understand of her longing and impatience." Harriet's soul is so fitful that after she dies her corpse comes back to life and continues pleading to be loved.

Liv Ullmann has a double role as the middle sister and as the Four mother. The sister is a Nine in denial ("I haven't any need of being burdened") who's married to a Fourish man who appears briefly before killing himself.

Then there's older sister Ingrid Thulin, an even more depressed Four (5 wing) married to an intolerant, insufferable One. Bergman often places nasty male Ones in his movies; they are invariably hostile to his sensitive Four heroes and heroines. The masochistic Thulin has a kind of breakdown: "Can you conceive how anybody can live with so much hate as has been my burden? There's no relief, no charity, no help, no nothing." In the background clocks are ticking while ghostly windswept howls echo down the empty halls.

The Fourth Man

Director Paul Verhoeven is very good at action films (*Total Recall, Robocop*). Earlier in his career he directed a warm-up to his *Basic Instinct* (see "Threes") called *The Fourth Man*. It's another morbid yarn about a woman under suspicion of murder.

Jeroen Krabbe plays a famous Four writer who gets involved with Two admirer Renee Soutendijk, a woman who keeps outliving her husbands. Krabbe's a self-indulgent fellow prone to bombastic statements about how artistic fantasy is the only reality. Well, *he* can't keep reality straight and the more he learns about Renee's past relationships, the more he fantasizes about what she might do to him. He eventually cracks up and is hospitalized.

The film gives Renee a hypnotic sexual allure and adds a sense of unstable menace so that we wait for her predatory homicidal instincts to suddenly emerge and lunge at Krabbe.

Except they never do. Unless I missed a scene while searching for a pencil, Renee hasn't done anything except marry three guys who died in accidents. She's a femme fatale who's not fatale. She has a 3 wing, is kind of vain, a little kinky, runs a glitzy hair salon, has flashes of ill-temper (low side of 8) but at bottom she's actually kind of *nice*. No matter, the film continues to blame her for Krabbe's collapse, as though she's a serial killer. At least she isn't gay ...

Verhoeven even ends the movie with lengthy close-ups of a female spider devouring her mate. Therapy could really help with something like this but I don't know what it would do to a film career.

The French Lieutenant's Woman, Out Of Africa

Every once in a while you come across a film character who so captures an Enneagram style that everything she says and does reveals it. So it is with the French Lieutenant's Woman (Meryl Streep), a character so chronically Fourish that the film's other characters take to psychoanalyzing the roots of her melancholy. She has, they conclude, "obscure melancholia," the kind which can't be explained, and observe that "it's as if her torture has become a true state of delight."

This film, heavily adapted by Harold Pinter from John Fowles's novel, interweaves two stories, one about a suffering Victorian governess and a Fiveish scholar (Jeremy Irons) and the other about the modern actors (Streep and Irons, again) who are portraying the Victorian couple in a film. The modern couple are probably both Threes; they are empty, hard-edged and engaged in a web of deceit. Their mutual vanity is contrasted with the more complex, passionate historical characters that they play.

The Victorian Streep first appears to Irons as a figure on a sea wall, staring into the stormy distance, alone, her face pale as wax. He gets intrigued by her and grows gradually attracted to comforting her in her melancholy. Here is a sampling of some of her more Fourish statements to him:

"I am nothing. I am hardly human anymore. I married shame; I am not truly like other women."

"You cannot imagine my suffering. I'm only at peace when asleep. When I wake the nightmare begins."

"I was lost from the moment I saw you. I have long imagined a day like this. I have longed for it."

"Now that I know that there was truly a day upon which you have loved me, I can bear anything. You have given me the strength to live."

Irons breaks off his engagement to another and finally makes himself available and committed to Streep. Guess what happens? Streep vanishes and Irons spends the rest of the film tracking her down. When he finds her she has grown some, and looking back on the past she says: "There was a madness in me, an envy. I suddenly realized that I must destroy what I love. It has taken me this time to find my own life."

This is a good film anyway, but it's highly recommended for Enneagram studies. Streep's character has a strong 5 wing and is a social subtype for the way she riddles herself with shame. The old woman she works for is a One.

Shortly after *The French Lieutenant's Woman*, Meryl Streep again starred as a Four in **Out Of Africa**. She plays Danish writer Karen Blixen (pen name Isak Dinesen). Now old, she's looking back on her years in Africa when she ran a coffee plantation and loved the unattainable Denys Finch-Hatton (Robert Redford). Her reminiscence is tinged with loss and melancholy and the film takes her romantic point of view.

Streep's character holds our sympathy but she's quite a sourpuss. She wears a pinched, disappointed look throughout the film and says things like, "When the gods want to punish you they answer your prayers," or, "I think God had a hand in it. He gave me my best crop and then He burned down the plantation."

This theme of finding endless loss and unfulfillment is mainly evident in her romantic attachments. Her husband Klaus Maria Brandauer is a feckless, adulterous Seven, while Redford is escapist and non-committal and also a Seven.

The story shows how Fours and Sevens can be both clashing and complementary styles. Both have a lot of imagination and tend to heighten mundane reality, Fours to enrich it and Sevens to escape it. When Streep and Redford first get together their favorite activity is to make up stories. Redford starts them and Streep embellishes. She's serious, he's light, she's morose, he cheers her up. "In the days and hours when Denys was home we spoke of nothing ordinary or small," she says.

That's probably the problem. Redford dances away from small, ordinary daily life with Streep. She complains chronically and has envy for his presence whenever he's gone. If Redford stayed around, though, chances are she'd find fault with him in other ways. She might notice hairs on his toothbrush or see his mottled skin close up.

Sevens sometimes fear this from Fours. The latter's capacity for lament can feel like a prison to a Seven. The Seven may want to keep life cheery and falsely upbeat while a Four can get locked into a sense of lack. The result is clashing defenses. If the Seven is escapist they may feel pulled down by the Four's negativity and irresponsibly dart off towards new options. In this film Redford has a plane and flies away into wild country whenever things get sticky with Streep.

The couple's arguments about commitment are supposed to typify conflicts between men and women but they're potentially typical for a Seven and a Four. In response to Streep's complaints about his lack of commitment, Redford delivers lines like:

"I won't love you more because of a piece of paper."

"I'm with you because I *choose* to be with you."

"I'll mate for life — one day at a time."

Both generous and noncommittal, Redford is described as someone who likes to give presents, but not at Christmas.

This movie is like a big, pretty coffee-table book; subjects like African race relations never sully its gloss. Streep, however, is superb and the film's Fourish tone is sustained to the point where it's eventually irresistible. Redford is stiff and awkward as if uncertain whether he's playing a man or an icon. He's a very Fiveish actor, so he gives his Seven role a stingy, solitary aura. Michael Kitchen, the villa owner from *Enchanted April*, plays another Nine here.

Streep played another Four with a 5 wing in the dull film *Plenty*. She's a real-life One so she's playing her connecting point in these movies.

From Noon Til Three

The same dynamic again. Charles Bronson and the late Jill Ireland star in a dark comedy-western that satirizes romance, commercialism and media mythmaking. Since it's hard to find in video stores, I'm going to tell you more of the story than usual. It plays very well as a cautionary tale about the excesses of Fourishness, but it also seems as if it might have been written by a Seven.

Ireland's character is a permanently nostalgic Four, a widow whose late husband's clothes are still laid out on the bed the way they were the day he died. This is introjection again — carrying someone absent around with you.

Bronson is a cowardly Seven bank robber who briefly hides out at her house, misrepresenting himself as a suave outlaw. For three hours he and Ireland have a romantic interlude before a posse comes and Bronson flees. Ireland takes him for dead and writes a romantic book called *From Noon Til Three* about their three glorious hours together. The book becomes an international best-seller, enthralling a vast audience with Ireland's gauzy distortions of Bronson's character and motives. It's a drippingly Fourish story of love tragically lost.

Myth so overtakes reality that when Bronson eventually returns, Ireland refuses to recognize him (the man in the book was six feet tall and amazingly handsome). The book has become so popular that there are now tours of Ireland's house, so that people can see where the great romance took place. There's a spinoff play based on the book and a hit song everyone is singing. Bronson even pays a dollar to visit his own grave.

Being a somewhat hedonistic Seven, Bronson simply wants to pick up with Ireland where they left off, but each time he tries to remind her of something that happened between them, she says, "You got that from the book!"

When Ireland does finally realize it's him (he drops his pants and shows her a scar), she offers him money to disappear again, citing the potential disappointment of her readers at his still being alive. In true Fourish style, she makes it clear that she would rather die than allow reality to undo her embellished memory of their brief romance. When Bronson threatens to go public about still being alive, hoping it will shake her awake, she instead shoots herself dead. Her fans later interpret the suicide as a desperate act of melancholy over Bronson's death ...

Stunned and disoriented, Bronson spends much of the rest of the film running around trying to convince everyone he formerly knew that he is still alive. No one believes him because he doesn't resemble the character in the book. Finally he lands in an asylum where the inmates are quite willing to believe he's the famous outlaw. In fact, Bronson's roommate is Abraham Lincoln and Napoleon lives there too.

This is an audacious little film that is worth searching for. Bronson shows an unexpected flair for light comedy and makes fun of his flinty tough-guy persona. The movie flopped completely with his fans.

THE TWO HAMLETS

OK, lovers of paradox: our subject is Hamlet as portrayed in two films — Laurence Olivier's 1948 version and the more recent Franco Zeffirelli film featuring Mel Gibson in the title role.

What's paradoxical? In the two films, Hamlet is portrayed as *two different Enneagram styles.* Olivier plays him as a Four and Mel Gibson as a counterphobic Six. The same play, the same lines, but two totally different emotional cores.

This just happens to correspond with Don Riso's and Helen Palmer's respective assessments in their books, *Personality Types* and *The Enneagram.* Shakespeare scholars I've polled would support Riso and fault Mel Gibson for getting Hamlet wrong. A further wrinkle is that Olivier was a Four in real life while nervous, loyal family man Gibson is a counterphobic Six. Gibson plays Sixes very well; his character in the *Lethal Weapon* movies is a near psychotic rendition of the same energy he brings to Hamlet.

Hamlet, 1948. "There's something in his soul on which his melancholy does brood." The traditional interpretation of Hamlet is as "the melancholy Dane," and Laurence Olivier plays him as moody, sullen and depressive.

This is Hamlet without the nerves — he lacks the basic terror that a Six would harbor. He's bitter and whiny, both tender-voiced and tragic-minded. His desire to slay the King (who killed his father) seems more a glum revenge for being abandoned than the issue of justice it would be for a Six. Olivier also adds a touch of vanity ("I am very proud ... ambitious"), making Hamlet a bit of a snob, afloat in an air of his own specialness.

Like *Wuthering Heights*, this black-and-white film is framed in brooding shadows and contains almost no humor. Hamlet as a Four is strangely more sympathetic than Hamlet as a Six. His dilemma is supported by the dark, romantic way the film is shot. Melancholy is made to be a tragic condition of existence rather than a function of personal neurosis. This aura of cosmic loss obscures the fact that, psychologically speaking, Hamlet is a Momma's Boy stalling at the gate of adulthood. (Turn to *Hamlet* under "Sixes.")

Impromptu

Bright, freewheeling comedy-drama about writer George Sand (Judy Davis) and her gallery of artist friends, including the composers Liszt and Chopin. Film affectionately spoofs their artistic temperaments, portraying them as a group of spoiled, passionate babies. They're a different species but not a better one.

This is especially evident during a stay in the country at the estate of a dim, well-meaning patron (Emma Thompson, hilarious as a Two). The cheeky, self-absorbed artists bicker and clash and bite Thompson's hand for trying to feed them. Their disdain for her money and her slowness at realizing their insults are very funny.

Chaos swirls around Davis as several people are in love with her even as she fancies Chopin (Hugh Grant) from afar. "She makes a great hash of her life but she's got a good heart," her publisher observes. A Four with a 3 wing, Davis is flamboyant, melodramatic and competitive but likable all the same. She burns with energy and is willing to put her life on the line for her ideals.

Chopin is a shy consumptive Five (4 wing) and it's a good portrait too. He spends much of the movie socially stricken and horrified by the brash, forward Davis. He fends her off, claiming that he is too ill and has too little energy to get involved with her. This is typical of how Fives think when defensive — they try and parse out their energy and emotional availability, measuring what each encounter will cost them. George Coraface plays one of Davis's ex-lovers, a jealous, volatile Two.

I've Heard The Mermaids Singing

Distaff Walter Mitty story follows a young aspiring photographer who keeps a video diary that we the audience see. She lands some temporary office work in an art gallery and punctuates her daily life with surreal daydreams of what she would do if she were brave. She's a meek Six (5 wing), played by Sheila McCarthy, and the film focuses mainly on her heroine worship of the gallery's curator (Paule Baillargeon), a glamorous, melancholy Four. The slight storyline tracks McCarthy's attraction and eventual disillusionment with the curator onto whom McCarthy has projected most of her own potential.

"I just loved how she talked and wanted her to teach me everything." McCarthy is first seen as socially graceless, not whiny, but nervous, gawky and young.

The curator, by contrast, is a skilled, poised fashion plate ("She was like a fairy tale"). She has a Four's appreciation of the art she sells and a 3 wing that lends administrative and public relations capacities. What she lacks, according to her, is true artistic talent. She asks McCarthy: "Do you know what it's like to want one thing all your life and know all your life that you'll never have it? A simple gift ... to make something beautiful is to be beautiful forever." At another point, when asked, "What do you want from life?" Baillargeon replies, "Universal respect, eternal youth, passion that never abates. I'd like to never get neurotic about growing old and some day make something breathtakingly beautiful that lasts forever and all time." (Nostalgia isn't what it used to be.)

When friends wish the curator well on her birthday, she asks, "Why do people insist on reminding me that I'm dying?" These sort of remarks are spoken with a quality of unreachable sadness and the heightened vanity in them is related to the curator's 3 wing.

McCarthy sets about trying to rescue the curator from her sadness, usually a mistaken thing to try with Fours. She also gives the curator her power; when Baillargeon unwittingly criticizes a few of McCarthy's photographs, the latter goes home and burns her own work. It's inevitable that McCarthy's heroine will disappoint her, and the film's one plot surprise hinges on the curator's 3 wing. When the moment arrives, McCarthy says, "But I believed you!" and lashes out violently. At film's end, some of McCarthy's power is being handed back to her through a small turn of events: Baillargeon comes to her house to apologize.

Several things are worthwhile about this film, but it's not all that good. McCarthy's character is made to be blandly likable as if inoffensiveness were a character strength. The film is coy and fey and more enchanted with itself than it should be. Still, the Sixish heroine worship is well captured and Baillargeon is quite an instructive Four. Sixes and Fours often befriend or marry each other in real life.

Moonstruck

Whimsical comedy about Italian American family dynamics and the uproar that's caused when Cher falls abruptly in love with her fiancé's brother. The brother, played by Nicolas Cage, is a Four, and throughout the film he makes hilarious, tormented speeches that are right in keeping with the style. One speech begins, "It's just a matter of time before a man opens up his eyes and gives up his dream, his one dream of happiness!"

When Cher initially balks at getting involved with him because "love ruins everything," Cage replies, "We are here to ruin ourselves, to love the wrong person, to break our own hearts!"

Cage, a bread baker who loves opera, lost a hand years earlier in an accident. He blames his brother for the loss and his sense of tragic deformity ("I have no life, my brother took my life"). When it's pointed out to Cage that, in truth, his brother had nothing to do with the accident, Cage yells, "What am I? A monument to justice? I don't care that it's not his fault! I blame him anyway!" Cage is a self-preservation subtype, a "dauntless" Four who advocates risk.

New York Stories

This trilogy of short films is a mixed bag. The first and best features Nick Nolte as a successful Four artist obsessed with a female assistant (Rosanna Arquette) who has gradually grown to hate him. The film shows again how a Four can abstract another person and relate to the *idea* of that person while ignoring them in reality ("I just wanted to kiss your foot. Sorry, it's nothing personal").

Nolte spends most of the time with a faraway, entranced look even when he's focused on Arquette. He has an upcoming art show and partly he uses the relationship to stir creative friction. As Arquette repeatedly rejects him, he throws himself into ever more splendid painting. External reality exists mainly to stimulate his inner creative drama. At a party in his honor, he ignores all the praise and, instead, worries about whom Arquette is talking to across the room. In the end when she leaves, he simply transfers the obsession to someone else.

Nolte has both 3 and 5 wings. He's competitive in relationship and solitary in work. His fixation on Arquette reflects a Four's connection to the low side of 1; it's as if he's pursuing a Big Idea that will save him. He's also critical like a 1. The other obvious connection is to the low side of 2 — Nolte's obsession is about dependency. He doesn't want to be left by Arquette and grasps at her like a man drowning. Nolte's a real-life Four, so this is Enneatype casting.

The third short film is by Woody Allen who plays his usual phobic Six character, Julie Kavner is a Nine, and Allen's mother a Two.

The Turning Point

Anne Bancroft and Shirley MacLaine star in what used to be called a "woman's picture." This 1977 movie is more like a 1940s soap opera about two friends who chose different life courses and now have regrets. Bancroft is a ballet diva Four who envies MacLaine's sedate domestic life — "If I were a man I could have had all the children I wanted and still danced." MacLaine's a mild Eight who's still bitter about giving up ballet and blames Bancroft.

Latter has a long list of Fourish complaints: she's growing old, can't dance as well, has ugly feet, never got married, never had children, etc. She's quite likable though and, despite a competitive streak (3 wing), she's honorable, accomplished and caring, a fairly healthy Four.

The story is enjoyably corny and well acted. The two angry friends finally have it out in a wild, funny scene. Tom Skerritt plays his usual persona, that of a Nine. Leslie Browne plays his daughter, also as a Nine. Martha Scott, the ballet's aristocratic director, is a One with a 2 wing. Anthony Zerbe pops up as an old flame of MacLaine's and he's a Seven.

OTHER MOVIE FOURS

John Barrymore, *Dinner At Eight*; Juliette Binoche, *Damage*; Ray Bolger (The Tin Man), *The Wizard Of Oz*; Jeff Bridges, *The Fisher King*; James Caan, *Chapter Two*; Maria de Medeiros, *Henry And June*; Gérard Depardieu, *Cyrano de Bergerac ('90)*; José Ferrer, *Cyrano de Bergerac ('50)*; Albert Finney, *The Playboys*; Greta Garbo, *Ninotchka*; Jeff Goldblum, *The Favor, The Watch & The Very Big Fish*; Marilyn Hassett, *The Bell Jar*;

Anjelica Huston, *The Addams Family, Addams Family Values*; Jeremy Irons, *Swann In Love*; Janis Joplin, *Janis*; Piper Laurie, *The Hustler*; Peter Lawford, *Little Women*; Vivien Leigh, *Ship Of Fools, A Streetcar Named Desire*; Steve Martin, *Roxanne*; Marcello Mastroianni, *Tchin*

Tchin (also called A Fine Romance); Jack Nicholson, *Five Easy Pieces*; France Nuyen, *The Joy Luck Club*; Gary Oldman, *Bram Stoker's Dracula*; Claude Rains, *The Phantom Of The Opera*; Vanessa Redgrave, *Howard's End*; Christopher Reeve, *Somewhere In Time*; Keanu Reeves, *My Own Private Idaho*; Jean Rochefort, *The Hairdresser's Husband*; Winona Ryder, *Beetlejuice*; Campbell Scott, *Dying Young*; Sissy Spacek, *'Night Mother*; François Truffaut, *The Green Room*.

FINER DISTINCTION NOTES

WINGS: Fours can have a 3 wing, a 5 wing or both wings.

Four With a 3 Wing

Fours with a 3 wing can sometimes seem like Sevens. May be outgoing, have a sense of humor and style. Prize being both creative and effective in the world. Both intuitive *and* ambitious. Good imaginations, often talented. Can be colorful, fancy dressers, make a distinct impression. Self-knowledge combines well with social and organizational skills.

When more entranced, often have a public/private split. Could conceal feelings in public then go home to loneliness. Or they could enjoy their work and be dissatisfied in love. Tendency towards melodrama and flamboyance; true feelings can often be hidden. Competitive, sneaky, aware of how they look. Some have bad taste. May be fickle in love, drawn to romantic images that they have projected onto others. Could have a dull spouse, then fantasize about glamorous strangers. Achievements can be tainted by jealousy, revenge, or a desire to prove the crowd wrong.

Real-Life Fours With a 3 Wing: Judy Collins, Neil Diamond, Martha Graham, Janis Joplin, Naomi Judd, John Malkovich, Mary McCarthy, Anaïs Nin, Nick Nolte, Laurence Olivier, Edith Piaf, Winona Ryder, Liv Ullmann, Robert James Waller, Tennessee Williams.
Movie Fours With a 3 Wing: F. Murray Abraham, *Amadeus*; Anne Bancroft, *The Turning Point*; John Barrymore, *Dinner At Eight*; Judy Davis, *Impromptu*; Jill Ireland, *From Noon Til Three*; Vivien Leigh, *A Streetcar Named Desire*; Winona Ryder, *Mermaids*.

Four With a 5 Wing

Healthy side of this wing brings a withdrawn, complex creativity. May be somewhat intellectual but have exceptional depth of feeling and insight. Very much their own person; original and idiosyncratic. Have a spiritual and aesthetic openness. Will find multiple levels of meaning to most events. May have a strong need and ability to pour themselves into artistic creations. Loners; can seem enigmatic and hard to read. Externally reserved and internally resonant. When they open up it can be sudden and total.

When entranced or defensive, Fours with a 5 wing can easily feel alienated and depressed. Many have a sense of not belonging, of being from another planet. Can get lost in their own process, drown in their own ocean. Whiny — tend to ruminate and relive past experience. Prone to the emotion of shame. Air of sullen, withdrawn disappointment. May live within a private mythology of pain and loss. Can get deeply morbid and fall in love with death.

Real-Life Fours With a 5 Wing: Diane Arbus, Marlon Brando, Jackson Browne, Leonard Cohen, Brian De Palma, Harvey Keitel, Sylvia Plath, Edgar Allen Poe, Anne Sexton, Vincent van Gogh, Virginia Woolf.
Movie Fours With a 5 Wing: David Andrews, *Cherry 2000*; Albert Finney, *The Playboys*; Claude Rains, *The Phantom Of The Opera*; Winona Ryder, *Beetlejuice*; Campbell Scott, *Dying Young*; Meryl Streep, *The French Lieutenant's Woman, Out Of Africa, Plenty.*

CONNECTING POINTS (Stress and Security)
Fours connect to the high and low side of 2.
Fours connect to the high and low side of 1.

Four's Connection to 2

Healthy connection brings interpersonal skills and the ability to voluntarily empathize with others. Can make good psychotherapists, teachers, ministers, parents. Teach others about the realms of subjectivity. Twoish capacity to identify with an audience. Good communicators, fine therapeutic skills. Can listen and accept, especially willing to understand the pain of friends. Less selfish. Will harbor and act upon ideals of service to others.

Low side brings dependency. Tendency to fixate on a loved one. Whiny demandingness and blame. Codependent melodrama when the real person behaves differently than the Four expects them to. Think they can't live without the other. Twoish capacity to empathize becomes compulsive. Four can't help but identify, especially with others' pain. Takes "beloved" person inside of their subjectivity, making that person their salvation. They may flee themselves by serving others. Prideful sense of specialness is also intensified. Hysterical illness possible.

Movie Fours who demonstrate this connection: Harriet Andersson, *Cries And Whispers;* David Andrews, *Cherry 2000;* Vivien Leigh, *A Streetcar Named Desire;* Nick Nolte, *New York Stories;* Claude Rains, *The Phantom Of The Opera.*

Four's Connection to 1

Healthy connection to 1 brings objectivity, balance and idealism. Helps Fours locate the objective world and connect to a factual reality that is independent of their inner feelings. Like finding dry land in a sea of subjectivity. Discipline of cleaving to the real world diminishes self-indulgence and melodrama. Practical problem-solving skills enhanced. Intense feelings smooth out, a kind of balanced equanimity takes hold. Will also be idealistic and willing to work hard out in the world for what they believe in. Become contributors instead of complainers.

The low side of this connection is that a Four can become fault-finding and nit-picky. Dissatisfied perfectionism may color their relationships. Get creatively blocked because nothing they produce is up to their own high standards. Induce shame in themselves with inner criticism. May tear down others out of jealousy. Sometimes latch onto a grandiose, obsessive Big Idea. Belief they are attuned to Absolute Truth. Idealistic and artistic pretentiousness possible. Sometimes can be rageful.

Movie Fours who demonstrate this connection: Anne Bancroft, *The Turning Point;* Nicolas Cage, *Moonstruck;* Judy Davis, *Impromptu;* Maria de Medieros, *Henry And June;* Winona Ryder, *Mermaids;* Campbell Scott, *Dying Young;* Meryl Streep, *Out Of Africa, Plenty.*

SUBTYPE THEMES

Self-Preservation

People with this theme are often advocates of risk. Can be reckless, court disaster or just flirt lightly with loss. Take chances to stir up emotional intensity, play out melodrama or to get attention. Sometimes they have a desire to punish other through hurting themselves. The logic is, "If I die then they'll be sorry and finally appreciate me."

Can seem like counterphobic Sixes in their behavior. With a 3 wing this subtype is more flamboyant and makes a show of their daring. With a 5 wing they grow more sullen and self-punishing.

Movie examples include: Nicolas Cage, *Moonstruck;* Meryl Streep, *Out Of Africa;* Judy Davis, *Impromptu.*

Intimate

Fours with this theme tend to be highly competitive in close relationships but also more generally. With a mate they are prone to jealousy. Want to be the most important person in mate's life. Could be jealous of a partner's past relationships, maybe want to be the only person the partner has ever loved. Related to the dependent side of 2.

More broadly can be consumed by professional envy. Long to best others in their work. Can jealously measure their contributions. Petty about keeping score. Want recognition for their uniqueness. Take away from successes of others when threatened. May seek revenge for a sense of defect. See F. Murray Abraham in *Amadeus,* Harriet Andersson in *Cries And Whispers,* Nick Nolte in *New York Stories.*

Social

Prone to shame because they compare themselves with the "normal" world around them. Can be highly self-critical and feel ashamed for their deviance from imagined group norms. Sensitive to criticism. May romanticize their defects but feel bad about themselves anyway.

If they have a 3 wing, may cover their shame with charm. Can also seek status or be driven to achieve to get revenge against those who once laughed at them (Danny DeVito, *Batman Returns*). With a 5 wing, can grow antisocial and depressed, bearing their shame in solitude (Meryl Streep in *The French Lieutenant's Woman*).

FIVES

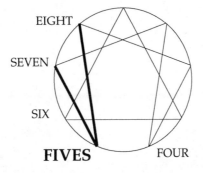

EIGHT

SEVEN

SIX

FIVES   FOUR

PEOPLE WHO PULL BACK FROM THE WORLD AND LIVE IN THEIR THOUGHTS. MAY BE WISE, FARSIGHTED AND KNOWLEDGEABLE OR ABSTRACT, STINGY AND SCHIZOID.

FAMOUS REAL-LIFE FIVES

St. Thomas Aquinas, Arthur Ashe, Playright Samuel Beckett, Author Paul Bowles, The Buddha, Director Tim Burton, David Byrne, Actor Richard Chamberlain, Agatha Christie, Montgomery Clift, Former CIA Director William Colby, Michael Crichton, Daniel Day-Lewis, René Descartes, Aviatrix Amelia Earhart, Thomas Edison, Albert Einstein, Author Loren Eisley, the cultural aura of England,

Chess player Bobby Fischer, E. M. Forster, Greta Garbo, J. Paul Getty, Author Graham Greene, Hildegarde of Bingen, Alfred Hitchcock, Anthony Hopkins, Howard Hughes, Jeremy Irons, Franz Kafka, Director Philip Kaufman, Jacqueline Kennedy Onassis, Director Stanley Kubrick, C-SPAN's Brian Lamb, John le Carré, Author Ursula K. LeGuin, Photographer Annie Leibowitz,

Vladimir Lenin, George Lucas, David Lynch, Author Norman MacLean, Reporter Robert MacNeil, Movie critic Leonard Maltin, Author Peter Matthiessen, Novelist Ian McEwan, Singer Natalie Merchant, Actor Sam Neill, Georgia O'Keefe, Al Pacino, Italian sculptor Paladino, Michelle Pfeiffer, Oliver Sacks, Author May Sarton, Ebenezer

Scrooge, Behaviorist B. F. Skinner, Poet Gary Snyder, Philosopher Susan Sontag, George Stephanopoulos, Actress Madeleine Stowe, Paul Tsongas, Max Von Sydow, Ludwig Wittgenstein, Reporter Bob Woodward.

INTRODUCTION

Fives, Sixes and Sevens share a general undercurrent of fear and form another "emotional Trio." Unlike Twos, Threes and Fours, people within this group are not confused about who they are or how they feel. Instead they tend to unconsciously anticipate the dangers of life and have a baseline habit of reacting fearfully. Fives, Sixes and Sevens are generally also thinkers — people who live more in their heads than in their bodies. They have specific struggles around taking action and asserting their wills in the world.

A Five's fears are specifically social — they habitually guard against being invaded or engulfed by other people. This is the most explicitly antisocial of the Enneagram styles. When defensive, Fives can be withdrawn and standoffish as a way to manage their hypersensitivity to others. Generally, they fear close relationship as it can lead to feeling overwhelmed, smothered or swarmed.

Fives generally live in their thoughts, in contrast to Fours, who live in their emotional imaginations. People with this style have well-developed abilities to analyze and synthesize knowledge. They may be perceptive, wise and objective, displaying an ability to stay centered and logical when others around them are losing their heads.

Awakened Fives usually strike some balance between interacting with the world and withdrawing from it. This style is frequently associated with knowledgeable competence and, sometimes, genius. When healthy, Fives express themselves in the world and actively offer the fruits of their knowledge. Teaching and writing are frequent occupations but whatever they do, healthy Fives seem to insist that their talent for knowledge count for something beyond itself. There is an idealistic quality to this drive that makes them willing and sometimes courageous contributors.

Healthy Fives can also practice what the Buddhists call "non-attachment." It's like being willing to play the games of life without being overly attached to results. As friends, they may be able to understand your point of view almost as well as their own. They are sympathetic, but able to view events from a distant enough perspective to avoid getting personally upset. This also contributes to a kindheart-edness that wishes others well.

More defensively, Fives can slide from nonattachment into disas-sociation, the inner state of being cut off from feeling. An entranced person with this style is hyperaware of the world's demands, and then passively responds by withdrawing. Most outsiders see a Five's capacity to pull back as a kind of independence. It's a defense as well; the Five is making a strong antisocial boundary to compensate for being overly sensitive in the first place.

Cutting themselves off then becomes a habit. The idea is, "If I can just learn to live with less I'll avoid the influence of others." This leads to the tendency to *hoard*, to keep and save what little they have in order to need less and stay withdrawn. Fives can hoard time, money, space, land, information, or emotional availability. It doesn't matter what is hoarded, the pattern is the same. The person tries to protect against flooding by stacking up supplies on their dry inner island.

Entranced Fives also stay distant from their own emotions by living in a world of information and ideas. The more they cut them-selves off, however, the more they struggle with feelings of emptiness, loneliness, and compulsive need. It's like trying to talk yourself out of being hungry. At this point a Five may be slow to know how they feel because they can only reach their feelings through a lengthy sequence of thought. Entranced Fives worship gods of reason and try to look distantly down on their own emotions. They may also act superior towards other people.

When Fives are deeply entranced, they may become schizoid and unpredictable, as though disassociated parts of them are taking turns talking. They can project an absent, vaguely shocked aura or be pointedly antisocial. A Five could sit through a party at which they said nothing and later claim that they had a good time. Or they might alienate others with nasty, sneering commentary and unpredictable aggression.

The habit of disassociating emotions becomes so developed that they lose basic touch with reality. They may develop weird phobias of invisible objects like germs. Aggressive episodes are possible, fol-lowed by bursts of acute paranoia.

The Five defensive tendencies of protection through isolation, observing from afar, and hoarding are all on display in the movies that follow.

FIVES IN THE MOVIES

There have actually been a number of Five performers who have movie star charisma but, like Fours, they are principally character actors and actresses. A limited list includes people like Montgomery Clift, Greta Garbo, Max Von Sydow, Anthony Hopkins, Michelle Pfeiffer, Al Pacino, Madeleine Stowe and Daniel Day-Lewis. Mostly these performers don't play Five roles but they have a basic aura that is pulled-back and enigmatic.

Actors like Steve McQueen, Clint Eastwood or Robert Redford (none of them Fives) lend their roles a Fiveish cast because holding back a little draws the audience towards the performer. You tend to wonder what they are thinking and feeling. Loner heroes and strong silent types frequently have this aura. Greta Garbo is the only female star I found who based her movie persona strongly on being a Five. It worked for her and there may be others, but I suspect that hard-to-reach females have a limited appeal to filmmakers.

Fives in the movies are generally not that common, probably because reclusive or intellectual characters aren't inherently dramatic. Their range of roles runs as follows: Professors & Scholars: Anthony Hopkins, *84 Charing Cross Road*; Peter O'Toole, *Goodbye, Mr. Chips*; Gena Rowlands, *Another Woman*; Robin Williams, *Awakenings*. Writers & Artists: Dirk Bogarde, *Darling*; José Ferrer, *Moulin Rouge*; Kerry Fox, *An Angel At My Table*; Glenda Jackson, *Turtle Diary*. Voyeurs: Michel Blanc, *Monsieur Hire*; James Spader, *sex, lies and videotape*. Recluses: Daniel Auteuil, *Un Cœur En Hiver*; Rutger Hauer, *A Breed Apart*; Michael Keaton, *Batman Returns*; Ben Kingsley, *Turtle Diary*; Andie MacDowell, *Green Card*; Ally Sheedy, *Only The Lonely*; Hugo Weaving, *Proof*. Robots: "Data," *Star Trek - The Next Generation*; Peter Weller, *Robocop*.

MOVIE REVIEWS

An Angel At My Table

"Too shy to mix, my only romance was in poetry and literature." This exquisite biography of New Zealand writer Janet Frame does a fine job of dramatizing the interior life of a socially paralyzed Five.

Partly this is done through voice-over — the film is based on Frame's autobiography — but mostly credit goes to lead actress Kerry Fox for the wonderful way she writes shyness and confusion all over Janet's face. The film is episodic and lifelike rather than eventful, even when we are shown incidents like Frame's hospitalization for schizophrenia.

The hospital episode is noteworthy because the diagnosis is totally wrong. Janet isn't schizophrenic — she's defenseless. She's an eccentric, withdrawn loner with poor social skills and overwhelming self-consciousness. During minor social encounters she goes stunned like a doe in headlights. As often as practical, she retreats from the world and hides in her books and writing. She refuses offers of food from others but then eats ravenously when alone (connection to 7). These bursts of secret appetite are related to other odd habits like hoarding and hiding bits of paper and trying not to smile because her teeth have gone bad.

We see a little of how she got that way. She grew up poor in a small, crowded home, straining for space. Frame was overshadowed by an older sister and frightened by her One father's angry outbursts. Life was sometimes rife with nasty surprise, and Janet is shown retreating into her imagination and books. Most Fives develop defenses against social exposure, unpredictability or loss of privacy. As an adult, Frame fears all three.

"I longed to be so full of secrets so that a man could discover them. But for so long I'd blocked all exits and entrances so that I felt as sexless as a block of wood." Nevertheless, Frame travels to Spain, has love affairs and gradually comes out of her shell. You get the impression that she will never marry but, by film's end, she is much more fully in the world and, through her writing, a willing contributor. She's a self-preservation subtype and defends herself by withdrawing.

A lovely, delicate, absorbing movie. The sister Isabel is an Eight.

Another Woman

Woody Allen movie about a stingy Five college professor (Gena Rowlands) who has retreated to a rented apartment to finish writing a book. She finds herself next door to a psychiatrist's office, and sound carries well through the walls. Rowlands gets voyeuristically distracted from her writing by the confessions of the doctor's patients, especially depressed, feelingful Mia Farrow. What Rowlands hears sets her on an internal quest to resolve the pain of her marriage to unfaithful, astringent Ian Holm (also Fiveish) and to examine the many ways she is haunted by regret.

If this sounds depressive and dry, it is. This is a movie about a lack of passion that itself lacks passion. The static, speechy screenplay forces the characters to act mannered and speak in the formal cadences of diplomats. The photography is darkly somber and reinforces a barren mood.

Caveats aside, *Another Woman* is quite informative about Fives. Most of the film's other characters are on to Rowland's defenses and make comments like, "She's led a cold, cerebral life and has alienated everyone around her," or "She's a little judgmental. She stands above people and observes them." Rowlands is another self-preservation subtype characterized by withdrawal. We see her refusing most social encounters and reading Rilke to disassociate after one upsetting confrontation. She also has a 4 wing, observable in her abstracted, off-center thinking and her somewhat melancholy yearning for a long-lost affair with decent, vital Gene Hackman.

Throughout the film she flashes back to scenes with him and inevitably realizes she was in love. The slowness of this dawning actually mirrors how disassociated Fives only gradually find their way into their feelings, usually through a lot of rumination.

The other realm Rowlands explores in flashback is her childhood family. John Houseman plays her elderly father, a stern, imperious One who makes a touching speech about his failures in a dream Rowlands has. Houseman was a real-life One and always played them. In another dream Rowlands remembers her father as a younger man, this time played by David Ogden Stiers. The character is still a One and Stiers always plays Ones too, most notably on the TV show *MASH*. Good Enneatype casting.

Betty Buckley and Sandy Dennis both appear in a few scenes as Twos.

Awakenings

Robin Williams stars as a meek Five in a rather good adaptation of a true story by neurologist Oliver Sacks. The year is 1969 and Williams/Sacks is hired at a state hospital to supervise a ward of apparently catatonic patients. They are the victims of a flu-like epidemic and Williams is hired to supervise the ward in which they are housed. The hitch is that Williams has no clinical experience — he's devoted the last ten years to research. In his job interview he cites an attempt to extract a chemical substance from the bodies of tons of earthworms. When the frowning hospital interviewer says, "But that can't be done," Williams beams proudly, "I know. We proved it!"

He's shown as a shy, absentminded professor throughout the film. His apartment is stacked with books, he turns down social invitations to stay at home alone with his piano. When he does venture out, he enjoys going to atriums. The two things that motivate him are the intellectual adventure of research and a basic kindheartedness that Fives sometimes have.

In his work, these qualities prompt him to question whether the catatonics — written off as incurable by the hospital staff — could be somehow helped. He experiments, follows his hunches and eventually finds a drug that works to awaken the patients, at least temporarily. The fallout from this event forms a story that could have been just sugary but instead comes by its sentiment honestly.

The disease, by the way, is a good metaphor for Nineyness. Robert De Niro, a sometimes dull actor, is splendid here as Williams's first test case. His character seems like a Nine but it's hard to tell because he is largely defined by the illness, as are the other inmates. Everyone's asleep. One nurse describes a patient as unable to walk alone: "But he'll walk with me. It's like he borrows my will." A good description of the unhealthy side of Nine.

John Heard plays Williams's administrative nemesis, a One. Julie Kavner is a Nine nurse and De Niro's mother is a Two. Williams is a real-life Seven so he's playing his connecting point.

Goodbye, Mr Chips (1969)

Peter O'Toole is the title character, a shy Five schoolmaster, and the film follows his life over a twenty year period. It's mainly a love story as he meets and marries Petula Clark, but the movie also shows a Five gradually growing into power.

As the story begins O'Toole is alone, lost in his work, disliked by his students, shy, haunted and elsewhere. He's so constricted socially that he can barely talk. At parties he goes stilted, formal and distant. He hides behind knowledge, uses academic terminology and priggishly corrects people's speech ("How you could ever imagine that a word like 'suitability' could prevail over a word like 'love,' I'll never know"). He's rather sweet in a hapless way; painfully earnest, honorable, gentle, flustered by a kiss on the cheek.

As the episodic story progresses nothing really happens. O'Toole marries, fights a few battles, gets promoted and grows. He becomes firm, committed, and socially comfortable. He's still a little stingy and grouses at the extravagance of his wife's anniversary presents to him. At film's end, though, he has stepped into his own social power in a way that is quite consistent with the Five "character arc." He's grown decisive and takes courageous stands in the world.

The movie is certainly worthwhile for learning about how Fives grow. I have two cautions about it: 1) It is sometimes, er, ... a musical ... and the songs are not so good; 2) The sex roles are very dated and figure awkwardly in the story. Otherwise, O'Toole is excellent and the film is warmhearted. It may be a little hard to find on video, but it does exist.

Petula Clark plays either a Nine or a Two, but it's hard to tell. Sian Phillips plays Clark's friend Ursula, a Seven with an 8 wing. O'Toole is a real-life Seven so he's also playing his connecting point.

Green Card

Andie MacDowell's Fiveish character in *Green Card* is named Brontë, a fact that's meant to tip you off. Not only does she love classical music, but her main interests in life are solitary. "Most women I've known have tried to crowd me, except you," an ex-beau tells her.

That's because Brontë, a botanist, is into plants rather than people. Although she does apply her knowledge socially — towards improving urban environments for children — what motivates her marriage to French stranger, George (Gérard Depardieu), is the desire for a really great garden. She needs to appear married to rent the apartment of her dreams, complete with atrium. He needs to seem married to qualify for a Green Card, a residence permit that allows him to live and work in America. They go through with the marriage but Brontë maintains her detachment: "I have no opinion of you, George. I'm just waiting for this to be over so I can start my life again." "You're like a plant — a cactus!" he replies.

Well, she is, but MacDowell's performance is not exactly assured. This is not as good a portrait of a Five as some of our other films, but it has moments. The comedy itself is not really funny and the romantic story is initially labored.

Depardieu is kind of a Seven with an 8 wing. Part of the film's problem is that it tries to make him lovable when he's actually domineering and demanding. He gets better, though, and the film does too. The last hour is quite tender. Remember that Seven and Five are connecting points for each other.

Monsieur Hire

"People don't like me but then I don't like people either. I like silence. I don't talk much." That's precise, dismissive Monsieur Hire talking. As played by Michel Blanc, he's the perfect embodiment of a Five expressing the low side of 8. He's nasty, punitive, standoffish — like Scrooge without the money. He erupts into yelling when threatened and is openly misogynistic. Part of the skill of the (excellent) film is to make us care for someone so willfully perverse and disagreeable. By film's end, Hire transcends his Fiveishness in quite a credible way and even becomes heroic.

This seems unlikely at first. Monsieur Hire is disliked by nearly everyone in the town where he has his tailor shop. He's stingy, aloof and displays an air of senseless superiority. He's also fastidious and almost unnaturally clean. Even when bowling, he rolls the ball with an arrogant precision.

He also has a past — a criminal record of indecent exposure that is related to the voyeurism that he still practices. At night, when alone, he dims the lights, plays one piece of music and spies on a beautiful neighbor (Sandrine Bonnaire). One day, he passes her on the street, smells her perfume and buys a matching bottle to sniff that evening at his window.

This practice becomes a perfect metaphor for Fiveish hoarding. There is no emotional risk in observing from afar and Hire can have the same experience each night, over and over, alone.

Within the story though, this kink makes him the prime suspect in the murder of a local young woman. A police detective is sure Hire did it and tracks him doggedly. Meanwhile, Bonnaire cottons on to being observed and turns tables on Hire. She seeks him out and wants detailed descriptions of his sexual fantasies about her. She's involved in something criminal and has several motives for courting Hire, but their relationship nonetheless develops a weird intimacy. Hire actually falls in love with her and his hoarding gives way to something like true generosity (connection to 7). Through the perversity comes real feeling and an accurate perception of who she is. In the end he gambles that the strength of Bonnaire's feeling for him will outweigh her other motives. Everyone's actual connection to the murder is also revealed. Bonnaire seems at first a Three and then a Six with a Three streak. Her Enneagram style was finally unclear, although the motive for her actions is loyalty. The detective after Hire is definitely a Four. He's preoccupied by the youth and beauty of the murdered girl and is haunted by his melancholy fantasies about her.

Only The Lonely

The script for this tame comedy-drama feels like a first draft. The thin story — lonely middle-aged nice-guy leaves home and gets married — is bulked up with a lot of fake ethnic goo. It is a virtual remake of the 1950s movie *Marty*, which featured identical characters who were Italian; this time they're Irish.

The types are good, though. The late John Candy plays the nice-guy Nine (1 wing). He's the guilty, peacemaking son of Maureen O'Hara, a domineering Two. She's *mean*, reflecting both a 1 wing and the low side of 8. Candy initially placates her bullying but into his life comes Five Ally Sheedy, a solitary mortician.

The new relationship starts out unpromisingly as the shy Sheedy speaks just ten words on their first date. The baffled Candy starts to excuse himself when Sheedy blurts:

"I had a wonderful time tonight."

"You did?" asks Candy, amazed.

"I have this thing ... this introverted kind of thing."

"That just means you're shy."

"No, it's worse than shy ... I guess it doesn't help spending eight hours a day with people who don't talk back to you. I'm trying to get past it."

With this assurance, things continue well until the couple's first meeting with Candy's mother. The jealous, hostile O'Hara tries to run over Sheedy while Candy minimizes and sues for peace. Sheedy stands up to O'Hara but then later gets angry at Candy for not protecting her. She promptly breaks off the relationship.

This might seem like a manufactured crisis for the film's under-nourished plot, but Sheedy's overreaction is also very Fiveish. She makes too strong a boundary to make up for having been vulnerable. This happens more than once before the film is over.

Nice-guy Candy finally has to take a stand ("Getting married is the only time in my life where I've made a decision without thinking of my family first"). O'Hara grows a little, lets Candy go, has an insight or two ("I'm not a lovable person but I can take care of myself"). It's a somewhat daring performance; O'Hara's character is, among other things, a racist. She gives the film a little life and Sheedy's Five character is worth a look. Latter plays a similar character in *The Breakfast Club*.

SCHIZOIDS

Here are two unrelated movies with identical character tensions related to Fives:

The Nutty Professor — Remember those Jerry Lewis movies where he bounced off walls and screeched like a gibbon? This isn't one of them. *The Nutty Professor* is Lewis's restrained, kind of cute version of *Dr. Jekyll And Mr. Hyde*. Lewis plays the Dr. Jekyll role as a nerdy, socially hamstrung Five (6 wing). He's a disorganized college professor who invents a potion that brings out what's latent in human nature. What's latent in him is his connecting point; when Professor Lewis drinks the brew he instantly turns from a Five into an Eight.

Latter character is obnoxious, overconfident and socially pushy. He's like a lounge lizard but brazen and loud. Lewis flips back and forth between the two styles, confusing and irritating the movie's other characters. Stella Stevens is good as a Oneish woman who fights with the Eight Lewis. Young kids would like this movie a lot.

Batman Returns is a sequel to the megahit *Batman* in which Jack Nicholson played a villainous Seven. This time out, Batman (Michael Keaton) is battling two foes, The Penguin and Catwoman, for the control of dank, surreal Gotham City.

Like Robin Williams and Peter O'Toole, Michael Keaton is a real-life Seven playing a Five. His Bruce Wayne is a rich recluse who is shy, absentminded, etc. He has a big mansion and a giant bat cave that is well stocked with computers. When crime strikes he jumps into his bat suit and becomes an avenging Eight. This back and forth dynamic is present throughout this movie as well.

The bizarre Penguin (Danny DeVito) is a Four. He's deformed, was abandoned at birth, and is on a melancholy quest to rejoin the world and find respectability. He's a social subtype, driven by shame. He tells Batman: "When it all comes down to it you're just jealous because I'm a genuine freak and you have to wear a mask."

DeVito's character has strong shades of The Phantom of the Opera. He has a Monster Complex and longs for the world's respect. DeVito overacts and his sequences go on too long, but the style is quite plain.

Michelle Pfeiffer steals the movie as the wild Catwoman. She too is schizoid, but her poles are between phobic and counterphobic Six (5 wing). By day she is fumbling, self-effacing and ambivalent. "How can you be so mean to someone so meaningless?" she asks her boss, Christopher Walken, an evil corporate Three. She's loyal to his abusive authority but turns on him (and men in general) when she becomes the rebellious counterphobic Catwoman.

Pfeiffer brings a lot of energy to the role(s) and she milks the contradictory nature of Sixes for a lot of humor. Catwoman is plainly drawn to Batman, but she can't let herself have him. She's just as self-defeating as her daytime alter ego, but in a more flamboyant way. Both sides of her have big authority problems, but as Catwoman she attacks what she's afraid of even when it means losing what she truly wants.

Michael Gough plays Batman's butler/confidant, and he's a One. The movie's director, Tim Burton, is also a Five (4 wing).

sex, lies and videotape

This is a great movie for students of the Enneagram. It is solely about the neurotic skews of a Nine, a Three, an Eight and a Five. Watching this film is a lot like the experience of doing therapy — the focus is close and tight on what's incongruent and accidentally revealing about everyone's behavior.

The Five, played by James Spader, is an aloof voyeur with a probing-yet-distant intensity. He has a hobby of videotaping women whom he has convinced to talk about their sexual histories. Socially, he maintains the withdrawn noncommittal role of interviewer. Alone, he replays the tapes, inhabiting a kind of secret garden of sexual fantasy in the emotional safety of solitude.

As events unfold, it becomes obvious that Spader's videotapes are a symbolic, abstract Fiveish attempt to understand why his last relationship went wrong years earlier. His defenses start to crumble when one of the other characters turns the video camera on him and says, "You've had an effect on my life, whether you like it or not." Spader confesses that he had spent years constructing his life so that he would have no effect on anyone. At the end, he acknowledges the failure of his defenses and starts to grow. He destroys the videotapes and commits to a real relationship in the world. The character has a counterphobic 6 wing and goes towards what he is afraid of.

Andie MacDowell plays a sexually repressed housewife whose Three husband (Peter Gallagher) is cheating on her. Much humor develops from her Nine style of minimizing and abstracting while she ignores the obvious emptiness of her life: "It seems so stupid talking about my problems when poor children are starving," or "Everything's just fine in my life but for some reason I keep thinking about garbage." Eventually she wakes up from her sleepy denial and becomes honest, focused and clear.

Laura San Giacoma plays MacDowell's younger sister, a tough Eight. She's having an affair with husband Gallagher behind her sister's back. She and Gallagher have a conflict that is probable for an Eight and a Three who don't like each other.

Writer/director Steven Soderbergh went on to make *Kafka*, a dull fictional film about the writer. The real-life Kafka was a Five and in the film he's played by real-life Five Jeremy Irons.

Turtle Diary

This low-key charmer must be the definitive Five movie. Glenda Jackson and Ben Kingsley star in a Harold Pinter story about two shy, lonely Fives who conspire to steal some sea turtles from a city zoo. Aided by an Eightish zookeeper, the plan is to release the turtles at the English coast where the Gulf Stream will take them to freedom. The execution of this caper generates some ironic suspense but the film's real pleasure is in watching the Jackson and Kingsley characters as they change and grow and bloom.

As the story begins, both are shown as quietly eccentric and restless with the sterility of their lives. Jackson is a reclusive writer of children's books and Kingsley manages a bookstore. They actually meet at the turtle aquarium where each spends solitary afternoons watching the animals dreamily swim.

Both characters are Fiveishly constricted but express it differently. Jackson's trouble seems more social; she is tortured, garbled and near-paralyzed when interacting with others. Underneath she has a spiritual anguish she can't articulate, but her night dreams are all of freeing the turtles. "They're imprisoned," she says simply, when asked why she wants to carry out the plan. The anguish is obviously for her own unrisked life and she conspires haltingly with Kingsley to free the turtles and somehow herself.

Kingsley's timidity is around action rather than interaction. Socially, he is secretive but finesseful; he bandies and repels and distances others with irony. But he's also impotent in a futureless job and when his loutish neighbor bullies him, Kingsley meekly tries to bury his anger in obsessive housecleaning. Springing the turtles becomes a metaphor for taking initiative. When he decides to carry out the plan he begins to display a delightful zest for living.

For both, the turtle jail break is a way of moving *towards* the world. Jackson quells her basic anxiety and risks falling in love. Kingsley becomes more self-assertive, going to the high side of 8. He handles his bully neighbor quite differently after the caper. He also gets more cheerful and expansive (high side of 7). At one point while transporting the turtles, Kingsley comments that he hasn't had a thought in several hours. Jackson knows exactly what he means; both of them are so involved in life that they aren't thinking *about* it.

The film gently sabotages our expectations that its two stars should get together romantically. They're actually wrong for each other. Both have the same dilemma and express two aspects of the Five style. Jackson has a 4 wing and Kingsley a 6 wing. Kingsley's other neighbor is a Two; her fate underscores the need to seize life today.

The Vanishing (Dutch version)

This is one of a thimbleful of films that features a Five villain. In 1965's *The Collector*, Five Terence Stamp kidnaps and imprisons a woman because he wants to possess her. His motivation is a metaphor for Fiveish hoarding, a desire to *have* gone mad. By contrast, *The Vanishing* features a Five serial killer whose actions are driven by a disassociated ideal of precision and a counterphobic desire to master fear.

The story hinges on one quiet event. An arguing young Dutch couple on vacation in France pull off at a truck stop. In bright daylight under utterly ordinary circumstances, the woman vanishes.

There are no clues, no residue and no case that the man, Rex Hofman (Gene Bervoets), can make to the police. They believe she simply jilted him. The case is eventually investigated but remains unsolved.

All would be over except that Rex Hofman is a melancholy Four who pines away for his lost love and grows obsessed with finding out what happened to her. He plasters France with missing person posters and goes on television to talk about the case and keep it alive. He's so haunted and preoccupied that his subsequent lady friend leaves him because she can't compete with the memory of the vanished woman. Hofman knows he's far gone but he's so morbidly romantic that he can't stop. An interviewer asks him: "Do you have hope (of finding her)?" "No," he replies. "Then why pursue it?" "It's a homage." (Introjection again.)

In parallel, we see scenes of Mr. Lemorne (Bernard Pierre Donnadieu), a precise, calm, solitary Five who is leading a double life. He's a family man with a wife and daughters who withdraws to a country house to plan out the specifics of his abductions of women. We see him rehearsing conversations with intended victims and timing steps with a stopwatch. He notes down the results of each practice session as if he were conducting a lab experiment, and indeed, he's a chemistry teacher in ordinary life.

This is a madness of detail and Lemorne speaks about it indirectly to his unsuspecting wife: "It has become a passion. You start with an idea in your head. You take the first step, then the second. Then you realize that you are up to your neck in something mad. But that doesn't matter; you persevere for the pleasure of persevering, for the satisfaction you get from it."

Lemorne is so confident in his ability to disguise that he subtly brags about his connection to the crimes. When he finds out that Rex is still searching for the lost woman, Lemorne sends him postcards and solicits a meeting. He eventually seeks out Hofman in Holland and offers him a ride back to France where he promises to explain everything about the vanishing. Hofman is so obsessed and Fourishly drawn to finding out what happened that he accepts the ride.

Along the way, Lemorne explains himself in matter-of-fact detail. He knows he's a sociopath and speaks of experiments and philosophical questions that have led to his secret habits. It becomes clear that he loves the detailed planning involved in his crimes, though he observes: "The best plan can be wiped out one moment to the next. That saddens me." The love of disassociated planning in Fives is related to the low side of 7.

Lemorne basically describes a history of dealing with fear by going against it. He has a counterphobic 6 wing and is obsessed with risk. He also describes in his calm, perverse way how a philosophical dilemma led to his first abduction. After one day saving a drowning child, Lemorne says, "my daughter was bursting with admiration. I thought that her admiration for me wasn't worth anything, unless I could prove myself absolutely incapable of doing anything bad. And since there is no white without black, I had, therefore, to conceive the worst thing that I could think of at that time."

This kind of logic reigning supreme is part of what's so chilling about *The Vanishing*. The film's style itself is Fiveish. It's dry, existential, and builds suspense from the accumulation of small details. There's not a wasted scene in the movie and, while it may spook you, there's little overt violence.

Be sure to avoid the dopey American remake of this story with Jeff Bridges and Kiefer Sutherland. Director George Sluizer redirected his original film, this time in a flat pedestrian fashion. It's as if someone had said, "George, the original was brilliant! Now how about a version that really bored, lazy people could enjoy?" Jeff Bridges plays a Five alright, but as a drooling weirdo, which robs the killer of his frightening ordinariness and completely telegraphs the story. This version even has a happy ending ... It's real dreck and deservedly flopped.

OTHER MOVIE FIVES

Kevin Anderson, *Liebestraum*; Daniel Auteuil, *Un Cœur En Hiver (A Heart In Winter)*; Alan Bates, *Zorba The Greek*; Dirk Bogarde, *Darling, Death In Venice*; Lothaire Bluteau (priest), *Black Robe*; Marlon Brando, *Reflections In A Golden Eye*; Richard Burton, *Who's Afraid Of Virginia Woolf?*; Robert De Niro, *Mad Dog And Glory*; Robert Donat, *Goodbye, Mr. Chips ('39)*; Colm Feore, *Thirty-Two Short Films About Glenn Gould*; José Ferrer, *Moulin Rouge*; Albert Finney, *Scrooge*; Laurence Harvey, *The Manchurian Candidate*; Rutger Hauer, *A Breed Apart*; Anthony Hopkins, *The Efficiency Expert, 84 Charing Cross Road*; Tommy Lee Jones, *Lonesome Dove*; Burt Lancaster, *Birdman Of Alcatraz*;

Fred MacMurray, *The Absent-Minded Professor*; John Malkovich, *The Sheltering Sky*; Steve McQueen, *Bullitt, The Getaway*; Sam Neill, *Hostage*; Judd Nelson, *The Dark Backward*; Al Pacino, *The Godfather Part II*; William Petersen, *Manhunter*; Robert Redford, *Jeremiah Johnson*; Mickey Rourke, *Wild Orchid*; Alastair Sim, *A Christmas Carol*; Terence Stamp, *The Collector*; George Stephanopoulos, *The War Room*; Dean Stockwell, *Tucker - A Man And His Dream*; Max Von Sydow, *Duet For One, The Passion Of Anna, Three Days Of The Condor*; Hugo Weaving ("Martin"), *Proof*; Peter Weller, *Robocop*.

FINER DISTINCTION NOTES

WINGS: Fives can have a 4 wing, a 6 wing or both wings. A Five's 6 wing can be phobic or counterphobic.

Five With a 4 Wing

The difference between the 4 wing and the 6 wing in Fives is like the difference between Art and Science. 4 wing brings an abstract, intuitive cast of thought, as though the Five were thinking in geometric shapes instead of words or realistic images. May be talented artistically and inhabit moods like Fours do. Combine intellectual and emotional imagination. Enjoy the realm of philosophy and beautiful constructs of thought. The marriage of mental perspective and aesthetics is the best of life for them.

When more defensive may seem a little ghostly, have a whisper in their voice. Fluctuate between impersonal withdrawal and bursts of friendly caring. Can get floaty and abstract. Act like they're inside a bubble, sometimes with an air of implicit superiority. Cliché of the "absentminded professor" applies especially to Fives with this wing.

Environmentally sensitive and subject at times to total overwhelm. Touchy about criticism. Can be slow to recover from traumatic events. Melancholy isolation and bleak existential depression are possible pitfalls.

Real-Life Fives With a 4 Wing: Samuel Beckett, Paul Bowles, Tim Burton, David Byrne, Agatha Christie, Daniel Day-Lewis, Albert Einstein, Jeremy Irons, Phillip Kaufman, George Lucas, David Lynch, Ian McEwan, Georgia O'Keefe, Max Von Sydow.
Movie Fives With a 4 Wing: Jeff Bridges, *The Fabulous Baker Boys*; Kerry Fox, *An Angel At My Table*; Glenda Jackson, *Turtle Diary*; Gena Rowlands, *Another Woman*; Dean Stockwell, *Tucker - A Man And His Dream*.

Five With a 6 Wing

The 6 wing brings an orientation to detail and technical knowledge, along with the tendency to think in logical sequence. Especially intellectual, far more analytical than Fives with a 4 wing. Can be loyal friends, offering strong behind-the-scenes support. Kind, patient teachers, skillful experts. May have a sense of mission and work hard.

Sometimes have an aura of sensitive nerdiness and have clumsy social skills. When defensive, they can be unnerved by the expectations of others. May like people more but avoid them more. Especially sensitive to social indebtedness. Could have trouble saying "thank you." Fear of taking action, develop "information addiction" instead. Ask lots of questions but don't get around to the decision at hand.

When more entranced, they develop a suspicious scrutiny of other people's motives but can also be blind followers. Misanthropic and Scrooge-like when defensive. More able to keep their feelings cut off in a constant way. Can be cold, skeptical, ironic, and disassociated.

Counterphobic 6 wing brings courage and antiauthoritarian attitudes. When defensive they may mock authority, or angrily tell others off. Tend to "push the envelope," experiment, find what the limits are.

Real-Life Fives With a 6 Wing: Arthur Ashe, Michael Crichton, Bobby Fischer (counterphobic), John le Carré, Michelle Pfeiffer (counterphobic), Oliver Sacks, George Stephanopoulos, Madeleine Stowe.
Movie Fives With a 6 Wing: Bernard Pierre Donnadieu, *The Vanishing*; Ben Kingsley, *Turtle Diary*; Peter O'Toole, *Goodbye, Mr. Chips*; Ally Sheedy, *Only The Lonely*; James Spader, *sex, lies and videotape*; Hugo Weaving ("Martin"), *Proof*; Robin Williams, *Awakenings*.

CONNECTING POINTS (Stress and Security)
Fives connect to the high and low side of 7.
Fives connect to the high and low side of 8.

Five's Connection to 7

The healthy side of this connection brings enhanced imagination and some social skills to a Five. It may spur them to seek adventure, whether intellectual, physical or social. Can have a positive outlook, be less self-conscious. A curiosity that helps them explore the world. May be quite funny, and display an engaging playful enthusiasm. Cheerful interest in things, stay mentally alive in old age. Capacity to savor the moment, yea-saying. Sometimes have a streak of generosity.

Unhealthy connection related to the way Fives can go abstract and schizoid. Social undependability and increased difficulty with commitment. May elusively jump around in their thoughts, scatter their attention into empty interests. Tendencies toward living in the future, greed and dilettantism. Use humor to disassociate or trivialize. Action taken sporadically and for strange reasons. React from different subpersonalities, lose their center. Play mind games for diversion, trying not to feel. Weird phobias and issues about appetite possible.

Movie Fives who demonstrate this connection: Bernard Pierre Donnadieu, *The Vanishing*; Kerry Fox, *An Angel At My Table*; Anthony Hopkins, *84 Charing Cross Road*; Tommy Lee Jones, *Lonesome Dove*; Ben Kingsley, *Turtle Diary*; Ally Sheedy, *Only The Lonely*; James Spader, *sex, lies and videotape*; Robin Williams, *Awakenings*.

Five's Connection to 8

Healthy connection helps Fives access raw instinctual energy and aggression. They take charge of situations that would otherwise overwhelm them. Lusty, pushy core of Eightishness helpful to withdrawn people. Brings sexuality and physicality, moral and social courage. They state their needs, initiate contact, get things done. Helps Fives translate knowledge into action. They take risks, become initiators instead of observers.

Low side of this connection reinforces antisocial hostility. Fives can get nasty, punitive and severe with others. Unhealthy Eightish tendencies toward sneering and ridicule may come into play and support a standoffish, go-to-hell attitude. Aggression in the service of maintaining distance. Protecting what little they have. Cold, disassociated behind-the-scenes control. Bursts of nastiness. Can also turn Eightness against themselves. Criticize, yell at and persecute themselves. Leads to stricken self-consciousness and paranoia.

Movie Fives who demonstrate this connection: Michel Blanc, *Monsieur Hire*; Jeff Bridges, *The Fabulous Baker Boys*; Albert Finney, *Scrooge*; Michael Keaton, *Batman, Batman Returns*; Jerry Lewis, *The Nutty Professor*; Peter O'Toole, *Goodbye, Mr. Chips*; Al Pacino, *The Godfather Part II*; Alastair Sim, *A Christmas Carol*.

SUBTYPE THEMES

Self-Preservation

Chief defensive tendency is to withdraw. Sensitive to feeling saturated by the world, Fives with this subtype lose their sense of privacy easily. Can feel knocked over by people's expectations. In isolation they refind their lost sense of balance and build up to the next round of social stresses. More alienated than the other subtypes. May hide in books, live alone or need their own room where they can close themselves off. Take little from others. Sometimes thin. Likely to hoard time and space. Have solitary hobbies and interests, seek comfort and solace alone. Examples include: Kerry Fox, *An Angel At My Table;* Gena Rowlands, *Another Woman;* Robin Williams, *Awakenings.*

Intimate

Intimate Fives trust only a few people but then do so totally. Friendship is based on the sharing of confidences. Intimacy is equivalent to exchanging secrets. Can go from enigmatic, deliberate distance to intense, unguarded openness. Seductive invitation to sharing secrets; seek a total merging. When entranced can be a little kinky.

A great movie example is James Spader in *sex, lies and videotape.* Sharing intimate sexual secrets is what he gets women to do on videotape. Both Monsieur Hire and Mr. Lemorne in *The Vanishing* show this theme albeit perversely. Ben Kingsley in *Turtle Diary* also enjoys secrecy and is a little more normal.

Social

Social Fives connect with groups of like-minded people. Enjoy living in the flow of a group interest, sharing knowledge and affiliations. May prefer specialized or esoteric areas of knowledge that exclude all but the initiated. Could live in high society, know the "right" people, belong to the best clubs. Might enjoy speaking a professional language that few people understand. Can be quite friendly but, at times, terrific snobs. Romanticize secret elitist group membership; concerned with titles, degrees, credentials, etc. Realm of academia.

Peter O'Toole in *Goodbye, Mr. Chips* is a good movie example. Also, Anthony Hopkins in *84 Charing Cross Road.*

SIXES

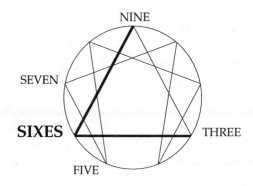

NINE

SEVEN

SIXES   THREE

FIVE

PEOPLE WHO ANTICIPATE THE WORLD'S DANGERS. MAY BE COURAGEOUS, LOYAL AND EFFECTIVE OR COWARDLY, MASOCHISTIC AND PARANOID.

FAMOUS REAL-LIFE SIXES

PHOBIC: Actor Jason Alexander, Woody Allen, Kim Basinger, Warren Beatty, Candice Bergen, Albert Brooks, George Bush, Actress Lynda Carter, Stockard Channing, Sally Field, Teri Garr, Cartoonist Cathy Guisewite, Philosopher J. Krishnamurti, Jack Lemmon, Comedian Richard Lewis, Actress/director Penny Marshall, Marilyn Monroe, Mary Tyler Moore, Bob Newhart, Richard Nixon, Actress Lena Olin, Director Sydney Pollack, Paul Reiser, Julia Roberts, Pat Robertson, Meg Ryan, Suzanne Somers, Bruce Springsteen, Meg Tilly.

COUNTERPHOBIC: Roseanne Arnold, Ellen Barkin, Photographer Peter Beard, U.S. Politician Jerry Brown, Comedian George Carlin, Carrie Fisher, Jane Fonda, Mel Gibson, Gene Hackman, Adolf Hitler, J. Edgar Hoover, Tommy Lee Jones, Director Spike Lee, David Letterman, NBC's Mary Matalin, Steve McQueen, Chuck Norris, Lee Harvey Oswald, Author Camille Paglia, Actress Rosie Perez, Robert Redford, U.S. Attorney General Janet Reno, Violinist Nadia Salerno-Sonnenberg, Steven Seagal, Sissy Spacek, Actor James Spader, Patrick Swayze,

Hunter S. Thompson, Ted Turner, Actress Sean Young, Russian extremist Vladimir Zhirinovsky.

INTRODUCTION

Six is the most explicitly fearful style in the Enneagram. People with this orientation are especially aware of life's dangers, and wary of the hazards that may lurk beneath everyday appearances.

There are two types of Sixes — phobic and counterphobic. Their reactions to being fearful are so different that outwardly they seem like separate Enneagram styles. This distinction is underrepresented in most writing about the Enneagram, so this chapter runs longer than the others.

When phobic Sixes sense danger, they lay low. They may act cautious, compliant or ambivalent in order to avoid potential attack. When a counterphobic Six senses danger, they often deliberately provoke it. They may act outspoken and aggressive, wanting to handle trouble before it handles them. Phobic Sixes can be charming, modest, and meek while counterphobes can seem tough, challenging and Eightish.

Some Sixes are absolutely phobic or counterphobic, but most exist along a continuum where they are more one than the other. Former U.S. President George Bush is basically an indecisive phobic Six who counterphobically went to war several times while in office. He often displayed a mixture of the two strategies; when his counterphobic episodes would pass, he returned to a baseline mode of cautious phobic inaction.

Sooner or later most phobic Sixes develop some counterphobic strategies anyway. The sheer difficulty of living daily with fear gradually motivates a more active form of coping. This doesn't mean that counterphobic is better than phobic — both are rooted in a habit of fearing that is itself distorted. All Sixes have an inner defense of doubting, of disbelieving reality and their own instincts. They *oppose* themselves in order to have a sense of control in a world that they believe opposes them anyway. When healthy, both types of Sixes tend to grow towards each other; phobics become more courageous and counterphobics more accepting.

Awakened phobic Sixes are steady, loyal and idealistic. They live the "truth of duty," but in a voluntary, dedicated way. They are usually committed to a group, tradition or cause beyond themselves. They fulfill their promises, work hard, and are honorable, protective friends.

Healthy phobic Sixes are often gracious and diplomatic. They put people at ease and are well liked for their discretion and manners. Often they are very funny and have vivid imaginations. Healthy Sixes handle power with integrity and may be fair-minded leaders because they sympathize with underdogs. They can affirm their personal value but also want others in their chosen group to get recognition. They're not pushovers and will take unpopular stands when necessary. Generally, though, they work toward solutions that benefit the group and allow everyone to win.

When more entranced, phobic Sixes can become more blindly dutiful even as they assume less personal responsibility. They might subtly shift their power onto an outside authority and begin to romanticize those who seem more sure of themselves. The Six strikes an unconscious bargain with their hero or heroine, a bargain that says, "I'll do what you want me to do if you'll protect me from danger." The Six then hides under an imaginary umbrella, pledging fealty to this outside force, growing addicted to the security that this arrangement seems to offer. The healthy Six capacity for deep loyalty is double-edged — when entranced, Sixes are often loyal to the wrong person.

When they give away their power, phobic Sixes start to chronically worry and feel more consciously helpless. To compensate, they get cautious and wary, trying to anticipate the motives of others. They may also try to check their own aggressive or powerful impulses, so that they don't deviate from the submissive role they have agreed to play. They could have trouble finishing what they start as they slide from doing into worrying about who will criticize the finished product. They may seem friendly but give off mixed messages as anger breaks through. Phobic Sixes can also be nervous, hesitant, skeptical, tense, indecisive, overreactive, vulnerable, and conservative.

When deeply entranced, phobic people become addled with fear and openly dependent upon others. They might surrender their life to work, becoming an abject slave to a job or a boss. They could act like weak, powerless losers, and yet demand coddling from friends.

Unhealthy phobic Sixes often tyrannize with their helplessness. They place strict, narrow limits on what they will risk or try. This forces others around them to handle what the Six is afraid of. If the others resent this arrangement, the Six will accept blame but no responsibility, reacting instead like a child being scolded by parents.

This dynamic is the seed of outright masochism. In very unhealthy scenarios, a Six could tolerate great abuse and still be loyal to their abusers. Being beaten up allows them to feel punished, defeated, and then absolved of a basic responsibility for their own existence. It's like a horribly painful way of trying to stay a child. Unhealthy phobic Sixes also avoid challenges, catastrophize, and may persecute others who deviate from norms. They can also be meek, cowardly, legalistic, petty, intolerant, melodramatic, and dogmatic.

When healthy, counterphobic Sixes are often courageous, willing to take a tiger by the tail and yank. They can be physically adventuresome, highly skilled and have a real gusto for living. If they participate in a tradition, it is usually in the role of constructive gadfly. Their underlying mission is to serve the tradition by stirring it up — they consider themselves team players who offer useful alternatives, using the old as a springboard to the new. To this end they may be energetic, honest, assertive, and have many good ideas.

If a healthy counterphobe is not serving a tradition, they are often creative and original. The Six ability to look past appearances and question assumptions leads them deeper into a unique point of view. Artistic expression is attractive as a core assertion of their own power and as a way to resolve a sense of alienation.

Entranced counterphobic Sixes often have an edgy, restless quality. Many channel their energies into physical activity; they can enjoy sports and tend to be more openly competitive than phobic Sixes. Counterphobes tend to hide their insecurities with cool or tough masks. The point of physical challenge is to expel fear by facing danger. Instead of being passively afraid, you take risks, stir up fear, and then beat it. If phobic Sixes are addicted to security then counterphobics would be addicted to insecurity.

If they are extroverted, entranced counterphobic Sixes can sound irritable and challenging like Eights. They are often defiant or rebellious towards authority and habitually find counterexamples to whatever others assert. The difference between an Eight and a counterphobe is that the Six has a core of fear and a hidden dependency on the very authorities s/he seems to dislike. Despite their attitude, they are often loyal, hard-driven workers and highly idealistic. They may feel more acutely as if the world is unfairly biased against them; some have a ranting Oneish quality, especially when they talk about governments and power structures. Many counterphobics are wryly funny and good at satire. If insecure, however, their humor can punch and bite.

When deeply entranced, counterphobes can be aggressive, unstable, and senselessly contentious. Because they take action compulsively — to quell their inner fears — they are prone to making bad decisions. When unhealthy, their preoccupation with risk can degenerate into a recklessness that borders on self-destruction.

The counterphobic's battles with authority might grow chronic or all-consuming. They often get caught in cycles of suspicion, endlessly testing other people's motives. When deeply entranced, they never reach conclusions about who to trust and just keep on testing.

They may also be fruitlessly hyperactive, as well as paranoid, accusative, belligerent, and vengeful. Some counterphobes prize their hatreds and can be aggressively unlikable or even dangerous. When inflamed they can adopt a vigilante-like mentality. Deeply entranced counterphobics generally act much worse than the authorities they accuse of abusing power.

SIXES IN THE MOVIES

Phobic and counterphobic Sixes are both represented in the movies although phobics are much more prevalent. A lot of phobic Sixes appear in comedies as nervous but lovable characters — anxious everymen and women who act out the audience's fears. These characters are often contradictory, worried and self-defeating.

Types of phobic roles include: timid underlings, wimps, Walter Mittyesque daydreamers, philosophically lost characters, hypochondriacs, detectives, cowards, paranoids, and innocent loyal protagonists who are faithful to a cause. There are also a number of "fish out of water" stories that put meek characters in an exceptional circumstance that brings out the character's latent courage.

Real-life phobic female Sixes tend to play to the likable aspects of the style. This makes them nonthreatening — women who are appealing for their vulnerabilities and nervous quirks. Some are portrayed as weak, helpless and needing rescue. Others can turn counterphobic and tough when need be so that they don't seem like complete wimps. Counterphobic Six actresses often play their own style as scared-but-brave characters who have a confrontational edge.

Real-life counterphobic actors, except for Mel Gibson, generally don't play their own style. Often they're good at playing tough guy Eights and otherwise seem to play their 5 or 7 wings. Occasionally a film will feature a counterphobic villain who is psychotic. Otherwise obvious male counterphobics are pretty uncommon.

MOVIE REVIEWS

The Apartment

In the original formulation of the Enneagram, Threes, Sixes and Nines are considered pure types, in the sense that they most deeply embody certain basic dilemmas. Threes, for instance, are most thoroughly preoccupied with image, although image-confusion is a problem for Twos and Fours. Fives, Sixes and Sevens all have an emotional core of fearfulness, but Sixes are the most consciously afraid. Nines are the most prone to self-forgetting and sleepy, angry oblivion, though Eights and Ones both have their own form of inner sleep.

These pure styles are well displayed in this biting Billy Wilder satire. The subject is Threeish corporate life circa 1960. Jack Lemmon plays the Six, a nervous, likable, cowed underling who romanticizes authority and harbors Threeish ambitions to rise to the top of corporate life, specifically to the statusy 27th floor of his company's building.

Lemmon's Three boss Fred MacMurray calls him "loyal, cooperative and resourceful." Masochistic is more like it. Lemmon strains to be ingratiating. He will do anything to court his bosses while rationalizing their poor treatment of him. Even when Shirley MacLaine stands Lemmon up for a date, he explains her behavior away and promptly asks her out again.

The film's title alludes to Lemmon's practice of allowing his bosses to use his apartment for extramarital affairs. This sordid arrangement leaves him little more than a pimp, one time catching cold on a windy park bench while waiting for a superior to finish with a tryst. Lemmon gets a promotion, though, and grows impressed with himself. In this way, he shows a Six's connection to the low side of 3. They can grow vain, competitive and deceitful.

Three boss MacMurray is a hard, insensitive liar — dim, fraudulent and cagey all at the same time. His second-in-command, Ray Walston, is exactly the same way. Shirley MacLaine plays a role that is both sexist and yet accurately Niney. An "Elevator Girl" in the corporate building and a self-described "happy idiot," MacLaine is portrayed as a passive-dependent slave to love. "Why can't I ever fall in love with anybody nice like you?" she asks Lemmon as she pines away for MacMurray. The latter won't leave his wife and gives mistress MacLaine $100 for Christmas, prompting a suicide attempt that Lemmon loyally covers up.

This film shows a Six struggling between his stress and security points. The low side of 3 tempts Lemmon greatly but the high side of 9 is what he chooses at film's end. He recovers his integrity, quits his job and chooses love over crass ambition. Actually he's still ambitious but he also wants honor.

More Enneatype casting as Jack Lemmon is a Six with a 7 wing in real life. He played Sixes many, many times before broadening his range in the 1970s and '80s. The man Lemmon plays in *The China Syndrome* (1979) could be seen as an older version of *The Apartment* character. He's a loyal company man who nevertheless keeps his integrity. Michael Douglas plays an Eight and Jane Fonda is something of a Three in this latter (terrific) film. Wilford Brimley has a small but pivotal role as Lemmon's Nine assistant.

Broadcast News

This story centers on the personal lives of three people who work in a TV news station. William Hurt plays a privileged, lucky, vacant Nine, rather like Dan Quayle. Albert Brooks and Holly Hunter both play Sixes — he phobic and she counterphobic — and the contrast between their two styles is very well done.

Brooks is whiny, dependent, loyal and anxious. Hunter is tough, driven, combative and anxious. He is openly self-doubting and addled with failure. She channels her fears into hyperactive work, succeeding despite herself while trying to compensate for her wobbly personal life. She could be mistaken for an Eight in some of the scenes, but the core of her aggression is fear and loyalty to the job. He fails at work, she fails at home.

The film itself is literate, intelligent, well-acted, yet somehow not really about anything. Brooks is a real-life Six and almost always plays them.

Class Action

Mary Elizabeth Mastrantonio is Gene Hackman's daughter in this nicely acted character study. They are rival lawyers representing opposite sides of an automaker's negligence suit. She's a yuppie-like counterphobic Six. Hackman's a flamboyant, politically radical Eight, so they are ideologically opposed as well.

Mastrantonio's character at first sounds like a One, but it soon becomes clear that her principles can be compromised by loyalty to the company, and she has a Threeish streak of ambition. She also has anxiety attacks, justice issues, and a certain nervous lovability. She's not quite her own person — watching her, you feel as if she's someone's daughter. This younger-than-their-years quality is very common with Sixes if their full adult power is still projected onto some outer authority. In this case it's the father; while loyal to her law firm, Mastrantonio is rebellious and counterphobic towards Hackman.

One of Hackman's legal assistants, Oneish Larry Fishburne, puts the daughter's dilemma beautifully when he says to her, "Your father *owns* you. If he stands up, you sit down. If he turns right, you turn left, even if you don't want to. Your biggest aspiration is to be the opposite of what he is. The problem is that you don't know what he is — that makes being *you* impossible!"

Later she tells Hackman, "I've spent my whole life being angry with you. It's been a constructive anger; I've gotten a lot done. You were my scapegoat. If anything ever went wrong I could blame you." This may not seem like a statement of dependency, but it is. In the end she recovers her own integrity and courage.

Gene Hackman is *extremely* good as a healthy Eight. His character goes from aggressive narcissism to unguarded tenderness by the film's end. In the process he learns to apologize, a useful thing for Eights.

The few scenes between Hackman and his wife are good, succinct examples of an Eight/One dynamic. She disapproves of his blustery defenses but loves his dedication to defending underdogs. He's afraid of her in the way John Wayne fears Katharine Hepburn in *Rooster Cogburn*. Hackman's a real-life counterphobic Six, by the way.

Colin Friels plays Mastrantonio's lover, another corporate Three. Mastrantonio's counterphobic Six has a 7 wing.

Crimes And Misdemeanors, Hannah And Her Sisters, Husbands And Wives

However you feel about Woody Allen's movies, they are chock-full of Enneagram styles. Allen is a Six in real life and it's possible to look at his body of films as a Six endlessly repeating variations on the same neurotic themes; "repetition compulsion," this is called in the trade.

Allen knows just enough about his characters to show how they don't know themselves. The results are films that accurately capture neurotic predicaments and therefore Enneagram skews. The same deluded conditions exist from movie to movie — there's rarely any resolution or awakening. Once in a while, Allen's own Six character learns something, but he's forgotten it by the next film.

It's not accurate or fair to evaluate an artist's productions solely in the light of their personality style — two or three of Allen's films are quite masterful and transcend his usual limits. But nearly every Allen story has Sixes in it and his recurrent themes always track back down to a basic fear of life.

Among Allen's more Sixish elements and themes: ambivalence in relationships; loving the wrong person and getting rejected; loving the right person and not realizing it; being unable to make up one's mind; fear of success; getting away with appalling deeds; avoiding personal responsibility; trying to find security in a dangerous world; trying to find moral certainty in an empty, impersonal universe.

Crimes And Misdemeanors is Allen's play on Dostoyevski's novel *Crime And Punishment*. In the book, the main character Raskolnikov commits a murder to prove his superiority to the laws of man, but he's gradually undone by his own latent conscience. In this film, the consequences are darkly reversed. Ophthalmologist Martin Landau is involved in a murder that he gets away with completely.

He's a Six (5 wing), full of conscious conscience and philosophical angst about the deed. He projects his guilt and responsibility onto an outside authority and imagines God is watching his every move. His expectation is that a cosmic moral force will swoop down and smite him for his deed. He searches for the moral certainty of punishment, flirting with the possibility of getting caught for an action he knows was born out of cowardice.

Landau is security-minded, and the murder is motivated by the possible loss of his home and family. He's had an affair with an "emotionally hungry" Two (Anjelica Huston) and she's threatened to expose both the affair and some of Landau's financial improprieties. "This woman's going to destroy everything I've built. Is what she's doing to me just? Is this what I deserve? I will not be destroyed by this neurotic woman." Landau twists the situation in his own mind so that *he* becomes the victim. Maintaining security is the issue; note that he's actually not grieving Huston's personal demise. Her death relieves him of one set of consequences but then he fears new ones.

Instead, nothing happens. The murder gets blamed on another

126 The Enneagram Movie and Video Guide

killer. Landau gradually goes back to his "protected world of wealth and privilege." After all his anxiety and crises of faith, in the end he sleeps fine.

Landau and Allen's Six character make an interesting contrast. Both are self-doubters, but Landau is successful (high side of 3) while Allen is a loser who continually shoots himself in either available foot. Allen's in dependent tension to a very Eightish Seven (Alan Alda), a warm, buffoonish TV producer who represents a shallow type of success that Allen's character both scorns and envies. Allen first gives power to Alda, and then is passive/aggressive and sabotaging. In the end, though, it's Allen who winds up self-defeated and bereft.

Jerry Orbach plays Landau's brother, an Eight upon whom Six Landau is dependent. Orbach is a hardened crook with soul-dead eyes and ties to organized crime that help him carry out the murder for his brother. Laudau gives him that power but then later blames him for the deed anyway.

Anjelica Huston's histrionic Two is crisply well-observed. She's gone demanding and vengeful (low side of 8) and is emotionally blackmailing Landau in the name of love. As she crosses boundaries — threatening to come to his house and talk to his wife — she seems selfish, prideful and guilt-inducing.

Sam Waterston plays a One Rabbi, a voice of moral certainty who ironically has an eye disorder and is going blind. Another moral force in the film is a Five philosopher whom Allen's character is filming for a biography. His fate is ironic too. Mia Farrow rounds out the cast as a likely Three. This is probably Woody Allen's masterpiece. However morally cynical it is, the film is excellent on every level.

Speaking of getting away with things, Michael Caine plays a successful married man who falls in love with his wife's sister and has a never-discovered affair in **Hannah And Her Sisters.** Caine's character fluctuates between Nine and Six, though he's mostly meant to be a Six. (During filming, Caine reportedly said to Allen, "Oh, I get it — I'm supposed to be a 6 foot 2 *you*.")

Mia Farrow plays Hannah as a nice Two and Barbara Hershey is the sister, sort of a Nine (she's mainly a male fantasy). The other clear styles include Dianne Wiest as another sister, an insecure Six. Max Von Sydow plays a crabby elitist Four, an artist who mostly communicates through faultfinding monologues. He's a jealous intimate subtype, which makes him sound like a One but he isn't.

The chief reason to see *Hannah* is Allen's character progression.

He plays his usual phobic role but the dilemma of Sixes is unusually distilled here. He's a hypochondriac who has a health crisis and a change in career. This leads to a self-doubting philosophical search for certainty which finally gives way to a kind of faith. "Why the hell don't I just stop searching for answers I'll never get and begin to enjoy life, since I'm going to die anyway?" he wonders. At the end he's calm, serene and congruent, like Woody Allen never is (high side of 9).

The rest of the film is a well-acted, if overpraised, soufflé. Kind of glib, kind of pleasant, just better than okay. Note that Caine's involvement with the two sisters is a metaphor for incest.

Husbands And Wives is Allen's next best movie, although it's nearly wrecked by constant, dizzying, hand-held camera work. Fortunately you can turn off a VCR and take breaks. It's worth seeing if only for the edgy, hilarious Judy Davis performance. She's a riot as a brittle, compulsive, counterphobic Six, a woman who alternates between modes of tactless self-absorption and crazed overcontrol. Woody Allen plays his usual Six character within the film and even *he* describes her as cerebral.

The story tracks two couples over several years as they variously divorce, reconcile, date others and crack apart. The humor ranges from rueful to bitter, as the characters swirl through a roundelay of attractions and repulsions. No one really knows themself and each has insights into their own behavior that are never quite right.

Film director Sydney Pollack plays Davis's husband, Gabriel, and he's pretty much a Three. He rationalizes like a Seven sometimes, but he's mainly characterized by a confused absence of feeling. He's not quite hard, but rather emotionally undeveloped and function-oriented ("Whatever works is the deal").

Davis gets involved with architect Michael (Liam Neeson), a brooding Four. Neeson's a romantic malcontent whose ex-wife told him he should have lived in another century. His heartfelt overtures are mostly wasted on the oblivious Davis. Later she describes to her therapist how she remained disassociated during sex with Neeson: "My mind just gets racing with thoughts. I thought that Michael was a hedgehog and Gabe was a fox. I thought about all the people I know and which were hedgehogs and which were foxes."

Neeson, in turn, is being chased by Allen's wife Mia Farrow, a whiny, contained Two. Juliette Lewis is rather like Barbara Hershey in *Hannah*, a Niney, indefinite, seductive, younger woman. Allen is attracted to her and then "virtuously" resists temptation. Mariel

Hemingway played a similar role in *Manhattan,* as a Nine teenager Allen falls for. This echoes Allen's real-life romantic involvement with his own stepdaughter. In a male Six, this pattern would be related to unresolved dependency on an emotionally incestuous mother. It also reflects how a Six could romanticize Nineyness.

Hamlet, 1991

A literary critic named George Steiner once wrote an essay called, "Is Tragedy Really Possible in a Democratic Society?" In it he argued that tragedy in literature is only possible if a character lacks personal freedom and is then victimized by a higher ruling power. In a democracy, where people theoretically have free choice, it is much harder to make a character's destiny seem inevitable and thus out of their own hands.

I thought about this idea while watching Mel Gibson (really pretty good) play Hamlet as a counterphobic Six. Director Franco Zeffirelli gives this version a colorful, sumptuous look, without the moody tones of Laurence Olivier's film. Stripped of melancholy and portrayed with a core of fear, this Hamlet starts to seem far less justified in his actions. Instead of being afflicted by a larger condition of existence, he sounds more like a vindictive Six who is simply refusing his own power.

"His will is not his own." Indeed, Gibson's power spins away from him while he goes in agitated circles. He quite aggressively drives Ophelia crazy. He seethes with anger, mainly towards older men. His humor is flippant and antiauthoritarian. He is caught in the vow of loyalty to his murdered father, but it's still somehow beside the point. Even the famous "To Be or Not To Be" speech sounds like a wonderfully phrased excuse, as if Hamlet is talking himself out of the need to do something productive with his life.

The King as played by Alan Bates is unusually sympathetic, which makes Hamlet's vindictiveness towards him seem even more infantile. Zeffirelli tries to compensate a little by making Mel Gibson hunky, but in the end this Hamlet is far less comfortable to watch than Olivier's. His actions nevertheless make far more human sense coming from a Six than a Four. What's interesting, though, is that both this film and Olivier's version work.

There is another Hamlet on video that doesn't. Nicol Williamson played the role controversially in the 1960s as — oops! — a One. He gives the character Oneish outrage over the king's slaying, which is fair enough. But then he holds the stance of righteous anger throughout the play. This gives Hamlet's actions and nonactions a moral dignity that doesn't square with the damage he does to everyone. Williamson's reading strains against the text, although his acting is technically flawless. The result is a performance that's interesting to watch yet hard to feel anything for.

Innerspace

Pleasant fantasy-comedy features Martin Short as a phobic hypochondriac. He works as a supermarket checker, is prone to panic attacks, and has recurrent nightmares of overcharging a customer with orange hair, who then takes out a gun and shoots him.

Short is accidentally thrust into danger when he is injected with the results of a miniaturization experiment. Military pilot Dennis Quaid is inside an experimental vehicle that has been shrunk to microscopic size and after the accident he is navigating around inside Short's body.

Quaid plays his usual persona, which is a Seven with an 8 wing, same as Jack Nicholson. His pilot is a rambunctious man of action, irresponsible, charming and wild. "When things are at their darkest, pal, it's a good man who can kick back and party."

Once injected, Quaid finds a way to communicate with Short and their interactions become a metaphor for the inner life of a Six. Quaid represents the instinctual, physically daring part of Short, which he gradually has to bring out during the story. With Quaid's coaching, Short changes from phobic to counterphobic and claims his own power to act decisively. By story's end, he's taking risks and really enjoying himself.

Lonely Hearts

This is a sweet, quirky Australian character study not to be confused with a recent American film of the same name. Latter is an SCT (Stupid Creepy Thriller) featuring Eric Roberts as a con-man Three and Beverly D'Angelo as a dependent, addictive Six. It's not too bad for its Enneagram styles but pointless otherwise. The Australian film — a gentle comedy — is much better and does not tell the same story at all.

The film opens with the first social gropings of an introverted piano tuner (Norman Kaye) stepping out after the death of his live-in mother. Seeking to live it up, he enrolls with a dating service and soon meets spinsterish Wendy Hughes. They date, fall in love, act in a play, break up and reconcile.

The story's main appeal is its characters. Kaye's a Nine (1 wing) who's breaking away from a dutiful low-profile life as a Good Son. He has a sense of fun, a few Bad Son habits (like shoplifting), and he routinely sabotages the wishes of his demanding Two sister. He has the sly, sleepy roguishness of a Walter Matthau.

Hughes, a normally beautiful actress, is scrubbed plain here. Kaye's sense of fun especially appeals to her shy, phobic Six character. She has a 5 wing and is shown to be timidly caught in a tense attempt to appease her elderly parents.

The family dynamic shown is one of several typical for phobic Sixes. Hughes's father is a domineering One with a 2 wing. He is bullying and overly protective, but a loving father from his point of view. He installs doubt and invites dependency with every remark, but he's convinced that the meek Hughes needs his guidance. The mother is a swarming Two who hysterically comments on everything that could go dangerously wrong in her daughter's life.

Hughes is, however, in her thirties and she has only just recently moved away from home. She's allowed her parents to keep her scared and self-doubting. She takes few chances and has trouble trusting people other than her mother and father. Early in the story she romanticizes them to Kaye and it's clear that she's loyal towards their oppression. She's afraid of the responsibility of taking steps on her own and instead hides dependently under their umbrella.

There's one telling scene where Hughes and Kaye bed down for the first time. She puts limits on the encounter and asks if they can avoid sex that first night. Kaye agrees but later, when they are drawn to each other, he gets carried away. Hughes leaps out of bed and flees as though running from attempted rape. She then refuses to see or speak to Kaye for weeks as she calms down her fears, builds a case against him and plans to avoid him for good.

All this might not be an overreaction, but Hughes is a virgin and *she never told Kaye*. As a Six she made the world more dangerous than it had to be and then fled the danger. Her lack of trust led to her concealing her inexperience which led to a worse but self-confirming result. She set herself up.

Of course, at film's end, she has to choose between Kaye and her parents. Of course, she plucks up her courage to live her own life. The way the film resolves is low-key and affectionate and a good example of a Six changing for the better. The director of the play that Kaye and Hughes act in is most likely a Seven with an 8 wing, though he sounds like a Two at first. Some Sevens do because both styles can be flamboyant and talk in grandiose ways.

Patti Rocks

I have a certain fondness for this comedy, but be warned that it's a scalding look at male/female relationships. The most controversial aspects of the script are the appalling, grotesque and pathetic monologues spoken by main character Chris Mulkey about women. He's an entranced Six with a strong 7 wing, and his bizarre observations are rooted in sexual dependency and irresponsibility. Some of the comedy is otherwise funny and Mulkey certainly gets what he deserves in the end.

The setup is that the married Mulkey has impregnated a woman he barely knows named Patti Rocks (Karen Landry). She lives some distance away, doesn't know that he's married, and Mulkey can't reach her by phone to talk her into having an abortion. He enlists friend John Jenkins, a One, to take a night drive in the middle of winter to help him clean up this extramarital mess.

Actually "help" is the wrong word. Mulkey wants Jenkins to talk to Patti *for him*. Mulkey is a whiny, dependent victim-of-himself who displaces responsibility onto anyone available. He moans, wheedles and pleads for Jenkins's help. When that doesn't work, he angrily guilt-trips him and keeps haranguing until Jenkins gives in. The pattern is repeated throughout the story whenever Mulkey tries to dance away from accountability.

As an anxious Six, Mulkey projects his power onto the sure-sounding Jenkins. The latter says no adamantly to each demand and gives Mulkey One-style lectures before giving in to the weaseling ("C'mon, please help me. You gotta. Please, I can't tell her. This is the last time!"). At one point, Mulkey even talks Jenkins into lending him his underwear.

Mulkey's most afraid of disappointing Landry, believing she will be angry to discover he's married. He needn't have worried; Landry has her own agenda and this fact forms the basis of Mulkey's emotionally brutal comeuppance. She's a Seven and quite similar to the Lena Olin character in *The Unbearable Lightness Of Being* (see "Sevens").

Jenkins is first seen as snappish and perfectionistic, and then more relaxed and playful (a One's connection to 7). Somehow he relates to Mulkey's monologues, which is not a good sign. Later Jenkins shows a little melancholy (connection to 4) during a scene when he tells Landry, "Somewhere down the line something went wrong and you spend the whole rest of your life trying to figure it out."

Send Me No Flowers

Before there was Woody Allen there was ... Rock Hudson. It was quite surprising to come across Hudson's old comedies and discover that his ongoing screen character was that of a phobic Six. *Send Me No Flowers* is a frothy little yarn. It may not be the best of Hudson's movies but it's an especially good showcase for his dour, fussy, anxious persona. He has a different look and manner than Woody Allen, of course, but that's part of the joke. Hudson was a big, capable-looking man in contrast to his character's comic cowardice. If you listen closely to both actors, though, you'll hear the same Sixish tendency: chronic anxious anticipation.

In *Send Me No Flowers*, Hudson plays a flaming hypochondriac, so the negative anticipation is about his health. The first hour of the movie is actually quite funny as it details Hudson's downward drive towards the goal of finding something wrong with himself. He starts over breakfast complaining to cheery wife Doris Day about a pain in his chest. When she dismisses it as probable indigestion, he starts in: "You can just sit there and laugh about it but men my age are dropping dead." "I'm not a hypochondriac. Someday when I'm lying in a hospital in my bed of pain you'll change your tune!" "I'd better cancel that lunch date the way I'm feeling." When Day asserts that he could probably risk a cup of tea, he muses: "Well, I don't suppose a cup of *weak* tea would be so bad ..."

By the time Hudson makes it to the doctor, he's in a fever of anxiety and suspiciously disbelieves the doctor's diagnosis of indigestion:

| Hudson: | "But what about this pain? You mean I can just live a normal life?" |
| Doctor (writing): | "You can just take one of those pills I gave you, right now if you want." |

Hudson:	"Right now! You make it sound so urgent! Is that my chart?
Doctor:	"Yes."
Hudson:	"Aren't you doing an awful lot of writing for indigestion?"

Hudson then focuses his anxieties on the results of a recent cardiogram, still being processed by another doctor ("He's certainly been ... studying it for quite a while"). This drives him to eavesdrop on a phone conversation his doctor has about a terminal patient, and Hudson mistakenly decides it's him ("Finally my hypochondria has paid off").

After the news of his supposed doom sinks in, Hudson sets about planning for his own death. He shows a behavior change very typical for Sixes facing tangible crisis — he gets calm. He makes secret funeral arrangements with mortuary director Paul Lynde (an effeminate male Two). With friend Tony Randall he begins to scout for a new husband for Day to succeed Hudson after his death ("I want a man who can afford to give Judy the things I went into debt for!"). He rejects a number of candidates ("Married to that cornball? Impossible! Why I'd ... I'd live first!") before the plot gets increasingly silly.

Clint Walker emerges as a rival for Day's affections and he's a Three. The other characters' styles are not so clear. Doris Day seems somewhere in the Three/Two range, though in real life she's an extroverted happy Nine. In her other films she tended to play Ones, her wing. Tony Randall is too busy reacting to Hudson's circumstances to have his own style, but he's a One in real life.

See if you can count the number of times Hudson, as a Six, finds some dark possibility in each new situation or idea. The pattern is present in nearly everything he says.

What About Bob?

"A multiphobic personality with acute separation anxiety and a strong need for family." That's how psychiatrist Richard Dreyfuss describes his client-from-hell, Bob, a phobic Six played by Bill Murray.

The story is simple. Frightened, helpless-acting patient follows his shrink on vacation and won't let him alone. The movie takes the dependent tendency within a phobic Six and magnifies the trait to comic proportions. Murray romanticizes Dreyfuss's power and authority while he flatters and cajoles his way into the latter's life.

While Dreyfuss — a vain, preening Three — loudly resents Bob's invasion of his life and boundaries, the clever screenplay reframes such reactions as unreasonable. Most of Dreyfuss's complaints are absolutely justified, but he's so unsympathetic that we don't care.

Basically, Bob is a stalker. It's a tribute to Bill Murray's comic skills that we don't really think about the hostility hidden within Bob's dependency. Lots of horror movies have been made from this exact same material. "Human Crazy Glue" is what Dreyfuss calls Bob, and this story has some similarity to *Fatal Attraction* and *Unlawful Entry*, two SCTs that feature maliciously dependent Twos.

That aside, the movie is pleasantly funny. Dreyfuss, the egotistical Three, has just written a self-help book and has a lot riding on its success. He's status-seeking, competitive and patronising. His glib therapeutic prescriptions to Bob are met with fawning idolatry and Dreyfuss's vanity hooks on Bob's adoration. He has a 4 wing and is less people-oriented than a Three with a 2 wing. He also shows a touch of envy.

Note that Dreyfuss has high expectations of his children; that they learn well and behave. Three parents can sometimes expect model children that reflect well on the parent's *image* as a good father or mother. Murray's Bob, of course, has great rapport with Dreyfuss's children precisely because he's a giant four-year-old himself.

Julie Hagerty plays Dreyfuss's Nine wife. She's a ditsy, good-natured minimizer. The more Dreyfuss objects to Bob, the more she misses the point. This, of course, serves the plot, but it's done in a very Niney way. Hagerty is a real-life Nine and always plays them.

This is one of those uncommon comedies that successfully sustains its tone. When you know Bill Murray's a Six, the film gets funnier and your kids will like it anyway.

OTHER MOVIE SIXES

Dan Ackroyd, *Sneakers*; Alan Alda, *A New Life*; Victor Bannergee, *A Passage To India*; Ian Bannen, *The Offence*; Ellen Barkin, *The Big Easy*; Kathy Bates, *Used People (counterphobic)*; Warren Beatty, *Heaven Can Wait, Ishtar*; Humphrey Bogart, *The Caine Mutiny, Treasure Of The Sierra Madre (counterphobic)*; Lorraine Bracco, *Medicine Man (counterphobic)*; Albert Brooks, *Defending Your Life, Lost In America, Modern Romance*; Nicolas Cage, *Honeymoon In Vegas*; Jill Clayburgh, *Starting Over*; Michael

Cole, *Nickel Mountain*; Karen Colston, *Sweetie*;

Billy Crystal, *City Slickers*; Keir Dullea, *David And Lisa*; Mia Farrow, *Alice*; Jane Fonda, *On Golden Pond (counterphobic)*, *Julia (counterphobic)*; Teri Garr, *Tootsie*; Philip Baker Hall (as Richard Nixon), *Secret Honor*; Julie Harris, *The Christmas Wife, The Haunting*; Dustin Hoffman, *Family Business, Straw Dogs, Tootsie (counterphobic)*; Anjelica Huston, *The Grifters (counterphobic)*; Timothy Hutton, *The Temp*; Ivar Kants, *The Mad Plumber (counterphobic)*; Diane Keaton, *Annie Hall, most any film*; Ben Kingsley, *Pascali's Island*;

Don Knotts, *No Time For Sargeants, The Shakiest Gun In The West*; Bert Lahr (The Cowardly Lion), *The Wizard Of Oz*; Christine Lahti, *The Fear Inside*; Jack Lemmon, *That's Life*; Mark Linn-Baker, *My Favorite Year*; Peter MacNicol, *Heat*; Karl Malden, *Nuts*; Steve Martin, *Parenthood*; Marsha Mason, *Chapter Two*; Marilyn Monroe, *The Misfits*; Mary Tyler Moore, *Just Between Friends*; Rob Morrow ("Joel"), *Northern Exposure*; Audie Murphy, *The Red Badge Of Courage*; Sam Neill, *The Picnic*; Paul Newman, *The Verdict*; Richard Nixon, *Millhouse: A White Comedy*; Nick Nolte, *The Prince Of Tides (counterphobic)*;

Anthony Perkins, *Psycho*; Michelle Pfeiffer, *Frankie And Johnny (counterphobic)*; Gena Rowlands, *A Woman Under The Influence*; Mercedes Ruehl, *Lost In Yonkers*; Meg Ryan, *When A Man Loves A Woman, When Harry Met Sally*; Martin Short, *Three Fugitives*; Maggie Smith, *The Lonely Passion Of Judith Hearne*; Sissy Spacek, *Carrie*; James Spader, *Bad Influence*; Meryl Streep, *Silkwood*; the robot "Threepo," *Star Wars*; Uma Thurman, *Mad Dog And Glory*;

Janine Turner ("Maggie") *Northern Exposure (counterphobic)*; John Turturro, *Barton Fink, Men Of Respect*; Gwen Welles ("Sophie"), *Eating*; Jack Weston, *The Four Seasons*; Frank Whalley, *Career Opportunities*; Gene Wilder, *The Producers*; Robin Williams, *Seize The Day*; Nicol Williamson (as Sherlock Holmes), *The Seven Percent Solution*; Henry Winkler, *Night Shift*; Billy Zane, *Dead Calm (counterphobic)*.

FINER DISTINCTION NOTES

WINGS: Sixes can have a 5 wing, a 7 wing or both wings.

Six With a 5 Wing

Sixes with a 5 wing are generally introverted and somewhat intellectual. When healthy, they often have many realms of interest as well as surprising competencies and skills. May have an original and idiosyncratic point of view. Can be bookish; some are interested in history or feel rooted in the past or related to a long tradition. Also good at predicting the future. May test potential friends for a long time but once you're in, you're in — a friend for life.

When more entranced, they may project a willed remoteness. Have a "tip of the iceberg" quality — they show little but you sense hidden dimensions, intensity and activity. Tension between needing to be seen and withdrawing for protection. Might act arrogant or cryptic or cynical when afraid.

When phobic, can be diplomatic and say things without saying them. Entranced counterphobics are either cool and loners or argumentative, tending towards violence. Can brood over injustices to them, entertain conspiracy theories, spend time alone building cases. Paranoia in private. May like secretive behind-the-scenes group activity. Sneaky vengeance, passive/aggressive toward others, self-attacking and self-destructive at home.

Real-Life Sixes With a Five Wing: J. Edgar Hoover, Tommy Lee Jones, J. Krishnamurti, Spike Lee, Steve McQueen, Richard Nixon, Lee Harvey Oswald, Robert Redford, Janet Reno, Steven Seagal, James Spader.
Movie Sixes With a 5 Wing: Keir Dullea, *David And Lisa*; Gene Hackman, *I Never Sang For My Father*; Rock Hudson, *Send Me No Flowers*; Wendy Hughes, *Lonely Hearts*; Ben Kingsley, *Pascali's Island*; Martin Landau, *Crimes And Misdemeanors*; Sheila McCarthy, *I've Heard The Mermaids Singing*; Sam Neill, *The Piano*; Anthony Perkins, *Psycho*; Michelle Pfeiffer, *Frankie And Johnny*; James Spader, *Bad Influence*; John Turturro, *Barton Fink*; Henry Winkler, *Night Shift*.

Six With a 7 Wing

Sixes with a 7 wing are generally outgoing and may appear more overtly nervous. More plainly want to be liked and will pursue others in contrast to 5 wing who pulls in. Can be charming, sociable, ingratiating. Have a faster tempo, stronger connection to 3. Often self-preservation subtypes, characterized by a personal warmth. Can have a cheerful, forward-looking drive and be disarmingly funny. Self-effacing, gracious and curious.

When more entranced, may be self-contradicting and seem as if they want two things at once. Sometimes test others overtly, drive you crazy with mixed messages. It may be hard to follow what they're saying. When threatened, one defense is to become impossible to please. When counterphobic, they tend to be accusative. Some get caught up in big plans that they hope will result in material security.

Also can be insecure, irritable, petty, irrational, chaotic. Subject to mood swings, inferiority complexes, runaway fears. May have hair-trigger flare-ups of paranoia. Falsely accuse others and then seem not to realize it. Other times they plead to be taken care of. Sometimes defensively conservative in their lifestyle. Some struggle with appetite.

Real-Life Sixes With a 7 Wing: Roseanne Arnold, Kim Basinger, George Bush, Mel Gibson, Diane Keaton, Jack Lemmon, Richard Lewis, Marilyn Monroe, Mary Tyler Moore, Camille Paglia, Rosie Perez, Sydney Pollack, Meg Ryan, Patrick Swayze, Sean Young, Vladimir Zhirinovsky.

Movie Sixes With a 7 Wing: Woody Allen, *most any film*; Victor Bannergee, *A Passage To India*; Billy Crystal, *City Slickers*; Judy Davis, *Husbands And Wives*; Teri Garr, *Tootsie*; Holly Hunter, *Broadcast News*; Diane Keaton, *Annie Hall*; Jack Lemmon, *The Apartment*; Steve Martin, *Parenthood*; Mary Elizabeth Mastrantonio, *Class Action*; Chris Mulkey, *Patti Rocks*; Bill Murray, *What About Bob?*; Sydney Pollack, *Tootsie*; Meg Ryan, *When Harry Met Sally*; Martin Short, *Innerspace*; Meryl Streep, *Postcards From The Edge*; Janine Turner, *Northern Exposure*.

CONNECTING POINTS (Stress and Security)
Sixes connect to the high and low side of 3.
Sixes connect to the high and low side of 9.

Six's Connection to 3

Healthy connection to 3 brings Sixes self-confidence, productivity and skillfulness. Often supports the will and focus to follow through on what they start. More able and willing to make decisions, leadership capacities can emerge. Emphasis on excellence — what Sixes do, they often do well. Can be proud of their achievements, self-affirming. Also, many have good organizational and administrative talents that are related to this connection. Highly capable, though not always confident.

When entranced, Sixes may descend into 3-like phoniness. Start projecting an image, wanting to be liked. Can go hard-hearted, charming, wear a mask to cover their anxiety. Some conceal their sense of deviance by attacking others who are different.

Disassociated ambition, can become compulsively competitive. More conscience than an unhealthy 3 but still may be mean, calculating, vengeful. Want to best others and feel superior but hide these motives to appear likable. Could stab you in the back, while feeling like *they* were the victim. Compensatory hyperactivity — they go in circles and do too much when under stress. Reach a point of exhaustion, then drop into a stupor (low side of 9).

Movie Sixes who demonstrate this connection: Judy Davis, *Husbands And Wives*; Dustin Hoffman, *Tootsie*; Anjelica Huston, *The Grifters*; Ben Kingsley, *Pascali's Island*; Jack Lemmon, *The Apartment*; Mary Elizabeth Mastrantonio, *Class Action*; James Spader, *Bad Influence*; Meryl Streep, *Postcards From The Edge*; Billy Zane, *Dead Calm*.

Six's Connection to 9

Healthy connection brings a calming, faithful, spiritual sense that helps a Six to trust life. They may begin to feel a part of the larger order of existence, in touch with the Big Flow. Helps them to develop a safer image of the universe and find their place in it. Begin to experience faith, not as a concept but in their bodies. Connection also contributes to an "internal reference," where the Six searches for their own true feelings about matters instead of relying on outside authorities. Trust themselves, grow more neutral and centered. Can humanly understand others who would ordinarily seem threatening. The Six sees through their own projections.

When more entranced, a Six may go numb, spaced-out, and lazy like an unhealthy 9. It's an escape chute from anxiety, a haze to shield against danger. May avoid responsibility, stick their head in the sand, procrastinate. Fractured, chaotic thinking. Go in circles; a 9 does this to avoid focused action whereas a Six wants to avoid independent action that may provoke attack. Can get habit-bound, rut-prone, cautious and stuck. Merge dependently with their environment, more passive with authority. Noncommittal or ambivalent in relationships.

Movie Sixes who demonstrate this connection: Woody Allen, *Hannah And Her Sisters*; Albert Brooks, *Broadcast News*; Mel Gibson, *Hamlet*; Jack Lemmon, *The Apartment*; Sheila McCarthy, *I've Heard The Mermaids Singing*; Michelle Pfeiffer, *Frankie And Johnny*; Gena Rowlands, *A Woman Under The Influence*; John Turturro, *Barton Fink*.

SUBTYPE THEMES

Self-Preservation

Self-preservation Sixes often display a personal warmth that is meant to defang the potential hostility of others. If they sense aggression or disapproval in the environment, they may counterphobically zero in on it. Use humor, charm, self-depreciation to make friends out of possible enemies. Can flatter like Twos, play themselves down, work to maintain other people's affection. Act vulnerable, invite rescue. Ingratiating, but more nervously dependent than other Six subtypes. Also less in touch with their own hostility.

Their home environment is sometimes important. May feel like their house is a fortress against the outside world's dangers. Worry about their ability to survive; have scary "worst-that-can-happen" fantasies. A good movie example is Bill Murray in *What about Bob?*. Also Teri Garr in *Tootsie* and The Cowardly Lion in *The Wizard of Oz*.

Intimate

Sixes with this subtype tend to act strong or seductive when insecure. They are much more likely to be counterphobic, especially the men. May seem like Eights, take risks, talk tough. Act powerful and in control at the times when they feel most frightened. Worry about looking weak, having their fears show (pave over feelings). May act arrogant but aren't really. Some study martial arts or seek a way of life that makes them strong.

Beauty is another focus; trying to seem attractive so as to contain fear, get approval, and distract others. May consciously hide behind a seductive mask. Unlike Threes, Sixes know they are hiding. Can act cool and patrician or be flirty. Some have a focus on aesthetics. This subtype often has a stronger connection to the vanity of 3.

Movie examples include: Humphrey Bogart, *Treasure Of The Sierra Madre;* Holly Hunter, *Broadcast News;* Anjelica Huston, *The Grifters;* Mary Elizabeth Mastrantonio, *Class Action;* Nick Nolte, *The Prince Of Tides;* Janine Turner, *Northern Exposure.* In *Batman Returns,* Michelle Pfeiffer turns from a meek phobic Six into a fiesty counterphobic Six. When phobic, she is a social subtype (see below). Her alter ego, the counterphobic Catwoman, is an intimate subtype.

Social

Social Sixes tend to be dutiful and especially dependent upon authority. More often phobic than counterphobic. Often dedicated to a cause. When acting alone they will still refer to others in their mind for safety and agreement. May want to see your opinion first before they will offer their own. Could change their mind to agree with you. Often align with a group or a cause and will follow the rules loyally, trying to please the boss. "Company men." Focus on a social or work context and try to be ideal within it. Could persecute others in the name of their group's ideals.

May imagine they can't live without the group's support: "If I don't play by the rules I'll be out on the street selling pencils." Later there's inevitable disillusionment. Then Six starts grumbling that they are not appreciated. Could go passive/aggressive, resent a boss they had romanticized. Connection to 9 is stronger with this subtype.

Movie examples include: Wendy Hughes, *Lonely Hearts;* Ben Kingsley, *Pascali's Island;* Martin Landau, *Crimes And Misdemeanors;* Jack Lemmon, *The Apartment;* Michelle Pfeiffer, *Batman Returns;* Sheila McCarthy, *I've Heard The Mermaids Singing;* Martin Short, *Innerspace.*

SEVENS

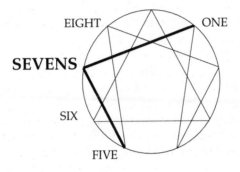

PEOPLE WHO LOOK FOR MULTIPLE CHOICES AND POSITIVE FUTURES. MAY BE WELL-ROUNDED, AFFIRMING AND GENEROUS OR NARCISSISTIC, ESCAPIST AND INSATIABLE.

FAMOUS REAL-LIFE SEVENS

Comedian Steve Allen, Comedian Tim Allen, Director Robert Altman, Desi Arnaz, Richard Avedon, Honoré Balzac, Humorist Dave Barry, Jack Benny, Actress Jacqueline Bisset, Poet Robert Bly, Sonny Bono, Comedienne Elayne Boosler, Musical comedian Victor Borge, Author Ray Bradbury, Football's Terry Bradshaw, Kenneth Branagh, Richard Branson, Jimmy Buffett, Michael Caine, Mythologist Joseph Campbell, Pierre Cardin, King Juan Carlos of Spain,

Chevy Chase, Maurice Chevalier, Buffalo Bill Cody, Joan Collins, Director Francis Ford Coppola, Filmmaker Roger Corman, MTV's Dan Cortese, NBC's Katie Couric, Singer David Crosby, Tony Curtis, Roger Daltry, Philosopher Ram Dass, Gérard Depardieu, Diderot, QVC President Barry Diller, Douglas Fairbanks Jr., Federico Fellini, Duchess of York Sarah Ferguson,

Physicist Richard Feynman, Errol Flynn, Peter Fonda, Malcolm Forbes, George Foreman, Bob Fosse, Michael J. Fox, Author Robert Fulghum, Clark Gable, Ava Gardner, Carlos Casteneda's Don Genaro, John Gielgud, Dizzy Gillespie, Jackie Gleason, Goethe, Ruth Gordon,

Cary Grant, Andre Gregory, George Hamilton,

Tom Hanks, Richard Harris, Goldie Hawn, Actress Marilu Henner, Abbie Hoffman, Pianist Vladimir Horowitz, Ron Howard, Lauren Hutton, Aldous Huxley, Self-help author Gerald Jampolsky, Derek Jarman, Magic Johnson, Architect Phillip Johnson, Dallas Cowboys owner Jerry Jones, Actress Carol Kane, Michael Keaton, John F. Kennedy, Ken Kesey, Comedian Alan King, Don King,

CNN's Larry King, CNN's Michael Kinsley, Comedian Robert Klein, Director David Lean, Timothy Leary, Director Barry Levinson, Puppeteer Shari Lewis, Artist Roy Lichtenstein, Singer Meat Loaf, Football's John Madden, Director Louis Malle, Author Henry Miller, Yves Montand, Dudley Moore, Robert Morley, Eddie Murphy,

Jack Nicholson, Leslie Nielsen, Donald O'Connor, Peter O'Toole, Blaise Pascal, Luciano Pavarotti, Author Joseph Chilton Pearce, Regis Philbin, Bronson Pinchot, George Plimpton, Vincent Price, Dennis Quaid, Anthony Quinn, Bonnie Raitt, Ron Reagan Jr., Basketball Coach Pat Reilly, Lee Remick, Filmmaker/Nazi propagandist Leni Riefenstahl, Jason Robards, Novelist Tom Robbins,

Ginger Rogers, Linda Ronstadt, Interviewer Charlie Rose, David Lee Roth, Economist Louis Rukeyser, Rosalind Russell, Susan Saint James, Director Martin Scorsese, Weatherman Willard Scott, Martin Short, Self-help author Bernie Siegel,

Steven Spielberg, Terence Stamp, Robert Louis Stevenson, Henry David Thoreau, Lily Tomlin, Tanya Tucker, Actress Janine Turner, Lana Turner, Peter Ustinov, Dick Van Dyke, Voltaire, Kurt Vonnegut, Eli Wallach, *Rolling Stone*'s Jann Wenner, Betty White, Robin Williams, Robert Anton Wilson, Jonathan Winters, Author Tom Wolfe, James Woods, Poet William Wordsworth, Director Franco Zeffirelli.

INTRODUCTION

Seven is the last style in the emotional trio that responds fearfully to life. Whereas Fives withdraw, and Sixes become self-doubting or suspicious, Sevens manage their fears in a much different way. People with this style tend to suppress and escape their fears by willfully focusing on the positive and imagining future plans, options and possibilities. Sevens are natural "reframers"— they look on the bright side of things, make lemonade out of lemons, and keep happily active. The defensive point of this is to avoid inner pain and be harder to hit as a moving target.

Healthy Sevens are often considered "renaissance" people and can be highly accomplished in many disparate realms of interest. Awakened people with this style are usually adventurous and multi-talented, with an authentic zest for living. Childlike but not childish, Sevens are great receivers. Most have a stimulating, positive outlook and can enthusiastically appreciate life's gifts, even the little ones. Many possess an endearing blend of charm and curiosity; they can be creative, outgoing, generous to friends, and progressively interested in new horizons. Sevens are usually highly resilient and bounce back well from loss and calamity.

At their healthiest, people with this style tend to look for long-range fulfillments and deeper satisfactions. To this end, they are able to accept the realistic necessity for both pain and commitment in their lives. The acceptance of life's painful dimension gives a Seven more depth and consequently enhances their joy. Many report that their willingness to make appropriate commitments gives their life an overall structure within which they can still find variety.

When more entranced, people with this style are prone to escapism, trying to avoid the pain in themselves and others. Commitment can become mistaken for confinement in the Seven's mind. They may control and sublimate their fears by running away into appetites. These can be for food, drugs, ideas, activity, people, new experiences, etc. Entranced Sevens eat life but don't digest it. They search out the new, trying to maintain a high by flavoring reality with their imaginations and fantasies of what will be. They can be dilettantish, impulsive, undisciplined, impersonal, glib, narcissistic and acquisitive. Sevens may entertain many interests, but indiscriminately. When defensive, their knowledge is extensive but not deep, rather like a jack-of-all-trades.

Many entranced Sevens have problems with completion. The word "execution" sounds less like it means finishing what you start and more like a kind of death. They tend to be strong on initiating action and weaker on follow-through. When defensive, they adopt what's called an "as if frame," where the Seven makes up positive fantasies about the future and pretends they are reality. "It's as if this wonderful adventure I'm planning is already happening."

Difficult present situations are sometimes avoided this way. A Seven can fantasize so much about a problem that they almost begin to believe they have solved it in reality. This eliminates the need to put themselves on the line, to struggle, to risk failure or have their actions judged. Most entranced Sevens have fears about their adequacy and tend to compare themselves with others. A Seven can feel inferior to someone they admire and then defensively act superior towards someone else to even the balance.

When Sevens are deeply entranced, the line between reality and fantasy loosens drastically. They often grow obsessed with grandiose visions and inflate themselves narcissistically. Very unhealthy Sevens may completely refuse responsibility and resist all realistic constraints on their behavior. They could act wild, impatient, chaotic, delusional, explosive. Tendencies toward addictions and manic-depressive cycles become quite strong. Appetites can't be permanently satisfied so the Seven plunges headlong into hedonism, seeking more to consume. Anyone who gets in the way of a manic Seven will be knocked down. All promises to others are broken. In extreme scenarios, unhealthy Sevens call legal forces down on themselves. The "world" has to restrain the antisocial behavior that's driven by a Seven's inner cravings.

SEVENS IN THE MOVIES

Popular commercial moviemaking is largely an escapist, that is to say Sevenish, medium. A huge number of film performers and many excellent directors have been Sevens. Most film comedy is generated by or around Sevens.

Movie Sevens often handle problems with wit and display grace under pressure. They show the audience how to take their own difficulties less seriously. Some Seven protagonists are capable, witty and debonair; other are little boys or girls acting out our fantasies. Even Sevens who refuse to accept adult responsibility are presented in an appealing light. Often they are disapproved of by unreasonable Ones, so the story is slanted in the Seven's favor. Female movie Sevens are often lively, inspiring characters who teach others how to enjoy life.

There are not many Seven villains; they are mostly antisocial maniacs driven by appetite. Some appear in tragic downfall stories about alcoholics or manic-depressives, but the portraits are still somewhat sympathetic.

Sevens can be found in the movies as jaunty lovers, adventurers, pirates, scoundrels, marginally criminal rogues, gourmands, male and female Casanovas, dreamers, drifters, charming scoundrels, con-men, wild men, lively Aunts, idealistic schoolteachers, drunkards, gluttons, visionaries, irresponsible parents and spouses, dance-away lovers and, in supporting roles, as the cheerful hedonistic friend of the stuffy hero.

MOVIE REVIEWS

AUNTIE MAMES

There are many stories of lively eccentric Aunt figures who are Sevens. This sampling begins with 1958's **Auntie Mame.**

"Life is a banquet but most poor suckers are starving to death!" This gluttonous metaphor is Auntie Mame's credo and she lives it every moment she can. Based on a memoir by Patrick Dennis, this film is adapted from a stage play that celebrated his aunt's eccentric vivacity.

What plot there is spins on how Mame (Rosalind Russell) upsets the Oneish mores and manners of those around her. Since these social conventions are extremely dated, the clash is only mildly amusing. Mame's Sevenness, though, stands out quite clearly. She writes a book called, "Live! Live! Live!" and is thoroughly disapproved of by a fussy, judgmental One banker (Fred Clark). He's Patrick's legal guardian and fights against Mame's corrupting influence ("I'm going to turn this kid into a decent God-fearing citizen if I have to break every bone in his body!").

Mame's a hyperactive extrovert — gregarious, grandiose, charming, fascinated by everything. It's interesting to see how the film presents her as a model of joyous vitality and love-of-living in stuffy upper-class 1957. Decades later she seems kind of tiresome. "You have given me a new interest!" she says rather often. Life is one glorious banquet after another. Without meaning to, the film portrays the sameness that results when a Seven seeks constant excitement and newness.

The portrait isn't entirely one-dimensional. Mame does have feelings and, while struggling through the depression, she sinks into pain and defeat at times. She's a self-preservation subtype and certainly cares about the people in her sphere.

In the end, though, she's unchanged, having taken Patrick's son under her wing. "I'm going to open doors, doors you never dreamed existed," she tells a nine-year-old boy, "Oh, what times we'll have, what vistas we'll see ... !" If you are not a Seven, you may want to lie down for a nap about this time. As a movie, *Auntie Mame* is talky and stagey but it presents an instructive portrait of the style.

Mame's sister Vera also seems like a Seven and Hermione Gingold plays a befuddled Nine. Mame has a 6 wing.

Watching *Auntie Mame* you suddenly realize that it's been re-made several times under different titles. Ruth Gordon played the character in 1971's **Harold And Maude**, the black comedy cult-favorite. This film's style is Sevenish and Maude, while robust and vivacious, is also distinctly impersonal as she seeks out new experiences.

Maude has a counterphobic 6 wing. She has a background as a political activist and is still a crusading antiauthoritarian. She steals cars, replants public street trees and enjoys outwitting the police. She "liberates" people from their attachments ("How the world still dearly loves a cage"), and is a blithe rationalizer ("Consistency is not a human trait"). Her suicide at the age of eighty — opting for death rather than a poor quality of life — seems at once courageous and escapist.

Harold (Bud Cort) is a Nine, although his habit of staging elaborate fake suicides at first seems Fourish. Harold's not a romantic, though; he's passive/aggressively punishing his Two mother for her self-absorption. Pretending to be dead is an apt metaphor for unhealthy Nineyness. Harold's military uncle is a Six. Naturally there's a dour One repressive Minister who's directly opposed to Maude's Sevenish high spirits.

A less romanticized Auntie Mame figure is Sylvie, played by Christine Lahti in 1987's **Housekeeping.** She's the eccentric itinerant aunt of orphans Lucille and Ruthie (Andrea Burchill and Sara Walker). After their mother commits suicide, Sylvie is called to live with the girls and be their surrogate parent.

Trouble is, Lahti's a flaming Seven and especially flighty (intimate subtype). She's so unsuited for adult responsibility that the girls begin "feeling like we were the parent and Sylvie was the child." They act that way too, especially Lucille, a budding One who gradually builds a firm judgmental stance (reaction formation) against Lahti. "I don't have to help the way I am," she says haughtily, "I'm not like Sylvie!"

This dynamic is very clear and well-drawn; you watch it grow from inception. Lucille intuitively knows that her adventurous, distractable aunt is only a peer. When the girls play hookey from school you can see them longing for Lahti to scold them and set limits. Instead their aunt tries to talk them into further truancy. Lucille eventually seizes responsibility and sets to work "improving" herself to compensate for the unstable circumstances. The house fills up with cans and newspapers, the yard gets overgrown, and, as Lucille says, Sylvie "just wanders away."

This is less objectionable to Ruthie, an introverted bookish Nine, who finds her lively aunt stimulating. It's not unusual for a Nine to take energy from being around a Seven — we just saw it in *Harold And Maude*. Ruthie's a future novelist and likes to narrate her adventures with Lahti — "Sylvie had no awareness of time; for her hours and minutes were the names of trains. We were waiting for the 10:52 ..."

There's a nice scene where we also see the Seven tendency to rationalize. Lahti "borrows" a rowboat so that she and Ruthie can visit a distant forest. The boat's owner chases them from the shore and Ruthie says to Lahti:

"That man is yelling at us."

"Oh, I know," Lahti says, breezily dismissive. "He always does that. If he thinks someone is watching he just carries on more. It's pitiful — he could have a heart attack someday."

Ruthie says, "It must be his boat."

"Either that or he's some kind of lunatic," Lahti replies. "I'm certainly not going back to find out!" She starts whistling as she rows faster.

Eventually Lahti calls down the forces of Oneness on herself. These are personified by church ladies, a policeman and various legal threats. Lahti panics and herself gets Oneish for a spell. She tries to act properly and cleans up the house. But in the end she resolves the dilemma in a very Sevenish way: she torches the house and hops on the next train. Good film.

Hugh Hefner: Once Upon A Time, Star 80

"A quite remarkable adventure" is how *Playboy* magazine publisher Hugh Hefner describes his rather preposterous life. "A lot of things in my life have seemed like fantasy," he adds, putting it mildly. This unusually sympathetic biography follows Hefner's story from his repressive Midwest upbringing through his swinging sybaritic decades to his later phase as a mellow, older family man crowding seventy.

It's quite easy to see Hefner's libertine Seven lifestyle as a reaction to the Oneishness in his background and within himself. His religious Midwestern mother is almost certainly a One and the family is descended from Pilgrims. The social forces that Hefner opposed and provoked are all represented by Ones in this film. William F. Buckley, fundamentalist ministers and feminist Susan Brownmiller all weigh in with objections. The men are distressed that *Playboy* is pornographic and Brownmiller emphasizes the magazine's objectification of women, a charge that Hefner truly does not comprehend.

Hefner himself has a strong 1 streak (connecting point); it's mainly obvious in his rebuttals to party poopers. He spouts ideas from the "Playboy Philosophy," a rambling manifesto that is both sincerely ethical and crazily warped. The film's cloying narration describes Hefner's life as a "quest for personal freedom and to liberate others from the past." This sort of logic reflects a Seven gone to 1. Hefner certainly has a point or two — sex ought to be less fraught with man-made rules, and moralistic repression is no answer — but his Oneness mainly seems a defensive reply to the world's wet blankets. Even Hefner wonders whether he might somehow "be coming full circle back to the values of my parents."

As a Seven, he's pretty flagrant. He sorts for beginnings and possibilities, acknowledges a lifelong problem with commitment and is an interested appreciator of each new day. As a child, he "turned to fantasies early, to escape into what I felt was a better world." As an adult he escaped his business woes by flying around the world in his jet. "*Playboy* is about the play and pleasure of life," he intones.

Hefner has a 6 wing that is somewhat counterphobic (his battles with authority), but also helps him be a loyal friend. He reveals, for instance, a genuine, touching anguish for the people he's lost in his life. He's a self-preservation subtype and has a large circle of acquaintances that he pals around with.

He also displays the kind of willed naïveté and deliberately positive outlook that Sevens have such a knack for. He calls a stroke he had his "stroke of luck," and talks only in terms of what he learned from the medical crisis. Hefner's good-hearted and, all in all, a hard guy to dislike (though he should never again sing in public).

The catch is appetite. Hefner is a sexualizing Seven, an orientation that arises out of problems with the mother. Usually the Seven child feels undernurtured and that sense of lack is converted into a kind of inner hunger. This can lead to addictive behavior, and in Hefner's case the addiction has been to erotic pleasure. The son's sense of distance from the mother later translates into an objectification of women and they become the source of sustenance for a possibly bottomless hunger. Since people generally resent what they are addicted to, the women tend to be worshiped and degraded by turns.

Of course, there are centuries of social tradition that support men's turning women into sex objects. But what Hefner has done with his magazine is also particular to the psychology of Sevens. As with the life of Casanova, another famous Seven, Hefner's story is about sexual gluttony.

Sevens, when defensive, tend to rationalize and offer illogical logic that bats away consequence. Thus being a libertine becomes "sexually enlightened," satisfying endless appetites becomes "freedom," and treating women as beautiful objects is reframed as "respectful admiration." The demeaning dark side of what Hefner has done is precisely what he deletes. At one moment he muses, "Can I honestly say that during all those years of adventure, which I regarded as a celebration of my life ... can I honestly say that someone wasn't hurt by what I did?" He pauses and you wait for him to connect, but he stops with, "I don't know."

For a harsher examination of the self-referential world Hefner created, you need to turn to another Seven. Choreographer/director Bob Fosse was quite successful on the stage before he turned to making films. He only made a few, but they were mostly splendid, notable for being both entertaining and dark-edged. *Cabaret* won awards and Fosse's autobiographical *All That Jazz* is quite a good, searing portrait of an addictive Seven with an 8 wing. Roy Scheider plays Fosse as both endearing and honest but hopelessly hooked on drugs, booze and sex.

Fosse, the man, died eight years later essentially from the lifestyle he so unsparingly showed in *All That Jazz*. A clause in his will left $25,000 to a group of his friends to "have one on me" and go out together for a big expensive dinner party.

With these credentials, the director made his last film, the tragic, little-seen **Star 80**, about the short life of *Playboy* centerfold Dorothy Stratten. Stratten haunts the Hefner biography partly because Hefner can't make any connection between the culture of his magazine and Stratten's murder. But Fosse sees it plain, and draws a line from Stratten's sleazy, ambitious husband directly to Hefner.

Eric Roberts (a great performance) plays the unstable husband who plucked Stratten (Mariel Hemingway) from a Dairy Queen and pushed and groomed her for centerfold stardom. As he succeeded, he lost her to Hefner's larger, more professional machine and the wider world of opportunity. Unable to let his "creation" go, he instead shot her and himself to death.

Roberts is playing a crazy, driven Three. He's star-struck, vain, competitive, and underneath narcissistically hostile. Hemingway's Stratten is a sweet, confused Nine with almost no point of view who allows herself to be molded. As Roberts grows increasingly dangerous, she minimizes and explains away his behavior. She also gets swept up in a world of image reflecting a Nine's connection to 3.

Cliff Robertson is ironically cast in a brief role as Hefner. It's ironic because Robertson is a real-life One and in the movies he has mostly played Ones. He makes a good Seven here (real-life connecting point) though he gives the role a Oneish aura. The film shows Hefner disparaging Stratten's husband ("He has the personality of a pimp") without the slightest inkling of their similarities. The *Playboy* machine puts a genteel sheen on the same mindset that Roberts expresses nakedly.

Star 80 is something of a horror movie, with Roberts as the monster, but it's darkly compelling and smart as almost a direct rebuttal to the Hefner hagiography.

Lillies Of The Field

Timeless, utterly charming story about a nomadic Seven, Sidney Poitier, traveling through the New Mexico desert. Low on cash he turns in at a nunnery hoping to find some quick work. There he encounters a group of German nuns led by Lilia Skala, a One.

Skala's what used to be called an "old battle axe." Tough, stubborn and determined, she has seen a vision of a new chapel in the desert. She decides that Poitier has been sent by God to build the chapel but he just doesn't seem to know it.

A good Seven, Poitier has other plans — Big Plans. He's cheerfully narcissistic about the grand future that he's traveling towards. The trouble in the present is that Skala won't pay him for his handiwork and he can't quite travel on without the money. Gradually it develops that the nuns, who barely speak English, are flat broke and stranded themselves. Poitier's Sevenish tag line, "But I'm just passing through!" sounds more and more feeble as he realizes the situation. For all his bravado, he's a kindhearted man with an active conscience (6 wing).

Skala sucks him into building the chapel by degrees. She maintains her rock-hard certainty that Poitier is heaven-sent and he gradually wilts before her will. The nun also has a 9 wing and is extremely impersonal. This gets to Poitier because he wants to at least be thanked for his contribution since no one will pay him. Skala sees no reason to thank a mere instrument of God and instead remains insulting and oblivious.

Within the Enneagram, Sevens have a mixed connection to One and Poitier shows it. At one point he becomes obsessed with building "his" chapel. This quality of fixation on an Absolute Idea is related, for a Seven, to the low side of 1. On the high side, Poitier shows great dedication and discipline that is also Oneish in flavor.

Skala also shows a little of the One's tension towards Seven as she resists Poitier's charm and playfulness. She manages to let her hair down once or twice as when he teaches the nuns to sing some rousing black spirituals. Again you see the Seven bent towards cheerful escapism directly opposed by Oneish tendencies towards serious, rule-bound commitment. By story's end, Skala and Poitier both reach a kind of middle ground, growing toward each other in small but significant ways.

This film looked like it would be sentimental and preachily Christian, but it's neither. The disarming, graceful comedy flows directly from the lead characters' Enneagram styles.

Mermaids

Winona Ryder plays Charlotte Flax, Cher's Four daughter in this mother/daughter character study. Cher plays a Seven, and the film presents another good contrast between the two styles. As a teenage Four, Ryder's Charlotte is the soul of romantic misery, fixated on a Niney local boy who is the gardener at a nearby convent.

Charlotte never knew her father but she thinks about him often, displacing feelings onto his myth (introjection again). She has a bit of a martyr complex and longs for an ideal purity to her life and motives: "I do so want to be good and virtuous." To this end she makes plans to become a nun even though she is Jewish. After meeting a real nun she says, "I desperately wanted to ask her what color her bra was and if she had pure thoughts every second of the day." At one point, Charlotte registers at a pregnancy clinic under the name "Joan Ark." Later in the story she takes up fasting.

The core of her behavior is a Four's longing in the face of abandonment, but Charlotte also shows the Four connection to 1. Her mother is a selfish, escapist Seven and though Cher tries to make the character memorably comic, Ryder's character has to compensate for feeling neglected. She will say, "Oh, Mrs. Flax is a really great mother," and then long to live someone else's life. Her romantic preoccupations keep her cushioned from Mom's abuse and Dad's absence.

Cher's Mrs. Flax is a Seven with an 8 wing. Her whole life is a pattern of flight, beginning with running away from home ("If you hate a place, you can get in your car and poof! you're gone!"). To Bob Hoskins, with whom she gets tentatively involved: "I'm never growing old." "But time catches up to you, what can you do?" he asks. "Keep moving," is the reply. Mrs. Flax is meant to be a comically lovable Movie Mother, but she is actually an aggressively undependable Seven — depersonalizing, selfish and glib.

The film soft-pedals Cher's neglect of her children but it's constant. She rationalizes, minimizes responsibility, and deflects criticism with sarcasm ("Oh, now we're going to play, 'Who's the Worst Mother in the World!'"). Her tone towards the children is often impatient and she mostly implies that they are too much trouble: "You're a kid and until you grow up, we're going to live *my* life *my* way!"

She's also a spectacular hypocrite. After her daughter has run away and returned, Mrs. Flax lectures, "Running away doesn't solve anything. I'm a grown-up. I don't run away. I just move on!"

My Dinner With Andre

When I first saw this film in a theater, perhaps a fifth of the audience walked out when they realized it was about a dinner conversation. Those who stayed laughed long and loud as the film is well acted, thought-provoking and joltingly funny.

Like *sex, lies and videotape, My Dinner With Andre* is somehow *about* Enneagram styles — neurotic skews and what's beyond them. The utterly alien world views of friends Wally (Wallace Shawn) and Andre (Andre Gregory) are contrasted at a reunion dinner that Wally attends mainly out of politeness.

The first part of the evening is dominated by Andre's rambling, fantastical account of a recent nervous breakdown and spiritual crisis. Andre's an intellectual Seven and he tells his tale with big, imaginative leaps that freely associate unrelated events. He's also a name-dropper and displays an implicit air of smug superiority towards Wally.

Andre has a 6 wing. At times he's full of guilty self-doubt and his initial story is about seeking answers from outside sources. Here and there his story sounds faintly paranoid. He's also angrily self-critical and has been seeking salvation through a Big Idea. Both of these are related to a Seven's connection to 1.

There's a spoof of artistic and New Age thinking in Andre's logic, but what's especially funny is watching Nine Wally lose his battle to stay politely disengaged while Andre painfully unravels. He tries to humor Andre, but is struck by the latter's anguish and sincere attempt to comprehend his condition. Also, Andre is making more sense than he first seems to be, touching nerves that Wally tries to keep deeply asleep.

Turning point comes when Wally blurts: "I don't really know what you're talking about! — I mean, I *know* what you're talking about, I just don't know what you're talking about!"

Wally then bursts out with a monologue on *his* philosophy of living. In contrast to Andre's kaleidoscopic style, Wally is studiously mundane. He's a self-preservation Nine and his defensive emphasis is on simple pleasures, maintaining routines and avoiding thorny questions. He's a minimizer: "Do you want to know my actual response to all this? I'm just trying to survive." Wally starts talking about his willed sense of purpose, the pleasure he takes in running errands and checking items off a daily list. If he wakes in the morning and "a roach hasn't died in my coffee cup during the night, I just feel incredible happiness."

About this time, Wally starts to unravel too as his defenses sound more arbitrary and absurd. Both friends keep unpeeling as Wally becomes more heartfelt and Andre less patronizing.

The conversation takes a new turn, as they talk less of their defenses and more about what an authentic life might be like. Andre wonders how he "could cut out all the noise, quit performing and start to listen to what's inside of me." Wally ruefully admits that he feels "adequate to *do* but not just to *be* a human being."

It's difficult to explain what finally happens in this film. The conversation keeps broadening and then dropping to new depths, and it's amazing how much ground is opened. When Wally and Andre finally go quiet, it's gently stunning. The friends and the viewer are left hovering above the tender, mysterious void that is beyond masks, defenses and illusions. Andre is far more sober and contained while Wally has come thoroughly awake to himself. The film is essentially the story of an epiphany.

The Night Of The Iguana

Excellent film of Tennessee Williams's play. Comedy-drama concerns an alcoholic defrocked Seven minister (Richard Burton), well out of luck and stranded at a seedy Mexican beach resort. How he got there has a lot to do with being a dissolute Seven with a 6 wing. He's sort of a screw-up, someone who pulls trouble down upon his own head. This is mostly driven by Sevenish appetite; Burton was bounced out of the priesthood for seducing women and drinking. Now a tour guide ("Tours of God's world by a man of God"), he courts disaster by staying drunk, letching after underage girls and infuriating a nasty, intolerant One passenger (the One/Seven tension again).

The latter gets Burton fired and the tour eventually clears out without him. He goes deeper into escapist alcoholic patterns, desperately, if cheerfully, flailing out of control. Part of what is highlighted is how an escapist Seven will not self-contain. It's everyone else's problem. One character eventually ties Burton up in a hammock and won't let him out till he's sober. This is a good metaphor for what Sevens sometimes force others to do — restrain them because they will not restrain themselves. Notice too how Burton goes quiet and contained when finally sober (connection to 5). Once his addiction is broken by outside forces, he returns to himself.

Ava Gardner also plays a Seven but with an 8 wing (her real-life style). She's lusty, aggressive and expansive. Deborah Kerr plays an eccentric, pious Two with a 1 wing ("What is important is that one is never alone"). She is very similar to Joan Cusack in *Men Don't Leave* (see "Twos"). Burton was an Eight in real life so he's playing his wing.

Nothing In Common

Seriocomic study of a young, successful advertising executive, a Seven, very well played by Tom Hanks. The film charts his struggle with emotional responsibility as he copes with the divorce of his aging parents.

Mom (Eva Marie Saint) is an oblivious Nine waking up to herself and how angry she has been while married. Hanks's real trouble, though, is with his ailing father, a grumpy, volatile Eight played by Jackie Gleason.

"Do you have any idea how much money I'm being paid to stay this immature?" Hanks asks a girlfriend to whom he cannot commit. He starts the story glib, cocky and juvenile. A boy-man, Puer Eternis. He is shown to be highly creative in his work and his abilities are clearly based on the fun-loving, imaginative Seven style of thinking.

As the movie progresses, Hanks has to deal with acute frustration and his own angry responses (he shows flashes of an 8 wing). As he copes with his father's medical needs and those of a difficult Eight advertising client, he goes through a rite of passage and believably begins to grow up. The film starts with a synthetic TV sitcom quality but turns into something both funny and unexpectedly touching.

Gleason is good as the father although the character is quite unpleasantly selfish. He does convey the fears and frustrations of aging, especially as they affect an Eight (7 wing). Sela Ward plays a corporate Three, the client's daughter with whom Hanks gets involved. She's crisp, efficient, a bit hollow, but nice underneath. Hector Elizondo is Hanks's nice-guy boss and he's a Nine. Eva Marie Saint is a Nine in real life. Jackie Gleason was a Seven with an 8 wing. Tom Hanks is a real-life Seven and almost always plays them.

Tucker - A Man And His Dream

Jeff Bridges is good in a role that glorifies being a Seven. He's a dreamer-in-denial automaker who tries to compete with the large auto companies by building a well-designed, unusually safe new car in 1940s America.

He fails. Based on a true story, the film downplays the fact that the real Tucker was squashed like an ant and died in jail for his efforts. Instead, the movie's tone is celebratory, cheering on a little guy with big dreams. Director Francis Ford Coppola is a Seven (8 wing) and *Tucker* failed at the box office, so there's some irony afoot here.

Bridges is shown as cheerfully ignoring everyone's advice against mass-producing a new kind of car. He has a Vision. This film shows a Seven fixated on the low side of 1, growing obsessed with a Big Idea. "What's the difference if we build 50 cars or 50 million? It's the *idea* that counts!" he says. Again, rationalizing is a defense for Sevens. Each time Bridges meets discouragement, he makes even bigger plans to suppress his own fears. He maintains a relentless enthusiasm, keeping a big frozen smile on his face (he practices in the mirror). When Bridges gets especially frustrated he throws tantrums and yells a lot. This also has a connection to 1— Sevens can get critical and enraged when opposed. The yelling also reflects an 8 wing.

Bridges gets monotonous and shallow after a while, but that's the point about narcissism. Note too how impersonal he can be in the service of the dream. He neglects his kids, for instance, because he can't quite snap out of the obsessive trance that he's in.

Martin Landau again plays a cautious, pessimistic Six (5 wing).

He's Bridges's loyal, skeptical accountant who is endlessly sorting for what can go wrong. Someone has to.

Dean Stockwell has a standout cameo as Five billionaire Howard Hughes. He's disassociated and weird, showing the abstract aura of a Five with a 4 wing. Joan Allen plays Tucker's wife and seems like a breezy Seven.

The Unbearable Lightness Of Being

This film, based on Milan Kundera's novel, centers on liaisons between a man and two women against the backdrop of the Russian invasion of Czechoslovakia in 1968. The man, Daniel Day-Lewis, marries Twoish Juliette Binoche but keeps Lena Olin, a Seven, on the side.

Olin is an artist and a generalist. She and Day-Lewis have a steamy affair that is both passionate and impersonal at the same time. She's a sexual epicure, at play in her artist's studio. She likes costuming and sexual posing; it's part of the sensibility that goes into her art. She certainly cares about people in the abstract but gets involved with unavailable men so that her personal options can stay always open.

"The only place we can find beauty is where the persecutors have overlooked it." Olin has some political conscience but, as she says, "I like to leave places." That's just what she does when the Russians invade; she flees to Switzerland, sets up a new studio, and gets involved with another married man. When the new married man falls in love with her and announces that he has left his wife, Olin reacts like a caged wolf. She packs up her apartment and overnight vanishes from view.

Later, back in bed with Day-Lewis, she muses, "Maybe I should have stayed — he was such a good man." This is spoken in a light, uninterested tone. You can tell that she has already blown off the involvement and rationalized her own responsibility. Soon after she moves to Marin County, California, which somehow seems fitting.

Olin is not playing an uncontained manic Seven like Auntie Mame, but the disassociated option-oriented style of thinking is just the same. She's an intimate subtype, because of the predilection for one-to-one relationships and the Don Juaness scenario she is living out.

Olin's a real-life Six so she's playing her wing. Day-Lewis is cast as a dashing, empty sex object. His behavior is also Sevenish but his Enneagram style was finally unclear, at least to me. Day-Lewis is a real-life Five, so it could be that he's playing a Seven in a very Fiveish way.

OTHER MOVIE SEVENS

June Allyson, *Little Women*; Alan Arkin, *Joshua Then And Now*; Richard Attenborough, *Jurassic Park*; Anne Bancroft, *84 Charing Cross Road*; Ian Bannen (grandfather), *Damage*; Alan Bates, *Duet For One, Women In Love*; Jacqueline Bisset, *Wild Orchid*; Joseph Bologna, *Chapter Two, My Favorite Year*; Klaus Maria Brandauer, *Mephisto*; Beau Bridges, *Heart Like A Wheel*;

Michael Caine, *Alfie*; Julie Christie, *Darling*; Glenn Close ("Maxie"), *Maxie*; Francis Ford Coppola, *Hearts Of Darkness*; John Corbett ("Chris"), *Northern Exposure*; Russell Crowe ("Andy"), *Proof*; Robert Culp, *Bob, Carol, Ted And Alice*; Kirk Douglas, *Lonely Are The Brave*; Melvyn Douglas, *Ninotchka*; Richard Dreyfuss, *Once Around*; Robert Duvall, *Lonesome Dove*; Anthony Edwards, *Mr. North*; Albert Finney, *Tom Jones*; Clark Gable, *The Misfits*; Andy Griffith, *A Face In The Crowd*;

Audrey Hepburn, *Breakfast At Tiffany's*; Dennis Hopper, *Flashback, most any film*; Bob Hoskins, *The Long Good Friday*; Tom Hulce, *Parenthood*; William Hurt, *Altered States*; Tommy Lee Jones, *Nate And Hayes*; Michael Keaton, *Beetlejuice, Clean And Sober, Gung Ho, Mr. Mom, Night Shift*; Val Kilmer, *Real Genius*; Alan King, *Memories Of Me*; Bruno Kirby, *City Slickers*; Kevin Kline, *Chaplin*;

Burt Lancaster, *Atlantic City, Local Hero*; Jean-Pierre Léaud, *Last Tango In Paris*; Jack Lemmon, *Bell, Book And Candle*; Kay Lenz, *Falling From Grace*; Hal Linden, *A New Life*; Viveca Lindfors, *The Sure Thing*; Andie MacDowell, *Object Of Beauty*; John Mahoney, *Barton Fink*; Ray Milland, *The Lost Weekend*; Matthew Modine, *Full Metal Jacket*; Zero Mostel, *The Producers*; Willie Nelson, *Songwriter*; Paul Newman, *Blaze, Butch Cassidy And The Sundance Kid, The Hustler*; Jack Nicholson, *Easy Rider, Heartburn, The Witches Of Eastwick*; Peter O'Toole, *My Favorite Year*, Al Pacino, *Frankie And Johnny*; Earl Pastko ("Satan"), *Highway 61*;

William Petersen, *Hard Promises*; Brad Pitt, *A River Runs Through It*; Robert Preston, *Finnegan Begin Again, The Music Man, Semi-Tough, Victor/Victoria*; Dennis Quaid, *The Big Easy, The Right Stuff, most any film*; Robert Redford, *Little Fauss And Big Halsey*; Jason Robards, *The Christmas Wife, Max Dugan Returns, The Night They Raided Minsky's*;

Susan Sarandon, *Bull Durham, Light Sleeper, White Palace*; Robert Townsend, *The Mighty Quinn*; Robert Urich, *Ice Pirates*; Dick Van Dyke, *Mary Poppins*; Jon Voight, *Conrack, Midnight Cowboy*; Fred Ward, *Henry And June*; Billy Dee Williams, *The Empire Strikes Back*; Robin Williams, *Concert Film, Good Morning, Vietnam, Toys*; James Woods, *Joshua Then And Now*; Ed Wynn, *Mary Poppins*.

FINER DISTINCTION NOTES

WINGS: Sevens can have a 6 wing, an 8 wing or both wings.
A Seven's 6 wing can be either phobic or counterphobic.

Seven With a 6 Wing

Healthy Sevens with a 6 wing are responsible, faithful, lovable, nervous and funny. They are generally more oriented to relationship and want to be accepted by other people. Can be steady, more willing to stick with commitments; the 6 wing brings a longer sense of time. Usually funny or enjoy a good laugh — an amazing number of comedians are Sevens with a 6 wing. More openly vulnerable, have an unguarded, tender sweetness. Some have trouble expressing anger even when they are justified. May evade or finesse authority but still aware of it like a 6. Canny and practical, they look for the deals and the loopholes.

When more entranced, may have surprise episodes of sensitivity and insecurity. Their feelings can be easily hurt sometimes. Sensitive especially to comparisons. May avoid putting themselves to the test. Grow dependent/addicted to other people, afraid to be alone, suspicious and skittish. Can feel guilt easily, may project their conscience onto to others and then act irresponsibly. Make themselves shallow, fall in and out of love easily. Sometimes breezily betray others by running away. Can be reckless, unstable, and self-destructive.

When Sevens have a counterphobic 6 wing their idealism can motivate a sincere desire for social reform. May work hard for a cause. Can be antiauthority, passive/aggressive, flippant, defiant. Some report hating to be told what to do. Clashes with Ones likely. May call down trouble on themselves. Complain about the status quo. The realm of hippie rebellion.

Real-Life Sevens With a 6 Wing: Dave Barry, Joseph Campbell, Chevy Chase, David Crosby, Peter Fonda (counterphobic), John Gielgud, Goldie Hawn, Magic Johnson, Timothy Leary (counterphobic), Rosalind Russell, Steven Spielberg, Lily Tomlin, Robin Williams, Jonathan Winters.

Movie Sevens With a 6 Wing: Richard Burton, *The Night Of The Iguana (counterphobic)*; Ruth Gordon, *Harold And Maude (counterphobic)*; Andre Gregory, *My Dinner With Andre*; Hugh Hefner, *Once Upon A Time*;

Audrey Hepburn, *Breakfast At Tiffany's*; Tom Hulce, *Parenthood*; Christine Lahti, *Housekeeping*; Rosalind Russell, *Auntie Mame*; John Shea, *Missing (counterphobic)*; Dick Van Dyke, *Mary Poppins*; Jon Voight, *Midnight Cowboy*.

Seven With an 8 Wing

When healthy, Sevens with an 8 wing are often generous, gregarious and expansive. Tend to be exceptionally loyal to their friends, especially when social subtype. Leap aggressively to the defense of those they care for. Might seem loud or boisterous although some are urbane and witty. Enjoy social celebrations, storytelling, jokes, food and travel. Generally have a strong self-confidence for worldly matters and getting what they want. Talent for making something out of nothing — entrepreneurial. Usually share what they have when healthy, want everyone to enjoy their sense of bounty and wide range of interests.

When more entranced, they may be demanding, displaying a selfish impatience and self-justifying narcissism. May want what they want right now. Aggressive, hasty drive to acquire money and material options. Can demand that the people in their lives say only what the Seven wants to hear — sugarcoated truth. Lash out angrily if reality doesn't meet their expectations. Often perfectionistic as parents (low side of 1). Moralize to others and then are themselves irresponsible. Amnesia for promises made in an expansive moment.   Particular difficulty with sexual fidelity.

Real-Life Sevens With an 8 Wing: Robert Bly, Joan Collins, Barry Diller, Ava Gardner, Jackie Gleason, Alan King, Larry King, Robert Klein, Henry Miller, Jack Nicholson, Anthony Quinn, Louis Rukeyser, Lana Turner, Jann Wenner, James Woods.
Movie Sevens With an 8 Wing: Klaus Maria Brandauer, *Mephisto*; Jeff Bridges, *Tucker*; Cher, *Mermaids*; Richard Dreyfuss, *Once Around*; Ava Gardner, *The Night Of The Iguana*; Andy Griffith, *A Face In The Crowd*; Bob Hoskins, *The Long Good Friday*; Michael Keaton, *Clean And Sober*; Ray Liotta, *Goodfellas*; Paul Newman, *Blaze*; Jack Nicholson, *Batman*.

CONNECTING POINTS (Stress and Security)
Sevens connect to the high and low side of 1.
Sevens connect to the high and low side of 5.

Seven's Connection to 1

Healthy side of this connection brings self-discipline, follow-through, and a certain idealism. There may be a principled persistence and sober critical faculties that help the Seven to get things done. Good at balanced evaluation; they're appreciative and sort for the positive but they're nobody's fool. Ethics can be important. Want to improve things, search for "win/win" solutions to problems. Start to take life seriously enough to do things well, finish what they start. The connection generally helps Sevens become more objective and committed in a way that they are comfortable with.

When more entranced, their discipline degenerates into a confining web of limits. The Seven projects their 1 streak and begins to react to the stuffy, pointless rules of others. May confuse discipline with repression, build a trap that they need to escape from, blame it all on you. Critical and dogmatic, can harbor perfectionistic ideals of what others should do. Start to think in black and white.

The other neurotic manifestation is when Sevens latch on to a Big Idea. This is an abiding principle or future possibility that the Seven is sure will resolve their present discomfort. Can grow quite deluded and obsessed. Eyes fix so completely on a future possibility that they excuse themselves from the consequences of present actions.

Movie Sevens who demonstrate this connection: Jeff Bridges, *Tucker*; Francis Ford Coppola, *Hearts Of Darkness*; Robert Duvall, *Lonesome Dove*; Andre Gregory, *My Dinner With Andre*; Hugh Hefner, *Once Upon A Time*; Dennis Hopper, *Flashback*; Tom Hulce, *Parenthood*; Sidney Poitier, *Lillies Of The Field*; Jon Voight, *Conrack*.

Seven's Connection to 5

Healthy connection to 5 helps a Seven take time to contemplate and internalize their experience. Often brings sobriety, perspective, and the power to digest the experiences they have "eaten." Helps Sevens slow down, calm down, detach, see the Big Picture. May also be more willing to accept their pain and chew through it. Develop a respect for inner turmoil and deeper emotional processes that can take time. May embark on a search for philosophical wisdom. Find more depth, learn how to be alone. Some Sevens have an almost aesthetic distaste for excess that is related to this connection.

When more entranced, connection to 5 supports escapism, stinginess, and depressive tendencies. Unhealthy Sevens will check themselves out of difficult situations, withdrawing into their mind like a 5. Depersonalize — may detach from other people with frightening speed. They then move on to the attractive and new. Addiction to information, ideas, mental fantasy. Tendency to intellectualize feelings and rationalize.

The Seven style is usually generous, but this connection can bring an incongruous "cheap streak." Could pinch pennies, complain about high prices, etc. When more entranced, this can take the form of a stingy selfishness; the Seven could be talking to you about *their* needs even as you are feeling abandoned or let down by their broken promises. Sevens are also prone to withdrawn depressions, especially as part of a cycle of highs and lows.

Movie Sevens who demonstrate this connection: Anne Bancroft, *84 Charing Cross Road*; Richard Burton, *The Night Of The Iguana*; Robert Duvall, *Lonesome Dove*; Hugh Hefner, *Once Upon A Time*; Lena Olin, *The Unbearable Lightness Of Being*; Robert Preston, *Finnegan Begin Again*; Robert Redford, *Out of Africa*; Fred Ward, *Henry And June*; James Woods, *Joshua Then And Now*.

SUBTYPE THEMES

Self-Preservation

Self-preservation Sevens are a little confusing since they tend to be highly social. Characterized by a drive towards family and shared group experiences. Enjoy operating within their real or chosen family, checking in with a group of like-minded people. Chronic sharing on a circuit. People in the group are the source of interesting information and stimulation. Don't feel burdened or trapped by duties like a social Seven. Loyal to family, often have a 6 wing. Defend their circle and castle. Barricade, find safety in numbers. This subtype goes with the image of the "party animal." Movie examples include Auntie Mame and, especially, Hugh Hefner in *Once Upon A Time*.

Intimate

Intimate Sevens tend to garnish and embellish reality with fantasy. Intimate relationships are often thought of as shared experimental adventures, and the Seven perceives their partner through a veil of imagination. Romanticize others as a way to avoid the limits and boredom of mundane life with the same old someone. Can be more involved with their fantasy of the partner than with the real person. Tentative, distractible, impersonal, may have a wandering eye. Some have great difficulty with commitment and seem fickle as they move on to the next fantasy projected onto the next new person.

More generally, intimate Sevens have a tendency to be suggestible. May especially seek the new with the fascinated enthusiasm of a faddist. Step into multiple futures to avoid the present.

Good movie examples include: Julie Christie, *Darling*; Tom Hulce, *Parenthood*; Christine Lahti, *Housekeeping*; Karen Landry, *Patti Rocks*; Lena Olin, *The Unbearable Lightness Of Being*.

Social

Social Sevens often feel a tension between duty to others and the desire to escape. Tend to feel responsible for the people around them and experience that as a confining burden. They then react against the weight of obligation, seeking variety and craving change. When entranced, can be highly irresponsible. When awakened, they make peace with commitment and sacrifice and are often very stable and generous. Often an idealism, sometimes a stronger connection to 1. Serving something beyond themselves, dutiful. Can be from a large family where they had lots of responsibility, eldest child. With an 8 wing they tend to fight the sense of burden harder.

Movie examples include: Beau Bridges, *The Fabulous Baker Boys*; Cher, *Mermaids*; Tom Hanks, *Nothing In Common*; Sidney Poitier, *Lillies Of The Field*, James Woods, *Joshua, Then and Now*. Also Christine Lahti in *Housekeeping*, though her basic subtype is intimate.

EIGHTS

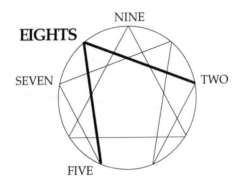

PEOPLE WHO NEED TO BE STRONG, TO PREVAIL OVER CIRCUMSTANCE. MAY BE POWERFUL, PROTECTIVE AND COMMITTED OR DESTRUCTIVE, EXCESSIVE AND SADISTIC.

FAMOUS REAL-LIFE EIGHTS

Lucille Ball, Charles Barkley, Humphrey Bogart, Charles Bronson, Football's Jim Brown, CNN's Pat Buchanan, Richard Burton, Johnny Cash, John Cassavetes, Fidel Castro, James Coburn, Sean Connery, Lawyer Alan Dershowitz, Danny DeVito, Football's Mike Ditka, U.S. Senator Robert Dole, Reporter Sam Donaldson, Kirk Douglas, Morton Downey Jr., Boxer Roberto Duran, Author Harlan Ellison, Hypnotherapist Milton Erickson, Moshe Feldenkrais, Director John Ford,

Indira Gandhi, Apache warrior Geronimo, John Gotti, George Gurdjieff, Director Howard Hawks, the culture of the Hell's Angels, Ernest Hemingway, Opera singer Marilyn Horne, Saddam Hussein, Director John Huston, Lyndon Johnson, Carlos Castaneda's Don Juan, Serbian leader Radovan Karadzic, Nikita Khrushchev, Rush Limbaugh, Ida Lupino, John Lydon (Johnny Rotten), the culture of the Mafia,

Norman Mailer, Musician Wynton Marsalis, Lee Marvin, Tycoon Robert Maxwell, John McEnroe, Golda Meir, Comedian Dennis Miller, Robert Mitchum, Actor Judd Nelson, CNN's Robert Novak, Director Sam Peckinpah, Sean Penn, Gestalt therapist Fritz Perls, Author/

producer Julia Phillips, Actress Julianne Phillips, Director Otto Preminger,

Anti-environmentalist author Dixy Lee Ray, Actor Oliver Reed, Geraldo Rivera, Axl Rose, Mickey Rourke, Telly Savalas, Baseball's Marge Schott, George C. Scott, the cultural aura of Serbia, Frank Sinatra, Grace Slick, Guardian Angel Curtis Sliwa, Joseph Stalin, CNN's John Sununu, Rip Torn, Donald Trump, Mao Tse-tung, Actor Ken Wahl, Barbara Walters, Denzel Washington, John Wayne, Director William Wyler, Zorba the Greek.

INTRODUCTION

Eights, Nines and Ones share a general undercurrent of anger and form another emotional trio. Remember Twos, Threes, and Fours are confused about who they are and how they feel. Fives, Sixes and Sevens react fearfully and are confused around taking action. Eights, Nines and Ones react from a baseline anger and have the most confusion in the realm of clearheaded thought. It may affect their feelings and actions but the area of disturbance is in the head. This difficulty is often described as a condition of mental sleep.

Eights, Nines, and Ones all have trouble with accurate mental conception, that is to say, thinking clearly. An Eight's thinking will tend to be distorted by narcissism and the need to be strong. Nines lose focus and get absorbed in the irrelevant. Ones distort their thinking when they reduce multidimensional reality down into simple moral catagories.

The anger in Eights is related to the desire to seem and feel strong. Most Eights mobilize their will to this end and are keenly aware of power. Nines tend to bury their anger or express it indirectly while Ones route their anger through judgment and disapproval.

Healthy Eights are often dynamic, strong and independent. When awakened, they can demonstrate the virtue of power, how to wield influence for constructive purposes. Many Eights are natural leaders who inspire others, protect the weak, and strive for justice. They may use their power to shake things up and have the courage and will to implement new ideas. They are generally honest, direct, and bring an energetic, lusty gusto to whatever they try.

Healthy Eights are often generous, loyal friends who protect what is soft and vulnerable in others. This is also a metaphor for how Eights relate to themselves; beneath their strong outer armor is a younger, more vulnerable part of them that they protect. This part is related to an innocence of perception that awakened Eights can have. They are sometimes able to see the world as if for the first time, with the eyes of a child. They may have a related love of nature that is a source of spirituality and evokes this innocent quality. Unguarded Eights often demonstrate the strength of gentleness — they are strong enough to be kind, open enough to be touched, secure enough to be wrong, rich enough to be giving.

When more entranced or defensive, an Eight's preoccupation with power begins to be tainted with self-interest. While still fairly free of self-doubt, entranced Eights cover up their vulnerabilities with aggressive displays of strength. They overidentify with being power-ful as a way to deny their softness and survive in a world that they think is full of dangers. They may also have a tendency to excess — staying up late, doing too much, driving too hard, indulging in addictions. This partly has the function of numbing their more vulnerable feelings.

Entranced Eights enjoy confrontation and try to make contact with others primarily through fighting. They push to measure others' motives and assess external threats. Eights may narcissistically inflate their presence and try to take up more than their share of space in a room. To protect the child within, they can act overbearing, arrogant, and insensitive. Underneath this intimidating shell the Eight may feel sensitive to betrayal, vulnerable to ridicule, or weak in a way that they are ashamed of.

Most entranced Eights don't quite realize how belligerent they seem. This is because they defensively deny feedback, especially about ways they might have been hurtful to others. Eights often specifically deny their guilt, covering it up with more aggression and pretending that they have nothing to apologize for.

In the movie *White Hunter, Black Heart*, Clint Eastwood's Eight character deliberately offends a number of people in a way that is very telling about this style. He doesn't just call them names, he sucks them into a dialogue or story that ultimately is insulting. Each time he does this, he takes out a sketch pad and draws the person as a *caricature*. This is very much a reflection of what Eights do in their minds when they are cruel to people — they make others into cartoons, two-dimensional objects that can then be skewered without conscience.

As with Twos, the healthy versus unhealthy expressions of the Eight style are unusually extreme. Their benign awakened use of power is corrupted drastically when Eights are deeply entranced. They can do immense damage — mostly to others — in the service of maintaining their grandiose image of an invulnerable self. A "get them before they get me" attitude thoroughly rules the Eight's behavior. To this end, they can be suspicious, bullying, vengeful, ruthless, psychopathic, or murderous. Many of the world's bloody dictators have been very entranced Eights, and their brutal excesses reflect how unhealthy people with this style may ultimately murder their own humanity.

EIGHTS IN THE MOVIES

Not surprisingly, unhealthy Eights make effective movie villains. The open aggression of the style photographs well and creates enough tension to drive many a story line. Eight movie villains are almost exclusively male. I don't think I found a single outright female example.

These types of roles start with the Bad-Bad Guy — a character who makes trouble just to throw his weight around or because he's obsessed with vengeance. Some are career criminals or mafiosos; others are avenging warrior figures, sociopaths or horror movie antagonists, especially Satan.

Then there are Bad-But-Appealing-Bad Guys, characters who still do evil things but have a sense of humor. They make trouble with gusto and are generally so pleased with themselves that the audience partly forgives them.

Up another notch are tragic, blindly destructive characters who don't intend to behave badly but do. These include deluded megalomaniacs, authoritarian bullies, tycoons, bad parents, angry kings, and male louts who are sexy but uncouth.

At the border of Good and Bad we find overzealous crusaders who are seeking justice. Also there are flawed cops who try to do the right thing but screw up because their rage gets in the way. Here's where the female Eights start to show up, often as tough independent women with hidden-away hearts. Usually they're good even though they act bad.

Eight protagonists are dynamic and adult in the sense that they take charge of situations and solve problems. Many are tough-but-tender and have an edge of narcissism or an endearing flaw.

The films reviewed in this chapter generally show Eights in a deeper light. Most are character studies and are surprisingly revealing of the strengths and sensitivities of the style.

MOVIE REVIEWS

The Andromeda Strain

Tense, terrific documentary-style thriller about a deadly virus that wipes out a small town in Arizona. A team of microbiologists goes to work in a top secret facility and discovers that the virus, dropped from space on a meteor, is like nothing they know.

The team is three men and a woman. The male characters are more faintly drawn, but the woman, Kate Reid, is a fleshed-out Eight and she provides most of the human interest and dynamism. She's rebellious, sarcastic and outspoken. Her first response to any procedure is to argue with it, then she complies. Close beneath the surface of this abrasiveness, Reid is vulnerable and rather sweet. Arthur Hill plays the by-the-book team leader, a One ("Our best hope is to be grindingly thorough"). James Olson is the psychiatrist, an irritable, introverted Five. David Wayne is the other, older man and a Nine.

The Doctor

Well-crafted, fact-based story about an arrogant and impersonal doctor who gets a taste of his own medicine when he becomes a cancer patient. William Hurt is the doctor, an Eight, and the film charts his journey from callousness to kindness as he learns to identify with his patients' suffering.

There are two striking contrasts relevant to the Enneagram. The first is the difference between Hurt's early bedside manner and that of *his* doctor, a Three. Both are insensitive and depersonalized but express it quite differently.

Hurt as an Eight is a subtle bully. He uses rough humor and caricature to stay disidentified with the pain of his patients. When a woman worries about her husband's reaction to her new surgery scar, Hurt jokes that she'll look just like a Playboy Playmate, complete with staple marks. She winces at his remark but he doesn't notice, thinking he's funny. Hurt then lectures his medical students on the professional virtue of not caring about the people you are cutting open. Denial of vulnerable feeling and the tendency to see others as caricatures are both specific defense mechanisms for Eights.

Hurt's Three doctor, by contrast, is crisp, efficient and mechanistic. She depersonalizes by seeing her patients as information. She deals with data and procedure and displays a technical fascination with Hurt's "case." She doesn't see him as a caricature but rather two-dimensionally, as a problem to be solved, a challenge.

The other thing to recognize is that the change Hurt goes through reflects an Eight's progression towards 2. Whereas a defensive Eight disidentifies, Twos have an exact opposite strategy of joining with others. When Eights change and grow, they sometimes develop Twoish strategies for fully identifying with others. Hurt gradually moves towards his wife (Christine Lahti) and declares his need of her. He also gets more thoughtful and introspective (connection to 5).

The film is low-key and naturalistic with bursts of melodrama. It presents an especially accurate picture of how an Eight might change and grow. Elizabeth Perkins is something of a counterphobic Six, but it's hard to tell because she's defined by the context of her illness and also a little romanticized.

The Fabulous Baker Boys

Precisely acted, near-perfect little character study of a two brother piano lounge act. Real-life brothers Jeff and Beau Bridges play respectively a nasty Five (4 wing) and a dutiful Seven (6 wing, social subtype). The brothers decide to spice up their piano routines by hiring a singer and into their lives comes Eight Michelle Pfeiffer.

She is one tough cookie. Almost everything she says is a preemptive strike, her best defense being a good offense. Her hardness is offset by an edgy insecurity which Pfeiffer shows is just beneath the surface. It's not fear, like a counterphobic Six would have. Rather, she's in a stand off with the world and has somewhere vowed to never be hurt again. When she and Jeff Bridges get involved, she starts by saying, "You're not going to wake up from dreaming about me and look at me like I'm a princess when I burp, are you?"

Bridges has his own problems with intimacy and has steel trap defenses for letting anyone into his solitude. He's essentially a Scrooge, so he and Pfeiffer keep triggering one another's hardness. Neither will take the risk of the first step. The story ends on a hopeful note, but both of them would have a long way to go. Nobody really grows much, but the film tartly evokes the lonely gulfs that can exist between overdefended people.

Gloria

Gena Rowlands gives a great performance in a mostly coherent John Cassavetes film. She's a retired Mafia gun moll who winds up protecting an orphaned ten-year-old whom the Mafia wants to kill. Her blunt Eightish hostility gradually softens into a gruff protectiveness of the boy. She is simple, rough-edged and will not back down. In the shocking action scenes she's a snarling, feral force of nature.

Rowlands is playing a self-preservation subtype, a woman who wants nothing more than to enjoy the modest pleasures of her retirement and have a little control over her environment. She initially resists the boy's plight and is decidedly unmaternal in her manner. She wants to be alone (connection to 5).

The connection to 2, however, gets the better of her; we see it in how she surrenders to taking care of the boy and also in a scene where she pleads his case before her mobster friends. She goes placating and seductive, like a weak wolf offering her throat. When this strategy fails, she turns rugged again and fearlessly shoots her way out of Mafia headquarters.

Rowlands was nominated for an Academy Award. The boy (Juan Adames) is meant to be lovably precocious, but at times he's just odd. It's as if he's playing some adult's warped memory of being a child.

I'm Almost Not Crazy

Take a break from all those fictional Eights and meet a real one in action. This documentary of the late actor/director John Cassavetes captures him at work making what was to be his last film. He's a bale full of contradictions — warm, impatient, humble, narcissistic, loving, bossy, funny. He also has passion without rage, which is a pleasure to watch.

Cassavetes has Eight-like problems with clear conception, as evidenced by his eccentric, rambling philosophy of moviemaking. If you've never seen his films, they are famous for their improvisational style and arrhythmic editing. Some are really good, some are just peculiar. A friend of Cassavetes tells a story of a film the director previewed that received a huge popular response. Cassavetes was so disturbed by the excited reaction that he reedited the film to his own inscrutable specifications. It later opened to bad reviews and flopped.

It's obvious that Cassavetes has gusto for what he's doing. He talks at length about wanting to make movies with authentic feeling ("All my work is about love"). He has an ethos of spontaneity and he shows an Eightish underdog sympathy for actors, advocating anarchy and freedom for them. What's not so clear is how this ethos relates to the finished product. You can see the film Cassavetes *thinks* he's making, but the result was a weird dud no one liked called *Love Streams*. With Eights, narcissism can compete with the best of intentions.

All in all, though, he's a sweetie, like a teddy bear with real claws. He would be a social subtype for his emphasis on love and responsibility as well as his enjoyment of the group process of filmmaking. Cassavetes involves everybody, and has genuine enthusiasm for the social chemistry of creating something with others. This also reflects an Eight's connection to 2.

The sad part of the film is related to Cassavetes's 7 wing. On the high side he shows excitement, great good cheer and abundant, if jumbled, imagination. The low side of a 7 wing for an Eight can include an almost virulent tendency to addiction, and unfortunately Cassavetes smokes and drinks his way through the film. He died of cirrhosis of the liver at the age of 59. Gena Rowlands, Cassavetes's wife, appears briefly and she's a Nine with an 8 wing.

Cassavetes, the actor, is showcased in Paul Mazursky's *Tempest*, a sometimes slow but surprisingly entertaining update of the Shakespeare play. The actor is an architect who has a mid-life crisis and retires with his daughter to a Greek island. There he slips into a Fiveish self-absorption that is both crazy and sane. Worth a look for how his Eight character changes and grows. He's lovably eccentric and again a social subtype. Raul Julia plays a Seven and Susan Sarandon has her usual persona which rides the border of Seven and Six.

Lean On Me

Morgan Freeman dominates every scene as school principal Joe Clark, a man who cleaned up and reformed a rough ghetto high school in New Jersey largely with the force of his personality. He wields a baseball bat, bellows through a megaphone, alienates teachers and superiors all in the name of tough love.

At first he seems like a One with an overriding sense of mission, willing to be abrasive for a good cause. Soon it becomes clear that he revels in his reformer role and can be egotistically unfair. This highlights the difference between Ones and Eights. Both styles can be overtly angry in manner, but a One does it in the name of principle while the Eight is glorifying the "strength" of the self. Clark can't openly admit he's wrong but can acknowledge the fact implicitly and indirectly, thus preserving his omnipotent self-image. His mission is opposed by Ones throughout the story. His saving grace is that he genuinely cares about the kids and they know it.

This movie is corny and overdone in places but Freeman is so good that it doesn't matter. For a more lethal variation of an Eight see Freeman's performance in the clever, underrated *Street Smart*.

Leaving Normal

As a film, *Leaving Normal* is a) crummy, b) stupid, c) phony, d) all of the above. For starters, there's too much music; it swells up sentimentally whenever the filmmakers think they have hit a Rueful Truth That Touches All of Our Lives. Usually the two lead actresses have just been shouting about philosophical sounding things and the music gets loud so that we know what they said was important. The actresses are traveling, so the film also has a lot of cute vignettes about things screenwriters imagine happen in rural places. You know, where those wacky country people with lovable eccentricities live.

Then there's the arty photography, the pretentious title, the ... oh, never mind.

The two reasons to see the film are Christine Lahti and Meg Tilly. They play an Eight and a Six respectively, and they do shout a lot, but they still ring true. And the dynamic between them is useful; Eights and Sixes can have trouble getting along because Eights tend to suppress their fears and act strong while Sixes sometimes fear strong, declarative people. In a highly unhealthy relationship an Eight could become sadistic and a Six masochistic.

Here Lahti's and Tilly's characters become good friends and we see the high side of such a union. Both share antiauthoritarian drives. Lahti extends a protective, loyal quality that includes challenges to Tilly's fears. Tilly is also loyal and is willing to confront Lahti on her denial, which Lahti first resents but finally appreciates.

At first they are more obvious in their styles. Lahti has a tough mouth and smokes, swaggers and swears. She's alcoholic, uneducated and has worked as a barmaid for too long. Tilly is breaking out of a short marriage with a man she barely knew but had romanticized (ie: gave him her power). She's apologetic, a little whiny and often beats up on herself. She has panic attacks and is superstitious, projecting lots of power onto outside forces. Lahti yells at Tilly for apologizing too much. Latter replies, "I'm sorry!"

Tilly's quite an active doubter: " I don't know if I should be doing this. How do I know I won't be making the same stupid choices again?" Later she loosens up enough for a romance with Lenny Von Dohlen, a shy, poetic truck driver, himself a self-doubting Six.

Malcolm X

Sweeping, seamless biography of black militant Malcolm X, splendidly played by Denzel Washington. He's an Eight and the film contrasts his grubby, rough, early life as "a junkie, a pimp, a convict" with his eventual religious conversion and career as a Muslim minister and firebrand.

The conversion occurs while Malcolm is in prison. His life is plainly not working and while he strikes defiant Eightish poses that get him harsh treatment, he's just about reached the limits of aggression for its own sake. He is repeatedly approached by a fellow prisoner Brother Bain (Albert Hall), an upright One, who asks Malcolm fierce, probing questions about his racial identity and what his life could count for. A slow unfolding of the spirit ensues, but what's also nice is the way Malcolm the Eight internalizes Brother Bain's Oneishness. It's as if the only cure for Malcolm's wild aggression is the absolute imposition of Oneish rules and precepts.   Eights sometimes internalize ethical Oneishness and it can work well for them.

Malcolm eventually joins the Black Muslim Organization of Elijah Muhammad (Al Freeman Jr.). Latter is a Nine with a strong 1 wing and the film shows both his strength as a spiritual leader and then later his welter of flaws. Freeman is a little like Ben Kingsley in *Gandhi*, "a sweet, gentle man" who is empowered by piety.

Malcolm's eventual disillusionment with Muhammad is first preceded by Eightish denial — he refuses to believe that Muhammad fathers children out of wedlock and is politically ruthless. When Muhammad reveals that it's true and blithely rationalizes the facts, Malcolm goes from denial to crushing disillusionment and says, "I could conceive death but I couldn't conceive betrayal." Actually betrayal is something Eights often fear. For some, it is worse than death.

By this time, too, Malcolm is powerfully committed to his cause, and the combination of Eight and One forms the basis of his take-no-prisoners preaching style. He's fiery, a little vengeful, and absolutely unsparing in his descriptions of white America's treatment of blacks. He's so controversial that he unnerves both the white establishment and his own organization which finally marks him for death. The film shows very well how an Eight could assume a leadership role and pursue it with unyielding commitment and courage. The portrayal is powerful and not the least bit sentimental. The film's epilogue — essentially a lecture — is so different in tone that it should have come after the credits.

Malcolm is an introverted Eight with both wings. In interviews Denzel Washington is very much the same way, so this would be Enneatype casting. The portrayal also shows an Eight's connection to the high side of 2 in Malcolm's devoted relationship to Muhammad and in his mellowing towards white people near the end of his life. The high side of 5 is evident in the way Malcolm becomes both studious and introspectively self-searching.

Reversal Of Fortune

Ron Silver plays real-life lawyer Alan Dershowitz who defended Claus von Bulow (Jeremy Irons) against charges of attempted murder of his wife, Sunny von Bulow.

Silver plays Dershowitz as a relatively healthy Eight (social subtype). Motivated by justice, he champions underdogs and defends poor people for free while charging the wealthy von Bulow full fee. "I've got to feel like some constitutional or ethical issue is at stake," he says, and it takes him a while to decide to defend von Bulow. "You have only one thing in your favor — everybody hates you."

Many movie Eights are villains, so it's nice to watch a productive one. He inspires his law students, takes risks, and pushily engages the world. He dislikes von Bulow and doesn't disguise the fact. He's honest, demanding and impatient. He also has a soft heart and a streak of insecurity. Silver gives a vivid, likable performance in a superb film.

Irons is most likely playing a Three with a 4 wing. He's subtly competitive, status-seeking and wears an enigmatic mask. His character is playing a role of himself. Glenn Close, though in a coma, is a Two.

September

Somber, whiny Woody Allen film about a group of depressed people spending an angst-filled weekend in a house in Vermont. Part of the problem is that everyone is in love with someone who's in love with someone else. Denholm Elliott loves Mia Farrow, a depressed, complaining Six, who loves Sam Waterston, a self-pitying Four. He thinks he loves the married, unavailable Dianne Wiest (Nine) who has gotten temporarily away from a life where she "was just going through the motions." Waterston the Four tells Wiest, "You haven't even left yet and I feel like I'm going to lose something that I'll never ever get back."

When Farrow's mother gusts into this stale atmosphere, things liven up considerably. She's an Eight, played by Elaine Strick, and she's loud, crass and delightful.

Strick would like to resolve her relationship with Farrow and this drives most of her behavior. She's secretly grieving her failings as a mother, but she covers her guilt with aggression, which is a defense for Eights. She offers Farrow unwanted opinions and simplistic homilies. She doles out criticism and then says, "Don't be so defensive!" when Farrow responds badly. Mom doesn't have a clue ...

She does try hard, though. She's basically good-natured, both well-meaning and gregarious. When she is unfair to Farrow late in the story, she apologizes and corrects her mistake. What she can't quite manage to do is switch places and identify with Farrow's feelings. Identification with others can sometimes be difficult for Eights, because of the tendency to caricature that I mentioned earlier. Eights avoid the weakness in others because it reminds them of their own.

By the way, the Strick/Farrow conflict in this film illustrates the different time orientations that Eights and Sixes can have. Strick lives very much in the present and the near future while Farrow is recycling the past. Strick is also keenly aware of aging and sums it up in this very Eightish way: "It's hell getting older. All the strengths that have sustained you all through your life start to disappear one by one."

Look for gruff Jack Warden, howlingly miscast as Strick's physicist husband. He almost always plays Nines and does here too.

The Shootist

Art imitates life in John Wayne's last movie. He plays an aging gunfighter who is dying of cancer, just as Wayne himself did a couple of years after the release of this film. Wayne was an Eight in real life and his gunfighter reflects a kind of mellowing that the actor himself publicly admitted just before dying.

"I won't be wronged, insulted or laid a hand on. I don't do these things to others and I require it from them." Vulnerable because of the medical diagnosis, Wayne's gunfighter is still tough, but he also reveals the tolerant, innocent goodwill that Eights can have when unguarded.

He has mixed feelings about what he has done for a living, but all in all says, "I've had a hell of a good life." He is without self-pity about his fate and genial beneath his crabby façade. He has enough conscience to put things right with the people he cares about and he decides on a death that is, to him, morally useful and dignified.

Wayne gives a fine performance in a movie that is more a character study than action western. James Stewart as his doctor and Lauren Bacall as his landlady are both Ones, and the Eight/One dynamic is really evident. Bacall partly disapproves of and partly admires Wayne's rough dealings. Wayne is rude and feisty towards her judgments but he also respects her.

Ron Howard plays Bacall's son, something of a Nine but it's not clear. He angrily stands up to Wayne's bossiness and, typical of an Eight, Wayne likes him for it. Hugh O'Brian has a cameo as a gambler-gunfighter and has a strong aura of a Three.

Twenty-One

This movie is luridly advertised as a frank, bold exposé of a sexually liberated young woman. Naaah — she's a blunt Eight (Patsy Kensit). Kind of a healthy one too, and the film is mainly a character study as Kensit finds her way through a difficult year and relocates from England to the U.S. Along the way, she talks into the camera about her life and her monologues are unvarnished and antiromantic ("For a while now in my life, sex and love have come in different packages ..." begins one). You can almost tell that she's an Eight from the assured way she walks and occupies space. But she also talks tough, has aggressive reactions and likes to play the Bad Girl.

Like our other Eights, she thinks in caricature and when she checks an aggressive response to someone in the film, she still says something judgmental to us. There's a lot of frank sexual content in what she talks about and this is related to the role lust plays in an Eight's life. It's also not unusual to find a female Eight who is outwardly mild-mannered but then has a profane, colorful mouth.

At bottom, Kensit's character is a genuinely nice person (high side of 2). She has a certain sense of propriety and a code of ethics that prevents her from acting out too harmfully. She loves her father in a tender, uncomplicated way. He is an amiable, befuddled Nine who is splitting from Kensit's Threeish mother. "I have a thing about pissing my father off," she says, "but if I were ever caught sexually molesting animals he'd defend me and there's no one in the world I trust more."

The family dynamics are consistent with the backgrounds of some Eights. Kensit's passive father and preoccupied, image-oriented mother make for a kind of power vacuum that an Eight child would tend to fill up with inflated demonstrations of strength.

Kensit's doomed affair with a drug addict (a dull passage since it's obvious what will happen) reflects the low side of the connection to 2, the tendency towards codependence. She tries to rescue him loyally even though his fate is really out of her hands.

The other thing to note is that Kensit has a 7 wing. She has a cheerful outlook and rebounds well from difficulty. "I don't think you should abolish morals and guilt, but I do think there's only one life and you'd better work out a way to enjoy it."

She has a woman friend who is only ever seen eating Chinese food and the woman is a Seven.

White Hunter, Black Heart

Clint Eastwood in an unusual, more or less true character study of film director John Huston and his obsession to kill an elephant during the making of the film *The African Queen*.

Huston's Eightness is the actual subject of the film and he's textbook — bullying, obnoxious, protective, profane, funny and, finally, humbled. "It's not a crime to kill an elephant, it's a *sin* to kill an elephant and that's why I want to do it." The sociopathic, antipuritan tendencies of the Eight style are well displayed. He won't do anything anyone wants him to precisely because they do. He favors underdogs and minorities yet his affection for them is self-serving. He enjoys cruel practical jokes and, in one memorable lengthy scene, he ruthlessly insults an anti-Semitic English woman.

Jeff Fahey plays Eastwood's screenwriter sidekick and he's in the Nine/One range. He has bemused tolerance for the director at first. As it grows clear that Eastwood is pathologically destructive, Fahey gets more and more Oneish.

White Hunter is talky and forced at first and it's odd to see the taciturn Eastwood with so much dialogue. But once the story gets rolling it builds to a strong, surprising punch. A brave, compelling, anti-macho tract.

OTHER MOVIE EIGHTS

Claude Akins, *Falling From Grace;* Alan Alda, *And The Band Played On, White Mile;* Idi Amin, *General Idi Amin Dada;* Philip Anglim, *Haunted Summer;* Kathy Bates, *White Palace;* Wallace Beery, *Dinner At Eight;* Tom Berenger, Platoon; Humphrey Bogart, *Casablanca, The Maltese Falcon;* Marlon Brando, *Last Tango In Paris, A Streetcar Named Desire;* Richard Burton, *Anne Of A Thousand Days;* James Caan, *Honeymoon In Vegas;* James Cagney, *One, Two, Three;* Cher, *Mask;* Lee J. Cobb, *On The Waterfront, 12 Angry Men;* Sean Connery, *Family Business, The Offence;* Barry Corbin ("Maurice"), *Northern Exposure;* Robert De Niro, *This Boy's Life, The Mission, Midnight Run, New York, New York, Raging Bull, The Untouchables;* Danny DeVito, *Other People's Money, Ruthless People;*

Melvyn Douglas, *Being There;* Michael Douglas, *Black Rain;* Robert Duvall, *The Great Santini;* Clint Eastwood, *Dirty Harry movies, Heartbreak Ridge, In The Line Of Fire, The Rookie;* Lee Ermey (Drill Instructor), *Full Metal Jacket;* Peter Falk, *A Woman Under The Influence;* Peter Finch, *The Nun's Story;* Linda Fiorentino, *Acting On Impulse, Vision Quest;* Laurence Fishburne, *What's Love Got To Do With It?;* James Garner, *Victor/Victoria;* Richard Gere, *Internal Affairs;* John Goodman, *Born Yesterday;* Gene Hackman, *Unforgiven;* Rutger Hauer, *Ladyhawke;* Wendy Hiller, *The Lonely Passion Of Judith Hearne;* Judd Hirsch, *Ordinary People;* Bob Hoskins, *The Lonely Passion Of Judith Hearne;* Joan Jett, *Light Of Day;* Alan King, *Just Tell Me What You Want;* Sue Lyon, *Lolita;*

Shirley MacLaine, *Used People;* Lee Marvin, *The Dirty Dozen, Gorky Park;* Mary McDonnell, *Passion Fish;* Viggo Mortensen, *The Indian Runner;* Craig T. Nelson, *All The Right Moves;* Paul Newman, *Hud, Harry And Son;* Jack Nicholson, *A Few Good Men;* Nick Nolte, *Q & A;* Tatum O'Neal, *Paper Moon;* Peter O'Toole, *Beckett;* Al Pacino, *Scent Of A Woman;* Jack Palance, *City Slickers;* Chazz Palminteri, *A Bronx Tale;* Estelle Parsons, *I Never Sang For My Father;* River Phoenix, *Dogfight;* Anthony Quinn, *Revenge;* T. Rex, *Jurassic Park;* Burt Reynolds, *Deliverance;* Jason Robards, *Parenthood;* Kurt Russell, *Backdraft;*

Roy Scheider, *The Russia House;* George C. Scott, *Patton, The*

Hospital; Martin Sheen, *Cadence*; Keifer Sutherland, *Stand By Me*, *Flatliners*; Kathleen Turner, *V.I. Warshawski*; Robert Urich, *Endangered Species*; Darth Vader, *Star Wars*; Diane Venora, *Bird*; John Wayne, *any of his films*; Peter Weller, *First Born*; Bruce Willis, *Mortal Thoughts*; James Woods, *True Believer*; Irene Worth, *Lost In Yonkers*; Robin Wright, *The Playboys*.

FINER DISTINCTION NOTES

WINGS: Eights can have a 7 wing, a 9 wing or both wings.

Eight With a 7 Wing

Awakened Eights with a 7 wing are often expansive, and powerful. Gregarious and generous, they may display a cheerful bravado. Can be forceful but with a light touch, funny. Often have a sense of humor about themselves. Generally more extroverted, ambitious and materialistic. May talk loud and be sociable partygoers.

Sometimes driven to bring the new into being. Can be visionary, idealistic, enterprising. Willing to take risks. May think more clearly than Eights with a 9 wing; 7 wing brings an intellectual capacity.

When more entranced, aggression combines with gluttony to form an almost virulent tendency to addiction. Many entranced Eights with a 7 wing have had drug and alcohol problems or tensions around addiction. Prone to temperamental ups and downs — can be moody, egocentric, quick to anger. Tendency to court chaos, inflate themselves narcissistically. Some are ruthlessly materialistic. Can use people up, suck them dry. Maybe be explosive or violent, prone to distorted overreaction.

Real-Life Eights With a 7 Wing: Lucille Ball, Sean Connery, Danny DeVito, Kirk Douglas, John Ford, Rush Limbaugh, Geraldo Rivera, Telly Savalas, Frank Sinatra, Grace Slick, Donald Trump, Zorba the Greek.
Movie Eights With a 7 Wing: John Cassavetes, *I'm Almost Not Crazy*; Michael Douglas, *Wall Street*; Robert Duvall, *The Great Santini*; Laura San Giacoma, *sex, lies and videotape*; Gene Hackman, *Class Action*; Christine Lahti, *Leaving Normal*; Ron Silver, *Reversal Of Fortune*; Elaine Strick, *September*.

Eight With a 9 Wing

Healthy Eights with a 9 wing often have an aura of preternatural calm, like they haven't had a self-doubt in decades. Take their authority for granted — queen or king of all they survey. May be gentle, kind-hearted, quieter. Often nurturing, protective parents; steady, supportive friends. Informal and unpretentious, patient, laconic, generally somewhat introverted. Sometimes a dry or ironic sense of humor. May have an aura of implicit, simmering anger rather like a sleeping volcano. Slow to erupt but when they do it's sudden and explosive.

When entranced, the 9 wing brings an Eight a kind of callous numbness. They can be oblivious to the force of their anger until after they've hurt someone. Calmly dominating, colder; may have an indifference to softer emotions. If very unhealthy, they can be mean without remorse or aggressive in the service of stupid ends. Paranoid plotting, muddled thinking, moral laziness. Can be vengeful in ill-conceived ways, don't know when to quit.

Real-Life Eights With a 9 Wing: Johnny Cash, Milton Erickson, Geronimo, John Huston, Lee Marvin, Golda Meir, Robert Mitchum, Dixy Lee Ray, Mickey Rourke.
Movie Eights With a 9 Wing: Robert De Niro, *The Mission*; Clint Eastwood, *White Hunter, Black Heart*; Rutger Hauer, *Ladyhawke*; Judd Hirsch, *Ordinary People*; William Hurt, *The Doctor*; Shirley MacLaine, *Used People*; Lee Marvin, *Gorky Park*; Jack Palance, *City Slickers*; Gena Rowlands, *Gloria*; John Wayne, *The Shootist*.

CONNECTING POINTS (Stress and Security)
Eights connect to the high and low side of 5.
Eights connect to the high and low side of 2.

Eight's Connection to 5

Healthy connection to 5 brings mental clarity. Begin to think coherently; Eights are more strategic and systematic when this connection is active. Develop an objective perspective that helps them depersonalize and pull back from narcissistic overreaction. Take the long view, think things through, pause before they react. Can grow philosophical. Sometimes studious and introspective. May develop an intellectual streak, especially with a 7 wing. Connection also helps take the edge off Eight's addictive tendencies. They consume less, keep their own counsel, grow more moderate in their behavior.

Unhealthy connection is characterized by morbid withdrawal and tendencies to paranoia, depression, and guilty brooding. Eights can isolate themselves and lapse into inaction. Often this comes after they have recognized their own cruelty or moral failures. Might experience crushing guilt, a feeling that they normally deny. Can then begin to cruelly self-punish, spiral into regret. Fears arise but not usefully. Go dead, feel powerless. Intellect is twisted in the service of self-hatred or heightened paranoia about betrayal by others. When deeply unhealthy there is a strong possibility of suicide.

Movie Eights who demonstrate this connection: Philip Anglim, *Haunted Summer*; John Cassavetes, *Tempest*; Robert De Niro, *The Mission*; William Hurt, *The Doctor*; Kate Reid, *The Andromeda Strain*; Gena Rowlands, *Gloria*; Denzel Washington, *Malcolm X*; John Wayne, *The Shootist*.

Eight's Connection to 2

Healthy connection to 2 helps Eights learn to change places with others. 2s are overidentified with others while Eights underidentify so this connection helps Eights learn how to empathize. Extend themselves, become better communicators. Connection helps them recognize their interdependence. Can become more compassionate and thoughtful, more open and willingly vulnerable. Sometimes have an ethos of love, in touch with the child within. May have therapeutic personalities in that they want to heal others, make things better. Display the strength of true gentleness.

Unhealthy connection to 2 brings codependence. An Eight may get overidentified with their partner and be unable to disengage. May defend their partner's weaknesses, even those that hurt the relationship. Compensate for other's limitations, make excuses.

Stronger tendency to overreaction, display a kind of hair-trigger hysteria. Can take the whole world personally like an unhealthy 2. Won't let go of slights and injustices, their pride is offended extra easily. More vengeful, act entitled, episodes of megalomania. Eight's narcissism is intensified and reinforced.

Could also develop an obsession re their partner. Compulsive clutching and possessive demands. Sometimes prone to jealousy, associated with unhealthy intimate subtype.

Movie Eights who demonstrate this connection: John Cassavetes, *I'm Almost Not Crazy*; Robert De Niro, *The Untouchables, New York, New York*; Gene Hackman, *Class Action*; William Hurt, *The Doctor*; Patsy Kensit, *Twenty-One*; Christine Lahti, *Leaving Normal*; Gena Rowlands, *Gloria*; Denzel Washington, *Malcom X*.

SUBTYPE THEMES

Self-Preservation

Self-preservation Eights often grow up poor or struggling. Food, home, money may be crucial. Generally seek control over their immediate environment and may worry about survival. Tend to value things over people. Maintaining order and material security are important. Eights with this subtype have a stronger connection to 5. Can be materialistic and feel deserving about it; more often have a 7 wing. Could be collectors or have prized objects.

Sometimes domineering towards those within their sphere. Might preach an ethic of selfishness — justify their bullying of intimates as necessary to "toughen them up" for the hard world outside. Survivalist mentality, territorial imperatives. Life is a jungle, only the strong survive. Hiding in and presiding over their castle.

Good movie examples include: Barry Corbin ("Maurice"), *Northern Exposure*; Robert De Niro, *This Boy's Life*; Peter Falk, *A Woman Under The Influence*; Jackie Gleason, *Nothing In Common*; Gena Rowlands, *Gloria*; Denzel Washington, *Malcolm X*.

Intimate

Want stability, loyalty and predictability in close relationships. May feel easily betrayed, and are prone to suspicion. Can love deeply, have a genuine close-up interest in and concern for spouse. Since life is dangerous they want to choose close allies carefully. Attached to the idea of being able to trust completely. Lots of testing of their partner's motives. If they pass the tests then the Eight relaxes.

When entranced, this can lead to possessive obsession, and a need to dominate and control partner. Intimate Eights can get codependent, jealous, hooked into the other. Sometimes can't let go; their partner's every move is (over)reacted to. When very unhealthy, spousal abuse scenarios are possible. Stalking, vengeful vows to follow other to the ends of the earth, etc. Connected to the low side of 2. Intimate Eights sometimes play socially rebellious "bad kid" roles.

Philip Anglim, *Haunted Summer*; Robert De Niro, *New York, New York, Raging Bull*.

Social

Social Eights are often loyal to a group and conceive of friendship as a pact of mutual protection. Want everyone to benefit; group's cohesion and welfare is most important to them. Often oriented to family, honest, hold themselves accountable to others. May be the group's protector or provider. Emphasis on cooperation.

When healthy, they are aggressively blustery but will back down and apologize when they've been unfair. More able to say the Three Little Words —"I was wrong." Stronger connection to 2, can emotionally switch places with others in their chosen group. As friends they want to protect what's soft or young in you and appreciate the same in return. Could be hostile towards anyone outside who threatens the group.

Movie examples include: Richard Gere, *Internal Affairs*; John Cassavetes, *I'm Almost Not Crazy, Tempest*; Gene Hackman, *Class Action*; Nick Nolte, *Q & A*; Ron Silver, *Reversal Of Fortune*; Elaine Strick, *September*.

NINES

NINES

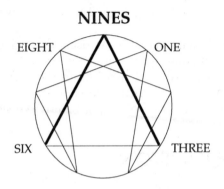

EIGHT | ONE

SIX | THREE

**PEOPLE WHO ARE RECEPTIVE TO THEIR ENVI-
RONMENT AND PLAY DOWN THEIR OWN PRES-
ENCE. MAY BE LOVING, MODEST AND TRUST-
ING OR STUBBORN, LAZY AND SOUL-DEAD.**

FAMOUS REAL-LIFE NINES

Actress Loni Anderson, Bruce Babbitt, the cultural aura of Bali, Anthropologist/author Gregory Bateson, Actress Annette Bening, Tony Bennett, Tom Berenger, Ernest Borgnine, Matthew Broderick, George Burns, Actress Kate Capshaw, Singer Belinda Carlisle, Art Carney, Actor Keith Carradine, Julia Child, U.S. Secretary of State Warren Christopher, Connie Chung, Bill Clinton, Tim Conway, Gary Cooper, The Dali Lama, Actor Jeff Daniels, Actress Lolita Davidovich, Doris Day, Designer Oscar de la Renta,

Clint Eastwood, Dwight Eisenhower, Queen Elizabeth II, Shelley Fabares, *Columbo*'s Peter Falk, Gerald Ford, Actor Dennis Franz, Buckminster Fuller, Annette Funicello, Mahatma Gandhi, James Garner, Chief Dan George, John Goodman, Tipper Gore, Actor Elliott Gould, Spalding Gray, Charles Grodin, Woody Harrelson, Gabby Hayes, Patty Hearst, Mariel Hemingway, Buck Henry, Audrey Hepburn, Barbara Hershey, Paul Hogan, Anjelica Huston, Actor Ben Johnson, Shirley Jones, C. G. Jung, Director Lawrence Kasdan, Grace Kelly,

Figure skater Nancy Kerrigan, Helmut Kohl, Actress Jennifer

Jason Leigh, Abraham Lincoln, Lyle Lovett, Andie MacDowell, Mr. Magoo, John Major, Novelist Thomas Mann, Ann-Margret, Dean Martin, Jerry Mathers, Actor Harry Morgan, Sancho Panza, Slim Pickens, the cultural aura of Poland, Actor Michael J. Pollard, Dan Quayle, James Earl Ray,

Ronald Reagan, Ralph Richardson, Psychologist Carl Rogers, Roy Rogers, Gena Rowlands, Actress Eva Marie Saint, Jerry Seinfeld, Garry Shandling, Wallace Shawn, Martin Sheen, Actor Tom Skerritt, Ringo Starr, Mary Steenburgen, Gloria Steinem, Actor Daniel Stern, James Stewart, Actor Eric Stoltz, Singer Andy Williams.

INTRODUCTION

Unlike Eights, who mobilize and directly express aggression, Nines take their underlying emotion of anger and tamp it down. Their central defensive strategy is to self-efface, to blend with and accommodate their environment. This tactic requires that Nines suppress their rough edges and conceal any part of them that might seem disagreeable. Most are angry about the consequences of this strategy — other people overlook Nines — but this anger comes out in indirect ways.

Since most Nines have taken on the coloration of their environment, there is a confusing variety to people with this style. Nines can have a wide range of occupations and outwardly appear much different from each other. What they share underneath, however, is a distinct tendency to fall asleep to their real inner needs. Remember when you are trying to identify a Nine that you are looking for the absence of something rather than an obvious definite quality that the person asserts.

Nines have sometimes been described as the "common people" of the Enneagram. When healthy, they possess a deep personal modesty and an elegant simplicity of thought. Awakened Nines are even-tempered, stable, unassuming, nonjudgmental and comfortable with who they are. They often have a cheerful Seven-like outlook, though they live in the present and not the future.

Many Nines have a calm, egoless, focused power that they bring to bear on whatever is important to them. This power is generally rooted in love whether the Nine thinks of it that way or not. Most healthy people with this style have a desire to contribute, to give to others freely, and to administrate their world in a way that benefits everyone they care about.

Nines are natural diplomats and mediators, and can be quite skilled at resolving conflict. Since they seek peace, union and harmony, it is often easy for a Nine to find points of agreement between warring parties. From there a Nine might patiently negotiate settlements that build on small positive steps. Awakened Nines are gently dynamic, suffused with a highly integrated sense of self and implicit mission. Most are also flexible and have the ability to state blunt, difficult truths in useful ways that somehow don't make others defensive.

When less healthy, a Nine's apparent simplicity becomes more like self-concealment. Entranced Nines begin to merge blindly with the wishes of others and the roles their environment wants them to play. In the process, they erase their own needs, priorities and ambitions. A Nine might give away his or her sense of initiative in order to have no opinion and thus keep an apparent peace. The more they absent themselves from their own life, the more passive, unfocused and ambivalent they become.

Entranced Nines tend to see all sides of a situation and identify equally with each outside perspective. They often focus on absurd or irrelevant details and lose the forest for the trees. They can be overly responsible but underperforming, obsessively complicating simple tasks even as they minimize the consequence of not getting important things done. Going in circles relieves them of the necessity to make decisions and personal choices, to take responsibility for having a self that they think might upset others.

Entranced Nines often have trouble overtly saying "no," but say it in other ways, usually through silent stubbornness and passive aggression. Nines usually blame others explicitly or indirectly for the life they feel they can't really have. Way deep down there's an angry, depressed nihilism in most unhealthy Nines. They have given up on their life and see no reason to stir themselves up to play at what they're convinced is an empty, fruitless game.

When deeply entranced, Nines can sink into depressed self-neglect and a kind of lazy oblivion that is an imitation of death. They may be apathetic, habit-bound, oblivious, or numb. They could talk incessantly about what they know they should do but then never bother to do it. They might try to avoid conflict but accidentally provoke it through bursts of disassociated nastiness. They might be disorderly, chaotic, cluttered and offer weird, ill-formed rationales for their irresponsibility. Deeply entranced Nines can do great damage to others while believing their actions have no consequence. Drug and alcohol addiction can be problems at this stage.

NINES IN THE MOVIES

Because of the passive nature of the style, Nines often play sidekicks or confused, indecisive characters or "common man" roles. When Nines are protagonists they tend to play the audience. They offer receptive characters with little overt ego with whom we identify and follow into the circumstances of the story. As events happen to the Nine they happen to us.

There have been a surprising number of Nine movie stars, most of them male. As in life, they vary tremendously, but Nine performers usually share an unfettered, truthful acting style. Clint Eastwood and the late Audrey Hepburn are both good examples, though, on the surface, they couldn't be more different. Both, however, have been described as modest, unpretentious people who would bring little personal temperament to their work. Audrey Hepburn played to the image-conscious, extroverted side of the Nine style (Grace Kelly did this too). Clint Eastwood is quite introverted and, by contrast, the only movie star in history who never combs his hair.

Eastwood the man is a Nine with an 8 wing and his screen persona is a blend of these two styles. He has flipped back and forth, although his most famous roles have been as Eights. Nearly all of his later films indict violence and explore the dark side of the heroic Eight character that he played for years. In the film *Unforgiven*, for instance, he is a Nine reluctantly drawn into battle with corrupt Eights.

Eastwood's predecessor in the movies was Gary Cooper, a real-life Nine who almost always played quiet, instinctual heroes. Eastwood has said that he openly modeled his minimal acting style on Cooper's. Other past Nine movie stars include James Stewart, Henry Fonda, Dean Martin and Ronald Reagan.

Lady Nines in movies tend these days to be impressive character actresses — Annette Bening, Barbara Hershey, Anjelica Huston, Jennifer Jason Leigh, Gena Rowlands, Mary Steenburgen. In the past, female Nines played sex objects who were beautiful, seductive, yet vague, a combination which allowed for maximum audience projection.

Partly because of the receptive nature of the style, many movie Nines are more clearly portrayed in relationship to other characters. Remember when you study this chapter that there are other good examples throughout the *Guide*. These include Woody Harrelson in *White Men Can't Jump*, Andie MacDowell in *sex, lies and videotape* and Wallace Shawn in *My Dinner With Andre*.

MOVIE REVIEWS

Antonia And Jane

Sometimes uproarious British comedy about two friends recounting different versions of their relationship in separate sessions with the same psychiatrist. Antonia and Jane are about to meet for an annual dinner and the occasion brings up insecurities in both of them. Each woman compares herself to her mistaken idea of the other.

The befuddled shrink struggles gamely, especially with Jane (Imelda Staunton). A hilariously obsessive Nine, Jane talks in rambling sagas and confused, dizzying circles. Here is a sample exchange:

Jane: "This week I asked myself, 'What do I really think about the poet Wordsworth?' But the question presupposes that I know who I really am — which I don't think I do."

Shrink (frowning): "There's no need to overcomplicate things, Jane."

Jane: "Okay, then assuming I do know who I am — which is a really big assumption — part of me thinks that anything I think about Wordsworth is completely beside the point!"

Shrink (lost): "What point?"

Jane (triumphant): "Ah! but is there a point?!"

Jane would be an extroverted Nine with both wings. She's very actively frustrated and has loud bursts of Eightish temper. Her antiauthoritarian attitude goes with the 8 wing, but her anger leads to absurd Niney courses of action and then more muddled thinking. At one point, Jane gets angry at her parents. In revolt, she marries an imprisoned drug dealer she barely knows and labels this act a political statement. Her 1 wing is evident in her receptive eagerness to please in relationships, plus a certain sweetness and idealism. Nines with both wings tend to flip back and forth between Bad Child/Good Child behavior.

The first half of the film takes Jane's point of view, and her image of Antonia is that of a Three. Antonia is beautiful, blond, waspish, and Jane's nightmare image of orderly, privileged success. Overcomplicating Nines sometimes see Threes as everything they are not.

The irony is that Antonia (Saskia Reeves) is actually a Six. Her life is just as confused as Jane's and she envies Jane's passionate disorder compared to her own bourgeois compromises. Antonia's life is coming apart anyway. She suspects her husband is having an affair and then counterphobically starts one herself. Her lover has pathetic, goofy sadomasochistic scenarios he wants her to play out; she tries hard to go along, but it's just too ridiculous. She has antiauthoritarian outbursts too and says at one point, "I've decided that everybody I know is part of a great conspiracy to make my life insupportable."

The Shrink is likely a not-so-bright Seven. She practices spin control and generally counsels with cheery platitudes like, "Try to regard everything as a delightful adventure" or, "Time's up for today. Just remember that whatever happens is a fresh challenge!" When Antonia's marriage really does bust up, the psychiatrist reasons with her, "Howard has left you; that is an existential fact. How you choose to react to that fact is up to you ..." To which Antonia replies, "I'd like to kill him!!!"

Back To The Beach

Adroit, good-natured spoof of those 1960s beach movies. Even if you never saw the originals, this movie is surprisingly funny and almost surreal. Annette Funicello plays a Nine with a 1 wing. She's a naïve, oblivious Goody Two Shoes, both endearing and simplistic. Described as "a woman who's been in a good mood for the last 22 years," she sweetly replies: "I just believe everything will turn out for the best."

While Annette is comic, it's quite true that some Nines are very cheerful. The ability to blank out trouble and difficulty and focus on the good is sometimes well developed. Think of Ronald Reagan, for instance.

Frankie Avalon plays Annette's husband, a nervous, excitable Seven (6 wing). Annette's a Nine in real life and I'm pretty sure Avalon's a Seven.

Carnal Knowledge

This bleak, excellent 1971 film plays like a pathology sheet, a rundown of diseases possible in relations between men and women. Story follows two college chums through decades of knotty, heartless love affairs. Their first involvement is with each other; they are forever talking in disassociated ways about women. What they say is generally rooted in contempt, so they wind up sounding like talking tumors.

Jack Nicholson plays his usual persona (Seven with an 8 wing), while Art Garfunkel is generally Niney. Garfunkel's character plays along with the more dynamic Nicholson, but has a streak of Oneish decency that emerges slowly. The story pretty much indicts both of them, though.

The middle third of the picture details Nicholson's live-in involvement with sweet, passive Nine, Ann-Margret. She's a nice person, but unmotivated by her own needs. She would be an intimate subtype for the way she longs for union with and commitment from Nicholson. She wants marriage and children but discovers that Nicholson is an unlikely prospect. Instead of dumping him, she goes inert and angry; she quits work, turns slovenly and pines away.

"You're more tired now than when you were working," he observes.

"The reason I sleep all day is because I can't stand my life."

"What life?" he asks.

"I sleep all day! Two years ago I slept 8 hours a day, a year ago it was 12, now it's up to 15, pretty soon it will be 24!"

It does seem as if she's sliding into death, although she has episodes of stubborn overt anger. Nicholson, the Seven, rails against her desire for commitment and especially feels trapped by her dependency ("For God's sake, I'd almost marry you if you'd leave me!"). Entranced Sevens frequently resent anyone acting dependent towards them; their anger is related to their own guilt over being undependable.

Ann-Margret's lazy sink into oblivion is very accurate to the style and subtype. Her character is very similar to Shirley MacLaine's in *The Apartment*, another intimate subtype.

Cynthia O'Neal has a small role as one of Garfunkel's paramours and she's a bossy, competitive Three.

The Last Picture Show, Texasville

"Ain't nothin' here, it's just flat and empty." That's a resident of Archer City, Texas, describing the setting for these two films, a tiny, dust-stripped town stuck to the earth a mile from the middle of nowhere. *The Last Picture Show* is a doleful, somber portrait of lives without futures. Most of the characters appear haunted or doomed and the film is partly about how to stay in or leave a place as optionless as

Archer City. This 1971 effort is considered a minor classic and it's still quite good, if overlong.

Texasville (1991) is a comedy, a kind of mirror image that revisits the same characters decades later and affectionately finds them mired in confusion. It turns out the characters did have futures that weren't quite so bleak, but no one in the town knows quite yet what they're doing. This latter film flopped but it's well-acted and literate if a little talky.

Leads Jeff Bridges and Timothy Bottoms are both Nines, though Bridges is more extroverted within the style while Bottoms is pulled into himself. In the first film, Bridges is cheerful and forward-looking and it's he who gets out of town by joining the military. Bottoms, by contrast, sinks into the deep sleep of his environment, looking increasingly dreamy and forlorn as the film continues. It's like he's slowly freezing to death.

Ben Johnson is on hand as the town's moral force and father figure to the boys. He's intriguing because he sounds like a One, seems like an Eight, yet he's most likely a Nine with strong wings. He has a basically receptive nature with moments of instinctual, almost mythic strength. Cybill Shepherd plays the town's flirtatious beauty, a Three with a 2 wing (intimate subtype). Her mother Ellen Burstyn is a Two with a 3 wing and it's interesting to see how outwardly similar they are yet essentially different. Shepherd's a status-seeking actress while her Mom's a fool for love.

In the sequel, Bridges has returned, gone into the oil business and is now $12,000,000 in debt. This takes the edge off his cheeriness and he tumbles through the film depressed and befuddled ("I don't understand anything any more. Everyone's gone crazy"). Described by newcomer wife Annie Potts (probable Eight) as having a "dour personality that's real reluctant to take a chance," Bridges washes around town in a stream of chaos. He's basically a passive witness to events, allowing situations to develop around him while remaining noncommittal ("It's hard to stay exciting for a whole lifetime.")

Bottoms has sunk further into Niney deep freeze, at the point now where people now worry about him. There's some indication that he might have brain damage but it's more intrinsic than that. He sees movies in the sky, forgets where he is and talks of suing the town for ruining his life. His sleep has turned into a kind of senility, complete with memory lapses, and he acts like an old man though he's only about forty.

Ben Johnson and Ellen Burstyn are both gone but two minor

characters from the first film have acquired Enneagram styles. Randy Quaid plays Bridges's banker, a climbing-the-walls anxious Six. Cloris Leachman has become Bridges's secretary and she's an opinionated One.

Cybill Shepherd's character has actually gone through an interesting transition. She left town too, became a movie actress and has returned to Archer City to grieve the loss of her parents and the death of a young son. She's a Three gone to 9 (see "Threes").

She's still a bit of a role-player — she toys with Bridges and maintains a capricious, mocking air — but she's in the process of acquiring some emotional substance. Her lost child haunts her and she's fascinated with community and family. She's aware of her roles: "I flirt a little, but that's my nature. Actually it's the ghost of my nature" — but in the end she breaks through to some deeper emotional connectedness via her grief. It's almost as though she's moving from her 2 wing to the high side of her 4 wing, getting in touch with sadness and a deeper dimension of feeling.

Little Murders

Dark, sometimes amazing satire of deracinated urban life. This 1971 story features alienated characters living distorted lives in a city where basic services are in breakdown. Gangs roam the streets and random shootings and power outages punctuate everyone's days.

Sound familiar? This film was so prescient that it doesn't seem dated now. The characters are exaggerated, even grotesque, but nearly all have vivid Enneagram styles. The script was written by cartoonist Jules Feiffer and has the depressive, comic Niney flavor of his drawings.

Elliott Gould plays Alfred, a Nine photographer whose chief defense against urban chaos is a stance of indifferent numbness. A self-described "apathist," we first see him passively resisting a gang beating. When future wife Marcia Rodd rescues him, he scolds her: "You shouldn't have done that. They were getting tired and about to let me go!" Rodd is a nice Two with a 3 wing ("Alfred, you've got to let me mold you"), though for much of the film she seems like a busy, administrative Three. She tries to inspire and motivate the slothful Gould:

She: Name something you enjoy.
He: Sleeping.

She: What about sex?

He: It makes me sleep better ...

Over the course of the story Rodd succeeds at bringing Gould partially to life ("I trust you. I really nearly trust you," he says). Nines will sometimes wake up for love, although this film illustrates their worst fear about what might happen should they start to care.

Gould's so nihilistic that he insists their marriage take place at the First Existentialist Church, presided over by hippie minister Donald Sutherland. Latter's ad-libbed marriage ceremony is an ideal specimen of rationalizing Seven logic: " You all know why we are here. Let me state that of the hundreds of marriages I've performed, all but seven have failed. The odds are not good. But nothing can destroy you if you don't see it as destructive. Any step that one takes is useful, is positive. Even the negation of the previous step. If you stay married, fine! If you don't stay married, fine! It's all right. Everything is an answer for someone. For Alfred, today's answer is Patricia. For Patricia, today's answer is Alfred."

Gould is also welcomed by Rodd's loony family. Father (Vincent Gardenia) is a flaming paranoid Six and mother (Elizabeth Wilson) is a weirdly normal Nine. Lou Jacobi plays a ranting One Judge that Gould and Rodd consult. Director Alan Arkin does a turn as a paranoid Six police detective, convinced that the city's random killings are part of a larger conspiracy to embarrass the police. This film is sometimes brilliant, generally interesting and very unusual.

Mr. And Mrs. Bridge

"I want a divorce and we can discuss it as soon as you've finished enjoying your beer." That's Mrs. Bridge (Joanne Woodward) talking to Mr. Bridge in a rare moment of open, if passive, discontent.

Mrs. Bridge is a ditsy, off-center Nine and Mr. Bridge (Paul Newman) is a thin-lipped, repressive One. The story of their life together is composed of small moments in which they mainly demonstrate their Enneagram styles. Nothing much happens, neither of them changes or grows. If anything, they get worse; that is, more entrenched and trapped within their limits.

Most of the time, Mrs. Bridge is lost to and passive to others. When Mr. Bridge proposes a trip to Paris, she says, "Just tell me what to read first. What do I know? I've never done anything, never been anywhere." Never *been anyone*, is what she's saying. Throughout the movie she displays a quality of busy, distracted sleep — the sleep of a self forgotten.

Mrs. Bridge's emotions surface in odd uprushes and the Nine style of minimizing conflict is obvious many times. At one point a suicidal Fourish friend (Blythe Danner) pours out her pain and Mrs. Bridge then changes the subject: "When you think about it, we really are awfully lucky ... would you like some tea?" Nines can be alternately sympathetic to others and then callously indifferent. Mrs. Bridge demonstrates how a Nine can do harm with neglect.

Late in the film, there's a telling scene. Mrs. Bridge backs her car out of the garage and it stalls in the narrow garage doorway. She can't get it started and realizes that the car doors won't open because they are blocked by the outer door frames on either side. So she sits. All day. She's neither determined nor resourceful — she just waits. This quality of passively tolerating an absurd situation can be very characteristic of sleeping Nines, as we saw in *Antonia And Jane*.

One other aspect to notice is how Mrs. Bridge is younger than her years; her passivity is a little childlike and even at sixty she seems like someone's younger sister. All her friends are younger too, and her counterphobic Six daughter is more astute about the scope of life than Mrs. Bridge is. Mother never does grow up.

Mr. Bridge, the One, is ramrod straight in both posture and behavior. He's from pioneer stock, tough, stubborn and radiating judgment. He speaks in clipped, measured cadences and his sense of humor is dry as dust. "I must confess I've never been able to find humor in smut," is his response to a colleague's racy joke. When Mrs. Bridge wistfully reminds him of the poems he once wrote for her (connection to 4), he replies, "For better or worse, I turned out to be an attorney and not a poet." This is partly an explanation for why he shows his wife little affection. He has a 9 wing and tends toward being plain and impersonal.

He is also domineering and has strong conflicts with his rebellious Six daughter. There's a hint of repressed incest in his disapproval of his daughter's sexuality and in her power over him. She's got something on him, though the film doesn't elaborate. Newman's character is also generally opposed to the irrationality of the women in his life.

NATIVE AMERICANS

American Indians endured countless racist portrayals in the early days of the movies. This changed a little in the 1960s when social paradigms shifted sufficiently to allow actual Native actors to play heroic or sympathetic roles. In some of the more recent stories the Indian characters are shown to be smarter and morally superior to the whites. I'm sure these portraits are sincerely intended and more accurate. What's interesting, though, is how the range of roles remains consistently limited. In terms of the Enneagram, movie Indians are only ever allowed to play Nines and Eights.

Why this happens I don't know. Part of it is likely an unconscious form of stereotyping — most of the films below have Anglo screen-writers or are adapted from novels written by whites. It could also say something about the cultural Enneagram styles of Native Americans, although there are many different tribes and cultures. This is obviously a minefield because judging groups of people on their social aura is the foundation of bigotry.

Cultures *do* have Enneagram styles in a certain limited way, however. In white America, Threeish ideals of success and wealth are unconsciously celebrated. In German Switzerland, a culture I know well, there is a group aura of Oneness and people often unconsciously strive to live up to orderly, correct One ideals. This doesn't mean that there are more Ones per capita in Switzerland. The culture does, however, teach individual Swiss how to think and act that way.

Not all but many Native American cultures have a Niney aura. The group style of thinking is holistic, nature-based and deep rooted in the notion that the individual is a small part of a natural order of Being. In the movies, sympathetic Nine Indians are often receptive and dignified. They are in touch with their instincts and possess a sensible simplicity that is unworldly but spiritually intelligent. Many of these characters are medicine men, while others are sidekicks to the white protagonist. Most of the portrayals are rouged with romanticism.

Native American Eights in movies are invariably warrior figures. In the westerns, they fiercely fight off the white invaders. In the present-day stories they are political militants. In most of the films the principal whites are Threes or represent Three forces and values.

The 1970 comedy-epic **Little Big Man** started the revisionist trend with its then-controversial portrait of General George Custer as a preening egomaniac Three. Dustin Hoffman plays a white boy raised by Sioux Indians who bounces back and forth between white and native cultures. He's essentially a Six, a cowardly survivor who's an unwilling participant in great events.

Chief Dan George is Hoffman's Nine grandfather, Old Lodge Skins. He's a medicine man, something of a seer but also earthy and unpretentious. He's clear-eyed and sarcastic in his appraisal of the invading whites, but ultimately he's accepting rather than bitter. The Dali Lama, a real-life Nine, displays a similar attitude toward the Chinese who have invaded his native Tibet. Real-life Nine Dan George wrote several sweet, thoughtful books that were testaments of his faith and serenity. In *Little Big Man* his character is based on the real-life Chief Black Elk, who was also very likely a Nine. The film holds up pretty well although it's sometimes pointedly sexist. Faye Dunaway turns up now and then as a cliché Two.

Chief Dan George's other best work was in Clint Eastwood's poetic film, **The Outlaw Josey Wales.** He has the sidekick role to Eastwood's loner hero, but Dan George steals the movie with offhand Niney comedy. He's clownish but dignified in an uncommonly good western. The late Will Sampson, a Nine in *One Flew Over The Cuckoo's Nest*, makes a brief charismatic appearance as an Eightish warrior chief with whom Eastwood negotiates. Sampson played Nines and Eights exclusively throughout his short career.

The contemporary heir to Dan George and Sampson is Graham Greene, who first came to prominence in 1990's **Dances With Wolves.** He gives a touching, funny performance as the Nine spiritual leader of the Lakota Sioux, a tribe that adopts another Nine, disenfranchised white soldier Kevin Costner. Greene is receptive, smart, moral (1 wing) and another holistic thinker.

Rodney A. Grant plays the Eight warrior role in *Dances*. He's fierce and hotheaded, but gradually grows loyal and protective of blood brother Costner. The Nine/Eight contrast is also evident in the movie's portrayal of different tribes. The Sioux as a whole have a Nine aura while their enemies, the Pawnees, are uniformly Eightish. Actor Wes Studi plays an aggressive Eight Pawnee and we'll see more of him.

Dances is very romantic and has peculiar paradoxes — Costner, for instance, "improves" the Sioux way of life by introducing them to rifles. The Pawnees were none too happy about their savage portrayal, either. The movie is otherwise well-crafted, moving, and extremely honorable.

Graham Greene plays a modern version of his *Dances* role on *Northern Exposure*, the TV show which is out on video. He is the shaman/mentor to series regular Ed (Darren Burrows), a young Indian Nine. Greene also played a dignified Nine in the movie *Ishi, The Last Of His Tribe.*

The actor jumped Enneagram styles for his next movie, a muddled amateur drama called **Clearcut**. Here he plays a nasty militant Eight who kidnaps a rich Eight lumberman in revenge for a crooked land deal that steals timber from Greene's tribal reservation. Along for the ride is the tribe's ineffectual white lawyer, a nervous-wreck Six. The stupid, buffoonish lumberman is meant to be an Evil White and the screenplay is larded with trumped-up polemics. Film is generally kind of lame.

Greene, however, has charisma galore and the courage to be a solidly unsympathetic warrior. The character is avenging his people, but he's thoroughly narcissistic and clearly enjoys sadism. He may have good politics but he's also a sociopathic and a nasty piece of work. Floyd Red Crow Westerman plays the requisite Nine medicine man, an enigmatic background figure who spiritually supports Greene's militancy.

Far more effective politically and dramatically is Greene's next effort, the intense, riveting **Thunderheart.** Story puts Threeish FBI Agent Val Kilmer onto a South Dakota Indian reservation to investigate a murder that looks politically motivated. All signs point toward a militant faction led by an Eight, played by real-life activist John Trudell. Kilmer also investigates a Nine medicine man in the background and clashes with tribal cop Greene. Latter is playing a Niney sidekick role but within that restraint he's a feisty, smart-assed Eight. Throughout the film he's astute, sassy, and bitterly funny.

This movie didn't do that well, which is a genuine mystery as it casts quite a subliminal spell. The FBI agent has a gradual spiritual conversion that undoes his Threeish efficiency and emotional hardness. Kilmer underplays this beautifully and the Nine medicine man is at the heart of the unfolding. Nonactor Chief Ted Thin Elk is another natural actor like Dan George was. His medicine man has a patient, lucid presence and he directs the unwitting Kilmer both spiritually and politically throughout the story.

Thunderheart's true villains have thoroughly Threeish aims. Sam Shepard plays Kilmer's Eight supervisor and Sheila Tousey is an Indian activist and seems a One. This is an engrossing thriller with tight intricate plotting — boy, it's good.

Also cinematically intense is 1992's **The Last Of The Mohicans** featuring real-life activist Russell Means in the title role. Means is an Eight in real life but plays a Nine with an 8 wing in this film. His character is receptive and wise but a man of action when necessary. The film's Eight warrior slot is capably filled by Wes Studi as Magua, a renegade avenger who has declared personal war on the invading whites. He's as rough and ruthless as Graham Greene in *Clearcut* and for basically the same reasons. Studi went on to play the title role in *Geronimo: An American Legend*. Studi played him as an Eight and, indeed, the real Geronimo was an Eight with a 9 wing.

The negative white forces in *Mohicans* are mostly represented by British Ones. At the center of the action is a love story between vague, indefinite Daniel Day-Lewis and vague, indefinite Madeleine Stowe. The performers are both real-life Fives and if you look closely it shows.

Finally there's the contemporary road comedy **Powwow Highway** which puts the two Indian roles together in the same car. A. Martinez plays an enraged militant Eight and Gary Farmer is the mystical, receptive Nine. Their styles are in constant comic contrast as they travel south from a Wyoming reservation to rescue Martinez's jailed, framed-up sister.

Martinez is prone to explosive rhetoric about Indian treatment by the whites but he's so angry that it's self-defeating. He's chronically eruptible and can't get out of his own way. He fights with everyone on real or imagined political grounds. The film endorses his spirit more than his methods.

Farmer's spaced-out, spiritually faithful character is a lovely guy and the road trip is part of a vision quest. He christens his battered Oldsmobile his "pony," and sets out to seek the spirits of his ancestors. Things keep working out well for Farmer, to Martinez's amazement and scorn. Even though Farmer's asleep in his own world, he handles each situation with comic ease and aplomb. By story's end, both characters are together in purpose and, in a way, represent the integration of faith and action.

Many of the friends' exchanges run like this:

Martinez: "Do me a favor. When the heat comes down don't start with the old legends and all that mystical horseshit. It will only make things worse."

Farmer: "Stop worrying. Trust the powers."

Farmer is a self-preservation Nine with a huge appetite for food. Film is offbeat, undemanding and enjoyable. Look for Graham Greene again in a cameo.

There are other movies where these same Enneagram dynamics are played out with white actors. In the absorbing, evocative **Emerald**

Forest, Eightish Powers Boothe finds his long-lost blond son (Charley Boorman), who's been raised in a Brazilian jungle by natives. The boy is a Nine and so is his adopted father, a medicine man. Their enemies are Threeish progress and another tribe called "The Fierce People" who all act like Eights. Boorman's Nine tribe is called "The Invisible People"(!)

The Emerald Forest has flaws, but it's as different a movie as you'll ever see. Charley Boorman gives a striking performance. 1985 film was a bit ahead of its time, as its real subject is the destruction of rainforests.

Paris, Texas

Harry Dean Stanton plays an amnesiac who wanders out of the Mexican desert after several years missing. Reunited with his brother in Los Angeles, he begins to reconstruct himself and to form a relationship with the young son he barely knows.

He's in what psychologists call a "fugue state" — a sort of shocked inner oblivion where he wanders, lost in a vague symbology. He's also a Nine — tender-hearted, good-natured, passive/dependent, asleep. The scenes of father and son bonding are exceptionally gentle and touching.

Over the course of the story, he slowly (mostly) awakens and deals with the long-repressed incident that led him to block out his memory. Amnesia is a defensive tendency for Nines under the best of circumstances, so it's a logical response to Stanton's trauma.

In the end he tries to do the right thing by everyone but only partly succeeds. He finds his missing wife but can't forgive her for her part in what happened. His resolution of the past is both right and wrong at the same time. It makes perfect sense if you remember that he's a Nine.

Dean Stockwell plays Stanton's brother, an exasperated but compassionate One. Stockwell's wife, French actress Aurore Clement, is a real nice Two.

Paris, Texas seems to be long and slow but I was surprised by its narrative tension. It has subtle, delicate performances and great music by Ry Cooder. A movie for anyone who's ever felt dispossessed.

The Whales Of August

Small-scaled old folks movie with Lillian Gish and Bette Davis as elderly sisters living at a beachfront home in Maine. Film is slow sometimes, but also poignant and Gish is especially good. She's a self-preservation Nine who lives each day in small, cheerful increments.

Gish stays busy with projects, paints landscapes and makes toys. She has principles and opinions (1 wing), finds the good in most events, and plays the calming peacemaker to her cranky sister. At this role she is mostly passive but she can get openly annoyed.

Davis is something of a Four, although she also sounds like a One. She finds fault with everything and is suspectible to plunges of melancholy ("I'm alright — just a touch of November in my bones"). She often blocks the forward-looking Gish's plans —"We're too old to be considering new things"— and makes comments like, "Everything dies sooner or later." To which Gish sweetly replies, "So you always say, dear."

Gish knows Davis is exasperating but you can almost see her deciding to cope with it. What the sisters have is reminiscent of a Four/Seven dynamic, where the will to find fault competes with the will to affirm the positive. Gish brings an unforced grace to her role, but adds enough irritation to keep the character believable.

Vincent Price drops in for tea and he seems a sunny Seven. Ann Southern also has a small role and she's a likely Two. Harry Carey Jr. plays the cantankerous plumber and he's a New England Yankee One.

OTHER MOVIE NINES

Rosanna Arquette, *Desperately Seeking Susan*; Peggy Ashcroft, *A Passage To India*; Lionel Barrymore, *Dinner At Eight*; Jeff Bridges, *Starman*; Richard Burton, *Beckett*; James Caan, *Brian's Song*; Sean Connery, *The Russia House*; Tom Cruise, *Risky Business*; John Cullum ("Holling"), *Northern Exposure*; Willem Dafoe, *Light Sleeper*; Rebecca DeMornay, *The Trip To Bountiful*;

Jeff Daniels, *Terms Of Endearment, Something Wild, Arachnophobia*; Brandon de Wilde, *Hud*; Sam Elliott, *Lifeguard*; Richard Farnsworth, *The Grey Fox*; Lou Ferrigno, *Pumping Iron*; Albert Finney, *Rich In Love*; Peter Fonda, *Easy Rider*; Morgan Freeman, *Driving Miss Daisy, Unforgiven*; Anna Galiena, *The Hairdresser's Husband*; Pamela Gidley, *Liebestraum*; Jack Gifford, *Save The Tiger*; Jeff Goldblum, *The Tall Guy*; Elliott Gould, *The Long Goodbye*; Spalding Gray, *Monster In A Box, Swimming To Cambodia*; Charles Grodin, *Midnight Run*; John Heard, *The Trip To Bountiful*;

Dustin Hoffman, *The Graduate*; Paul Hogan, *Crocodile Dundee*; Bob Hoskins, *The Favor, The Watch & The Very Big Fish, Mona Lisa*; John Hurt, *The Elephant Man*; Wilfred Hyde-White, *My Fair Lady*; Jeremy Irons, *Damage*; Alex Karras, *Victor/Victoria*; Kevin Kline, *Silverado*; Alice Krige, *Haunted Summer*; Jessica Lange, *Tootsie*; Kyle MacLachlan, *The Hidden*; Ann-Margret, *A New Life*; Ross McElwee, *Sherman's March, Time Indefinite*; Don McKellar, *Highway 61*; David Morse, *The Indian Runner*;

Bill Murray, *Tootsie*; Jack Nicholson, *The King Of Marvin Gardens, Missouri Breaks*; Leslie Nielsen, *The Naked Gun*; Annette O'Toole, *Cross My Heart*; Al Pacino, *Sea Of Love*; Sarah Jessica Parker, *Honeymoon In Vegas*; Mandy Patinkin, *Alien Nation*; Sean Penn, *At Close Range*; River Phoenix, *My Own Private Idaho, Running On Empty*; Michael J. Pollard, *Bonnie And Clyde, Little Fauss And Big Halsey*; William Powell, *Mr. Roberts*;

Stephen Rea, *The Crying Game*; Christopher Reeve, *Street Smart*; Burt Reynolds, *Starting Over*; Ralph Richardson, *Greystoke*; Peter Riegert, *Local Hero*; Gena Rowlands, *Light Of Day, Once Around*; Bruno S., *The Mystery Of Kaspar Hauser*; Michael Sacks ("Billy Pilgrim"), *Slaughterhouse Five*; Marianne Sägebrecht, *Bagdad Café*; Peter Sellers, *Being There*; Tom Skerritt, *The Turning Point, Getting Up And Going Home*; Charles Martin Smith, *Never Cry Wolf*; Maureen Stapleton, *Nuts*;

Mary Steenburgen, *Parenthood*; Daniel Stern, *City Slickers*; Eric Stoltz, *Mask*; David Strathairn, *Sneakers, Passion Fish*; Donald Sutherland, *Ordinary People*; Oleg Tabako ("Oblomov"), *Oblomov*.

FINER DISTINCTION NOTES

WINGS: Nines can have an 8 wing, a 1 wing or both wings.

Nine With an 8 Wing

Awakened Nines with an 8 wing have a modest, steady, receptive core. They are charged by the dynamism of 8 — when focused on goals they often have great force of will. Get things done, make good leaders. May have an animal magnetism of which they are only partly aware. Can seem highly centered, take what they do seriously but remain unimpressed with themselves. 8 wing can bring a strong internal sense of direction. Relatively fearless and highly intuitive. Generally not intellectual unless they have it in their background.

When more entranced, they manifest the contradictions of the two styles expressing them *in sequence.* Could be passively amiable like a Nine and then turn horribly blunt like an 8. One moment they are opinionated or nasty, next moment kindly and supportive. Often don't hear their voices when angry. Can have a sharp, grating edge. May be slow to anger and then explode. Or angry but don't know it; may confuse being assertive with being rude. Placidly callous — both styles support numbness. Tactless and indiscriminate and indiscreet. May be unwittingly disloyal, spilling everyone's secrets. Sexual confusion, sometimes they are driven by lust.

Real-Life Nines With an 8 Wing: Clint Eastwood, Peter Falk, Gerald Ford, James Garner, John Goodman, Elliott Gould, Woody Harrelson, Helmut Kohl, Carl Rogers, Gena Rowlands, Gloria Steinem.
Movie Nines With an 8 Wing: Richard Burton, *Beckett*; Sean Connery, *The Russia House*; Clint Eastwood, *Tightrope, Unforgiven*; Sam Elliott, *Lifeguard*; Elliott Gould, *The Long Goodbye*; Woody Harrelson, *White Men Can't Jump*; Bob Hoskins, *Mona Lisa*; Ann-Margret, *A New Life*; Al Pacino, *Sea Of Love.*

Nine With a 1 Wing

Tend to have been "model children." Instinctively worked to please their parents by being virtuous, orderly, and little trouble. When awakened, they have great moral authority plus good-hearted peace-making tendencies. Often have a sense of mission, public or private, that involves working hard for the welfare of everyone they are committed to. Principled expression of love. Desire to contribute, do little harm. May be well-liked, modest, endearing, gentle yet firm. Some have great grace and composure with bursts of spontaneity and sweetness. Elegant simplicity.

When entranced, they tend to be self-neglectful. May go passively dead and operate from a dubious, fractured morality. Dutiful to what they shouldn't be. Play the good child, disappear into contexts, settle for being overlooked or just partly recognized. Passive tolerance of absurd or damaging situations. One-sided relationships where the Nine gives too much. Rationalize, minimize, tell themselves they had a great childhood, everything's fine. Placid numbness creeps over them. Intolerance of their own emotions. Gradually deaden their soul.

Real-Life Nines With a 1 Wing: Annette Bening, Tony Bennett, Warren Christopher, Connie Chung, The Dali Lama, Annette Funicello, Mahatma Gandhi, Charles Grodin, Patty Hearst, Audrey Hepburn, Anjelica Huston, Grace Kelly, Nancy Kerrigan, Ann-Margret, Martin Sheen, James Stewart.

Movie Nines With a 1 Wing: Tom Cruise, *Risky Business*; Annette Funicello, *Back To The Beach*; Chief Dan George, *Little Big Man*; Graham Greene, *Dances With Wolves*; Audrey Hepburn, *Robin And Marian*; Eva Marie Saint, *Nothing In Common*; Wallace Shawn, *My Dinner With Andre*; Tom Skerritt, *The Turning Point*; Harry Dean Stanton, *Paris, Texas*; Donald Sutherland, *Ordinary People*; Joanne Woodward, *Mr. And Mrs. Bridge*.

CONNECTING POINTS (Stress and Security)

Nines connect to the high and low side of 6.
Nines connect to the high and low side of 3.

Nine's Connection to 6

The high side of this connection brings several qualities, among them courage. Whereas healthy Sixes develop the courage to *do*, Nines find the courage to *be*. Connection helps them challenge fears and take risks. Expose the inner self they usually disguise with self-effacement. Can also be especially loyal friends, faithful and committed to those they love. Connection brings tenacity and a willingness to see things through. Realistic, more able to acknowledge what can go wrong.

More entranced, they develop a nervous, agitated quality. Can overanticipate new events, start to doubt themselves. Obsessive worry distracts them from the need to take useful action or see the obvious. Go scatterbrained. Nine's laziness is reinforced by 6's tendency to procrastinate. Nines put off what is specifically important to their well-being.

Dependency often an issue — will hand over responsibility, then blame others for making the decisions that the Nine won't make. Cowardice, may wimp out on agreements. 8 wing and this connection can make for antiauthority attitudes.

Movie Nines who demonstrate this connection: Jeff Goldblum, *The Tall Guy*; Andie MacDowell, *sex, lies and videotape*; Wallace Shawn, *My Dinner With Andre*; Imelda Staunton, *Antonia And Jane*; Donald Sutherland, *Ordinary People*; Joanne Woodward, *Mr. And Mrs. Bridge*.

Nine's Connection to 3

High side brings a kind of clarity of the heart. Can suddenly see clearly and prioritize on their own behalf. Take decisive deliberate steps towards goals important to them personally. Steady persistence — when focused, Nines are unstoppable. Connection brings energy and industry and helps with appropriate social presentation. Willing to dress up and voluntarily play roles in the service of goals.

Unhealthy connection brings tendencies towards role-playing, vanity and hyperactivity. Can allow themselves to go false and be defined by a milieu. Play out roles based on the expectations of others. May get caught in vanity and take pleasure in being mistaken for an image. Can have a prince or princess-like quality, act a little entitled. Proud of what others praise, but secretly know it isn't who they really are. Underneath the image, a Nine may feel indefinite and numbly unworthy. Can be fascinated by phoniness in others, want to break through or tear it down. Their unfocused hyperactivity is a busy, active form of sleep.

Movie Nines who demonstrate this connection: Richard Burton, *Beckett*; John Cleese, *A Fish Called Wanda*; Tom Cruise, *Risky Business*; Willem Dafoe, *Light Sleeper*; Jeff Daniels, *Terms Of Endearment*; Sam Elliott, *Lifeguard*; Jeremy Irons, *Damage*; Andie MacDowell, *sex, lies and videotape*; Peter Riegert, *Local Hero*; Imelda Staunton, *Antonia And Jane*; Donald Sutherland, *Ordinary People*.

SUBTYPE THEMES

Self-Preservation

Preoccupied with physical comfort, maintaining habits and satisfying appetites. The image of the lazy couch potato goes with this subtype. Strategy for getting along is to ask as little of life as possible. Can have a love of the minimal and enjoy the repetition of known routines. Distract themselves with pleasant domestic activities. Live conservatively. Consume food and drink for anaesthesia. May have large appetites, drug addictions, be physically slow moving.

Many good movie examples including Gary Farmer, *Powwow Highway*; Albert Finney, *Rich In Love*; Lillian Gish, *The Whales Of August*;

Elliott Gould, *Little Murders;* William Hurt, *The Accidental Tourist;* Wallace Shawn, *My Dinner With Andre.*

Intimate

Focused on an ideal of romantic union. Get lost in one relationship or in the yearning to have one. High expectations of partner. Sometimes sound melancholy like a Four. Prone to jealousy. May settle on someone and then grow critical and have a wandering eye. Can also deny their partner's flaws and idealize them to stay in union.

Another scenario involves multiple relationships, searching from one person to the next. Sometimes the Nine can't decide between two people. Triangulation. Paradoxically, this subtype can be fickle because they are so easily disappointed.

Good movie examples include: Andie MacDowell, *sex, lies and videotape;* Ann-Margret, *Carnal Knowledge;* Shirley MacLaine, *The Apartment;* Joanne Woodward, *Mr. And Mrs. Bridge.*

Social

Social Nines tend to gravitate toward groups and then have conflicts about joining or staying apart. Can enjoy group energy and interests but may be also aware of the group's expectations. These the Nine will both play along with and resist.

When immersed in a group, social Nines can lose themselves, trying to become all things to all people. Gregarious but may start to resist being too heavily influenced, to compensate for their sense of lost identity. Can sometimes resent how the group doesn't really see them. May fixate on what others think of them. Or resent the group and make fun of it. Some social Nines stay basically uninvolved but hang out at the group's edge. Frequently there's lots of activity. May get caught up in roles — a stronger connection to 3 goes with this subtype.

Movie examples include: Jeff Bridges, *Texasville;* Sean Connery, *The Russia House;* Tom Cruise, *Risky Business;* Imelda Staunton, *Antonia And Jane.* Bill Clinton would be a real-life social Nine.

Bibliography

Baron, Renee & Elizabeth Wagele - *The Enneagram Made Easy.* San Francisco: Harper & Row, 1994.

Beesing, Maria, Robert J. Nogosek & Patrick O'Leary - *The Enneagram: A Journey of Self-Discovery.* Denville, New Jersey: Dimension Books, 1984.

Callahan, William J. - *The Enneagram For Youth.* Chicago: Loyola University Press, 1992.

Condon, Thomas - *The Everyday Enneagram.* Bend, Oregon: The Changeworks, publication date December 1st, 1994.

Hurley, Kathleen V. & Theodore E. Dobson - *What's My Type?* San Francisco: HarperSanFrancisco, 1992.

Keyes, Margaret F. - *Emotions and the Enneagram: Working Through Your Shadow Life Script.* Muir Beach, California: Molysdatur, 1990.

Linden, Anné & Murray Spalding - *The Enneagram and NLP: A Journey of Evolution.* Portland, Oregon: Metamorphous Press, 1994.

Naranjo, Claudio - *Ennea-Type Structures: Self-Analysis for the Seeker.* Nevada City, California: Gateways, 1990.

Olson, Robert - *Stepping Out Within.* San Juan Capistrano, California: Awakened Press, 1993.

Palmer, Helen - *The Enneagram: Understanding Yourself and Others in Your Life.* San Francisco: Harper & Row, 1988.

_____ - *The Enneagram in Love and Work.* San Francisco: Harper & Row, 1994.

Riso, Don R. - *Personality Types: Using the Enneagram for Self-Discovery.* Boston: Houghton Mifflin, 1987.

_____ - *Understanding the Enneagram: The Practical Guide to Personality Types.* Boston: Houghton Mifflin, 1990.

Rohr, Richard & Andreas Ebert - *Discovering the Enneagram.* New York: Crossroads, 1991.

Zuercher, Suzanne - *Enneagram Companions.* Notre Dame, Indiana: Ave Maria Press, 1993.

These and many other products available through the Changeworks Catalog.

INDEX

INDEX of MOVIES with MULTIPLE ENNEAGRAM STYLES

INCLUDES VISIBLE DYNAMICS AND CONFLICTS BETWEEN STYLES.

224

(4/9 dynamic, 4/1 conflict)
Crimes & Misdemeanors
Woody Allen - 6
Martin Landau - 6 (5 wing)
Anjelica Huston - 2
Alan Alda - 7 (8 wing)
Jerry Orbach - 8
Mia Farrow - 3ish
Sam Waterston - 1
(6/2 conflict, 6/7 conflict,
6/1 dynamic)
The Crying Game
Stephen Rea - 9 (1 wing)
Jaye Davidson - 2
Miranda Richardson - 3ish
Forest Whitaker - 2ish
(9/2 dynamic)

D

Darling
Julie Christie - 7
Dirk Bogarde - 5
Laurence Harvey - 3
(5/7 conflict)
Diary Of A Mad Housewife
Carrie Snodgress - 9 (1 wing)
Frank Langella - 8
Richard Benjamin - 3
(9/3 dynamic, 9/8 dynamic)
Dinner At Eight
Jean Harlow - 3ish
John Barrymore - 4
Lionel Barrymore - 9
Lee Tracy - 2
Wallace Beery - 8
The Doctor
William Hurt - 8
Hurt's Doctor - 3
Christine Lahti - 2ish
Elizabeth Perkins - 6ish
(8/3 conflict)
Dragnet
Dan Ackroyd - 1
Tom Hanks - 7
(1/7 comic conflict)
Driving Miss Daisy
Jessica Tandy - 1

Morgan Freeman - 9
(9/1 dynamic)
Dr. Jekyll & Mr. Hyde
Fredric March - 1 & 7
(1/7 conflict)
Duet For One
Julie Andrews - 1
Max Von Sydow - 5
Alan Bates - 7
(1/7 conflict, 1/5 dynamic)

E

Enchanted April
Josie Lawrence - 6 (7 wing)
Joan Plowright - 1 (2 wing)
Miranda Richardson - 9 (1 wing)
Alfred Molina - 3
Richardson's husband - 7
Michael Kitchen - 9 (1 wing)

F

The Fabulous Baker Boys
Jeff Bridges - 5
Beau Bridges - 7
Michelle Pfeiffer - 8
Family Business
Dustin Hoffman - 6
Sean Connery - 8
(8/6 conflict)
A Few Good Men
Tom Cruise - 3
Demi Moore - 1
Jack Nicholson - 8
(3/1 conflict, 3/8 conflict)
A Fish Called Wanda
Jamie Lee Curtis - 3
Kevin Kline - 7
John Cleese - 9
Michael Palin - 6
Cleese's wife - 1
(3/9 dynamic)
Flashback
Dennis Hopper - 7
Kiefer Sutherland - 1
(7/1 conflict)
The Four Seasons
Alan Alda - 1

Jack Weston - 6
Len Cariou - 7
Carol Burnett - 8ish
Bess Armstrong - 9ish
Sandy Dennis - 9
The Fourth Man
Jeroen Krabbe - 4
Renee Soutendijk - 2 (3 wing)
Frankie & Johnny
Al Pacino - 7 (6 wing)
Michelle Pfeiffer - 6 (counterphobic)
(5 wing)
(7/6 dynamic)
From Noon Til Three
Charles Bronson - 7ish
Jill Ireland - 4
(4/7 dynamic)

G
Glengarry Glen Ross
Jack Lemmon - 3 (2 wing)
Al Pacino - 3 (4 wing)
Alec Baldwin - 8
Alan Arkin - 9 (1 wing)
Jonathan Pryce - 9
The Grifters
Annette Bening - 3 (2 wing)
John Cusack - 3 (4 wing)
Anjelica Huston - 6 (counterphobic)
(3/6 dynamic & conflict)

H
Hannah & Her Sisters
Michael Caine - 6ish
Woody Allen - 6
Dianne Wiest - 6
Max Von Sydow - 4
Mia Farrow - 2
Barbara Hershey - 9ish
Harold & Maude
Ruth Gordon - 7 (6 wing)
Bud Cort - 9
Vivian Pickles - 2 (1 wing)
Harold's Uncle - 6
Minister - 1
(9/2 conflict, 7/1 conflict
& 7/9 dynamic)

Haunted Summer
Philip Anglim - 8
Alice Krige - 9
Eric Stoltz - 4ish
(9/8 dynamic)
Henry & June
Fred Ward - 7 (8 wing)
Maria de Medeiros - 4
(7/4 dynamic)
Honeymoon in Vegas
Nicolas Cage - 6
James Caan - 8 (going to 2)
Sarah Jessica Parker - 9
Housekeeping
Christine Lahti - 7 (6 wing)
Andrea Burchill - 1 (2 wing)
Sara Walker - 9
Sheriff - 1
(7/1 conflict, 7/9 dynamic)
House Of Games
Joe Mantegna - 3
Lindsay Crouse - 9
Lilia Skala - 2ish
(9/3 dynamic)
Hud
Paul Newman - 8
Melvyn Douglas - 1
Brandon De Wilde - 9
(8/1 conflict)
Husbands & Wives
Woody Allen - 6
Judy Davis - 6 (counterphobic)
Mia Farrow - 2
Liam Neeson - 4
Sydney Pollack - 3ish
Juliette Lewis - 9ish (8 wing)
The Hustler
Paul Newman - 7
Piper Laurie - 4
George C. Scott - 3
(7/4 conflict)

I
Impromptu
Judy Davis - 4 (3 wing)
Hugh Grant - 5 (4 wing)
Emma Thompson - 2 (3 wing)

George Coraface - 2
(4/5 dynamic)
The Indian Runner
David Morse - 9
Viggo Mortensen - 8
(8/9 dynamic)
I Never Sang For My Father
Melvyn Douglas - 1
Gene Hackman - 6 (5 wing)
Estelle Parsons - 8
(6/1 dynamic & conflict,
6/8 dynamic, 8/1 conflict)
Innerspace
Martin Short - 6 (7 wing)
Dennis Quaid - 7 (8 wing)
(6/8ish dynamic)
In The Line Of Fire
Clint Eastwood - 9 (8 wing)
John Malkovich - 3 (4 wing)
(9/3 conflict)
I've Heard The Mermaids Singing
Sheila McCarthy - 6 (5 wing)
Paule Baillargeon - 4 (3 wing)
(6/4 dynamic)

J
Just Tell Me What You Want
Ali MacGraw - 3
Alan King - 8
Peter Weller - 9
Myrna Loy - 1
(3/8 dynamic)

K
Kiss Of The Spider Woman
William Hurt - 2 (3 wing)
Raul Julia - 1 (9 wing)
(2/1 dynamic)

L
The Last Picture Show
Jeff Bridges - 9
Cybill Shepherd - 3
Timothy Bottoms - 9
Ben Johnson - 9ish (both wings)
Ellen Burstyn - 2
Leaving Normal

Christine Lahti - 8 (7 wing)
Meg Tilly - 6
Lenny Von Dohlen - 6
(8/6 dynamic)
Lillies Of The Field
Sidney Poitier - 7 (6 wing)
Lilia Skala - 1 (9 wing)
(7/1 conflict)
Little Fauss & Big Halsey
Robert Redford - 7
Michael J. Pollard - 9
(7/9 dynamic)
Little Murders
Elliot Gould - 9
Marcia Rodd - 2 (3 wing)
Donald Sutherland - 7
Vincent Gardenia - 6
Elizabeth Wilson - 9
Lou Jacobi - 1
Alan Arkin - 6
(9/2 dynamic)
Lonely Hearts (American)
Eric Roberts - 3
Beverly D'Angelo - 6
(3/6 dynamic)
Lonely Hearts (Australian)
Wendy Hughes - 6 (5 wing)
Hughes's father - 1 (2 wing)
Hughes's mother - 2
Norman Kaye - 9
Kaye's sister - 2
(6/9 dynamic, 6/1 dynamic)
The Lonely Passion Of Judith Hearne
Maggie Smith - 6 (5 wing)
Bob Hoskins - 8
Wendy Hiller - 8
(8/6 dynamic)
Long Day's Journey Into Night
Ralph Richardson - 1 (2 wing)
Katharine Hepburn - 2 (3 wing)
Jason Robards - 6ish
(2/1 dynamic)
The Lost Weekend
Ray Milland - 7 (6 wing)
Philip Terry - 1
Jane Wyman - 2ish
(7/1 conflict)

M

Malcolm X
  Denzel Washington - 8
  Albert Hall - 1
  Al Freeman Jr. - 9 (1 wing)
  (8/1 dynamic)
The Manchurian Candidate
  Laurence Harvey - 5
  Frank Sinatra - 8ish
  Angela Lansbury - 2
  (2/5 conflict)
A Man For All Seasons
  Paul Scofield - 1
  Wendy Hiller - 1
  John Hurt - 6
  Robert Shaw - 7 (8 wing)
  Nigel Davenport - 8
  (1/7 conflict)
Man On A Swing
  Cliff Robertson - 1
  Joel Grey - 2
  (1/2 conflict)
Mary Poppins
  Julie Andrews - 1 (2 wing)
  David Thomlinson - 1 (9 wing)
  Dick Van Dyke - 7
  Ed Wynn - 7
  Glynis Johns - 2
  (1/7 dynamic and conflict)
Men Don't Leave
  Jessica Lange - 9
  Joan Cusack - 2
  Kathy Bates - 8
  Arliss Howard - 9
  (8/9 dynamic, 9/2 dynamic,
  9/9 dynamic)
Mermaids
  Cher - 7 (8 wing)
  Winona Ryder - 4 (3 wing)
  Bob Hoskins - 9ish
  (7/4 conflict and dynamic)
Midnight Run
  Robert De Niro - 8
  Charles Grodin - 9
  (8/9 dynamic)
Missing
  Jack Lemmon - 1 (9 wing)

John Shea - 7 (6 wing)
Sissy Spacek - 6
(1/7 conflict, 1/6 dynamic)
The Missouri Breaks
  Marlon Brando - 3 (4 wing)
  Jack Nicholson - 9 (8 wing)
  (3/9 conflict)
Monsieur Hire
  Michel Blanc - 5
  Sandrine Bonnaire - 6ish
  Detective - 4
Mr. & Mrs. Bridge
  Joanne Woodward - 9 (1 wing)
  Paul Newman - 1 (9 wing)
  Blythe Danner - 4ish
  Daughter - 6ish (counterphobic)
  (1/9 dynamic, 1/6 conflict)
Mr. Johnson
  Pierce Brosnan - 1
  Maynard Eziashi - 2
  (1/2 dynamic)
My Dinner With Andre
  Wallace Shawn - 9
  Andre Gregory - 7
  (9/7 dynamic)
My Favorite Year
  Peter O'Toole - 7 (6 wing)
  Mark Linn-Baker - 6
  Joseph Bologna - 7 (8 wing)
  Lainie Kazan - 2
  (7/6 dynamic)

N

Nate & Hayes
  Tommy Lee Jones - 7
  Michael O'Keefe - 1
  (7/1 conflict & dynamic)
Network
  William Holden - 1
  Faye Dunaway - 3
  Peter Finch - 6
  Robert Duvall - 8
  (1/3 conflict)
A New Life
  Alan Alda - 6
  Ann-Margret - 9
  Hal Linden - 7

John Shea - 2
(9/2 dynamic)
The Night Of The Iguana
   Richard Burton - 7 (6 wing)
   Ava Gardner - 7 (8 wing)
   Deborah Kerr - 2ish
   Angry passenger - 1
   (1/7 conflict, 7/7 dynamic)
North Dallas Forty
   Nick Nolte - 9 (8 wing)
   Mac Davis - 3
   G. D. Spradlin - 1
   Steve Forrest - 7
   (9/3 dynamic)
Nothing In Common
   Tom Hanks - 7 (8 wing)
   Jackie Gleason - 8 (7 wing)
   Eva Marie Saint - 9 (1 wing)
   Hector Elizondo - 9
   Sela Ward - 3
   Barry Corbin - 8
   (7/8 conflict, 7/9 dynamic)
Nuts
   Barbra Streisand - 8 (7 wing)
   Richard Dreyfuss - 6ish
   Eli Wallach - 1
   James Whitmore - 1
   Karl Malden - 6
   Maureen Stapleton - 9
   (8/1 conflict)

O

The Offense
   Sean Connery - 8
   Ian Bannen - 6 (5 wing)
   (8/6 dynamic)
The Official Story
   Norma Aleandro - 1 (2 wing)
   Hector Alterio - 1 (9 wing)
   (1/1 conflict)
Oklahoma Crude
   George C. Scott - 9 (8 wing)
   Faye Dunaway - 1 (9 wing)
   Jack Palance - 5ish
   (9/1 conflict)
Old Gringo
   Gregory Peck - 1

Jane Fonda - 6ish
Jimmy Smits - 8
(8/1 conflict)
On Golden Pond
   Katharine Hepburn - 7
   Henry Fonda - 1 (9 wing)
   Jane Fonda - 6
   (1/6 conflict, 7/1 dynamic)
One Flew Over The Cuckoo's Nest
   Jack Nicholson - 7 (8 wing)
   Louise Fletcher - 1 (9 wing)
   Will Sampson - 9
   (7/1 conflict)
Only The Lonely
   John Candy - 9 (1 wing)
   Maureen O'Hara - 2 (1 wing)
   Ally Sheedy - 5
   (9/2 dynamic, 5/9 dynamic)
Ordinary People
   Mary Tyler Moore - 3
   Donald Sutherland - 9 (1 wing)
   Timothy Hutton - 6ish (5 wing)
   Judd Hirsch - 8
   (3/6 conflict, 3/9 dynamic,
   8/6 dynamic)
Other People's Money
   Gregory Peck - 1
   Danny DeVito - 8
   (8/1 conflict)
Out Of Africa
   Meryl Streep - 4
   Robert Redford - 7
   Klaus Maria Brandauer - 7
   (4/7 dynamic & conflict)

P

Parenthood
   Steve Martin - 6ish
   Mary Steenburgen - 9 (1 wing)
   Jason Robards - 8 (7 wing)
   Rick Moranis - 3
   Tom Hulce - 7 (6 wing)
   (6/9 dynamic, 7/8 dynamic)
Paris, Texas
   Harry Dean Stanton - 9 (1 wing)
   Dean Stockwell - 1 (2 wing)
   Aurore Clement - 2

Pascali's Island
  Ben Kingsley - 6 (5 wing)
  Charles Dance - 3 (4 wing)
  (6/3 dynamic)
Patti Rocks
  Chris Mulkey - 6 (7 wing)
  John Jenkins - 1
  Karen Landry - 7 (8 wing)
Picnic
  William Holden - 7ish
  Kim Novak - 9
  Rosalind Russell - 1
  Cliff Robertson - 1
  Arthur Hunnicutt - 9
  (7/1 conflict, 9/1 dynamic)
The Playboys
  Robin Wright - 8
  Albert Finney - 4
  Milo O'Shea - 7
  Aidan Quinn - 9ish
  (8/4 conflict)
Postcards From The Edge
  Shirley MacLaine - 2 (3 wing)
  Meryl Streep - 6 (7 wing)
  Streep's grandmother - 8
  Dennis Quaid - 7
  Gene Hackman - 8ish
  (2/6 dynamic & conflict)
Proof
  Russell Crowe (Andy) - 7
  Hugo Weaving (Martin) - 5
  (7/5 dynamic)
Pumping Iron
  Lou Ferrigno - 9
  Arnold Schwarzenegger - 3
  (3/9 dynamic)
Punchline
  Tom Hanks - 4 (3 wing)
  Sally Field - 6 (7 wing)
  John Goodman - 9ish
  Mark Rydell - 2
  (4/6 dynamic)

R

Reflections In A Golden Eye
  Marlon Brando - 5 (4 wing)
  Elizabeth Taylor - 2

  Brian Keith - 8ish
  Zorro David - 2
Reversal Of Fortune
  Ron Silver - 8 (7 wing)
  Glenn Close - 2 (3 wing)
  Jeremy Irons - 3ish (4 wing)
Ride The High Country
  Joel McCrea - 1 (9 wing)
  Randolph Scott - 3 (both wings)
  Ron Heck - 6 (counterphobic)
  James Drury - 7
  L. Q. Jones - 1
Risky Business
  Tom Cruise - 9 (1 wing)
  Rebecca DeMornay - 3
  (9/3 dynamic)
Rooster Cogburn
  Katharine Hepburn - 1 (9 wing)
  John Wayne - 8 (9 wing)
  (1/8 dynamic)

S

Save The Tiger
  Jack Lemmon - 3
  Jack Gifford - 9 (1 wing)
  (3/9 dynamic)
Seize The Day
  Robin Williams - 6
  Joseph Wiseman - 1
  (6/1 conflict)
September
  Elaine Strick - 8 (7 wing)
  Mia Farrow - 6
  Sam Waterston - 4
  Dianne Wiest - 9
  Jack Warden - 9ish
  (6/8 conflict, 4/9 dynamic)
sex, lies & videotape
  James Spader - 5
  Andie MacDowell - 9
  Peter Gallagher - 3
  Laura San Giacomo - 8
  (5/9 dynamic, 9/8 conflict,
  3/8 dynamic)
The Shootist
  John Wayne - 8
  Lauren Bacall - 1

Lena Olin - 7
Daniel Day-Lewis - 7ish
Juliette Binoche - 2ish
Unforgiven
Clint Eastwood - 9 (8 wing)
Morgan Freeman - 9
Gene Hackman - 8
(9/8 conflict)
Unlawful Entry
Ray Liotta - 2
Madeleine Stowe - 6 (5 wing)
Kurt Russell - 8 (7 wing)
(2/6 dynamic & conflict,
2/8 dynamic, 8/6 dynamic)
The Untouchables
Kevin Costner - 1 (9 wing)
Sean Connery - 8
Robert De Niro - 8 (7 wing)
(8/1 conflict)
Used People
Shirley MacLaine - 8
Jessica Tandy - 1
Kathy Bates - 6 (counterphobic)
Marcello Mastroianni - 2
(8/2 dynamic, 6/8 conflict)

V

The Vanishing
Bernard Pierre Donnadieu
("Mr Lemorne") - 5 (6 wing)
Gene Bervoets ("Rex Hofman") - 4
(4/5 dynamic)
Victor/Victoria
Julie Andrews - 3ish
James Garner - 8
Robert Preston - 7
Lesley Anne Warren - 2
Alex Karras - 9
V. I. Warshawski
Kathleen Turner - 8
Jay O. Sanders - 8
Little Girl - 8
(8/8 dynamic)

W

Wall Street
Charlie Sheen - 3

Michael Douglas - 8 (7 wing)
Martin Sheen - 1 (2 wing)
Hal Holbrook - 1
(3/8 dynamic, 8/1 conflict,
3/1 dynamic)
The Whales of August
Lillian Gish - 9 (1 wing)
Bette Davis - 4
Ann Southern - 2
Vincent Price - 7ish
The Plumber - 1 (9 wing)
(9/4 dynamic)
What About Bob?
Bill Murray - 6 (7 wing)
Richard Dreyfuss - 3 (4 wing)
Julie Hagerty - 9 (1 wing)
(6/3 conflict)
White Men Can't Jump
Wesley Snipes - 3
Woody Harrelson - 9 (8 wing)
(3/9 dynamic)
A Woman Under The Influence
Gena Rowlands - 6
Peter Falk - 8
(8/6 conflict)
The World According To Garp
Glenn Close - 1 (2 wing)
Robin Williams - 4
John Lithgow - 7
(4/1 dynamic)

Z

Zelly & Me
Isabella Rossellini - 2
Glynis Johns - 2
Alexandra Johnes - 4ish
(2/2 conflict)
Zorba The Greek
Anthony Quinn - 8 (7 wing)
Alan Bates - 5ish
Lila Kedrova - 2
(8/5 dynamic)

THE CHANGEWORKS CATALOG

The Changeworks publishes a free catalog containing hundreds of quality self-help products. The catalog includes:

* dozens of Enneagram books and audiotapes

* A wide range of NLP-based products

* Thomas Condon's books and tapes on the Enneagram

* Best-selling Multi Evocation tapes with Ericksonian Hypnosis

* Upcoming workshops with Thomas Condon

To order the free catalog or additional copies of *The Enneagram Movie & Video Guide* call toll-free 24 hours a day

1-800-937-7771

The Enneagram Educator

is the only information source for the rapidly expanding world of the Enneagram. It features a wide range of articles, news, workshop information and new product reviews. Thomas Condon continues to write regular columns. The *Educator* comes out quarterly. Price is just $15 a year.

To Subscribe call 1-800-333-7373